RECLAIMING OUR SCHOOLS
A Handbook on Teaching Character, Academics, and Discipline

Edward A. Wynne
The University of Illinois at Chicago

Kevin Ryan
Boston University

Merrill, an imprint of
Macmillan Publishing Company
New York

Maxwell Macmillan Canada
Toronto

Maxwell Macmillan International
New York Oxford Singapore Sydney

To the thousands of practicing and aspiring teachers and school administrators who provoked, advised, and informed us during our classes and research. We hope this book fairly reflects their major concerns and helps them in their important work.

Cover art: Nancy Doniger
Editor: Linda Sullivan
Production Editor: Julie Anderson Tober
Artist: Jane Lopez
Art Coordinator: Peter A. Robison
Photo Editor: Anne Vega
Text Designer: Jill E. Bonar
Cover Designer: Cathleen Norz
Production Buyer: Pamela D. Bennett
Electronic Text Management: Ben Ko, Marilyn Wilson Phelps

This book was set in ITC Century by Macmillan Publishing Company and was printed and bound by Arcata Graphics/Martinsburg. The cover was printed by New England Book Components.

All photos by Edward A. Wynne.

Macmillan Publishing Company
866 Third Avenue
New York, NY 10022

Macmillan Publishing Company is part of the
Maxwell Communication Group of Companies.

Maxwell Macmillan Canada, Inc.
1200 Eglinton Avenue East, Suite 200
Don Mills, Ontario M3C 3N1

Library of Congress Cataloging-in-Publication Data
Wynne, Edward.
   Reclaiming our schools: a handbook on teaching character,
academics, and discipline / Edward A. Wynne, Kevin Ryan.
     p. cm.
   Includes bibliographical references and index.
   ISBN 0-02-430755-0
   1. Moral education—United States. 2. Classroom management—
United States. I. Ryan, Kevin. II. Title.
LC311.W96 1993
370.11'4'0973—dc20   92-13342
                                                                CIP

Printing: 1 2 3 4 5 6 7 8 9   Year: 3 4 5 6

Foreword

by

James S. Coleman
President, American Sociological Association
1991–1992

The act of educating another is a moral act: Whatever part the concern with their own needs plays in the lives of educators, it shares its place with their concern for those they teach. Thus teaching is itself a part of the moral message transmitted by a teacher to a child. And the school is the social agency that organizes such transmission. That moral message may be strong and clear if the teacher is dedicated to the task of teaching, or distorted if the teacher has largely given up on that task.

But the moral message contained in the act of teaching is only part of the values teachers and schools transmit. Teachers and schools, like parents and families, cannot avoid teaching values. And as schools come to encompass an increasing part of most children's lives, the values transmitted by schools come to be a larger part of the cultural heritage that the younger generation receives from the older. Yet this teaching of schools often goes unnoticed, unintentional and unreflexive.

Sometimes, however, it is not. In recent years, the recognition that schools inevitably teach values has become widespread. As a result, attempts to teach values have arisen, along with controversies about what values are taught. Often the recognition and the controversy have led to a frightened drawing back, resulting in the teaching that "all values are equally meritorious," a form of moral relativism that undermines the very values inherent in the act of teaching. Sometimes it is teaching of values about what others do, or are doing wrong. This includes teaching about the wrongs that governments do, the wrongs that corporations do, the wrongs that others in authority do. What is taught most broadly is that those in authority or those in power do wrong. This is not all bad. One is never too young to learn the lesson of Lord Acton, that "Power corrupts; absolute power corrupts absolutely." But such values have a serious defect as an aspect of moral education. They provide no guides for one's own action; they are not values about what one should and should not do.

Edward Wynne and Kevin Ryan have responded differently. They are not reticent about what values are to be taught in schools by teachers. Nor do they advocate focusing on the wrongs that others do. They are concerned with each child's personal values, those that will guide the child's own actions. Their unhesitating answer is that it is traditional values that schools should teach. This book is designed to be an aid for those who agree with that answer.

They do not provide an explicit argument to persuade those who do not agree with them or who are uncertain about what values to transmit. Their argument is implicit in much of what they have written, but a few points may be added.

What is most striking about traditional values is their similarity from one culture to another. The values of respect for others, taking responsibility for one's own actions, helping others in need, keeping promises (and not making promises that one cannot keep), honesty, and putting forth one's best efforts are all widely shared among cultures, primitive and modern, on every continent. There is no imposition of these values by one cultural group on another; in every culture, there is an attempt by the adult generation to impose these values on the young.

Why the similarity? The answers, I believe, must lie in the fact of society itself, and the demands that the proper functioning of a society imposes on its members. Every society has its members whose actions do not uphold the traditional values stated in the preceding paragraph. But if the society were largely made up of members who were dishonest, did not keep promises, did not help others in need, and ignored the other traditional values, the society would hardly function well.

Thus it is not accidental that these traditional values are so similar in different cultures. These values are important to the functioning of a society. Yet this leads to the question: Why doesn't the "society of the school itself" (for the school is a small society, with its values, norms, taboos, and heroes) induce this socialization by the very demands it makes on its members? I believe the answer is that the school does so to some degree, but much less than it might if it were a different kind of society. The society of the school is a partial society, a dependent society, a society largely without common goals. A child does not live with the other children in a school, but spends only some hours each day there (and those hours with others of the same age). Therefore, it is easy for children to escape helping others in need, easy to escape the consequences of dishonesty and of breaking promises. The children and youth in school are under the supervision of a staff, like inmates of a prison. As a result, their values can become to be biased in the direction found in all dependent societies: collusion in cheating, norms against working hard, lack of responsibility for their actions. Because this society of the young has mostly the individualistic goals of individual achievement and few common goals (except interscholastic athletics), the values of helping one another, of contributing to a joint effort, and of respect for others have little means for encouragement.

The typical organizational deficiencies of a school prevent it from being a society in which the values that can sustain a society's functioning are learned in the very process of interaction. Yet if the school is to function well, and if its students are to be fit for the society they will inhabit as adults, these values must be transmitted. How this can come about in a school, how its teachers and principals can bring it about, is the focus of this book. I commend it to your attention.

Preface

This is a handbook for educators and other citizens interested in ways morals can be taught in schools and classrooms. It will show readers how to conduct such instruction and help them evolve a better understanding of what teaching morality really means. It will also propose and justify a practical definition of moral instruction. Even readers who disagree with elements of that definition should find many of the insights in the book useful.

By *morals*, we mean such long-honored educational concerns as teaching character, academics, and discipline. We will show the many moral ramifications of effective academic teaching and learning. In a sense, such concerns are the traditional emphases that have prevailed through thousands of years of education. And we are unabashed about using the word *traditional* in discussing moral education.

Morality is not a novel educational concern. Many good ideas about how to teach it have been around for a long time. Indeed, we are not reluctant to recommend education policies and practices that were successfully employed long before our country was founded, e.g., expecting students to work hard at learning. Obviously, not all things that happened in the past were good or desirable. However, it is equally likely that many novel educational practices are probably unsound. Unfortunately, contemporary education literature typically gives an extraordinary emphasis to what was allegedly invented yesterday. In such an intellectual environment, it is fair to say our perspective is much more sympathetic to tradition than that of many other authorities. Our sympathy is not unqualified. Still, this sympathy with the past is, at this time, a considerable innovation. It is probably the most notable intellectual contribution of this book.

Our cumulative research and teaching over 40 years assure us that many contemporary educators share our interests in traditional morality—including some who do not even realize the unique nature of their priorities. The handbook is first addressed to such educators. It will also engage academics who want to understand these themes more fully or inform their students about an important educational issue. The book's focus is essentially secular, or nonreligious. However, many educators in religious schools will find its materials useful. Finally, the handbook, with its essentially nontechnical language, can be useful to laypersons concerned with education.

We believe that too much educational writing during the past three or four decades has been pervaded with sentimentality. Readers accustomed to such sentimentality may find our analysis upsetting. However we do not propose to take sentiment out of education. Love, dedication, and caring will always be vital components of good teaching. We merely want to mix such sentiments with a moderate dose of prudence. This blending can be in the interest of both students and the commonweal.

As for prudence, we do not think that education regularly is, or should be, fun. Nor do we believe that everybody can become an A student. However, we do not imply that anyone's moral worth is dependent on attaining that difficult academic goal. Furthermore, we do not believe that 50 percent or more of our young people should aim to obtain a four-year college education. Indeed, there are undoubtedly even a number of young people who should not aim to complete an academic high school program, especially by proceeding straight through school. Many of such youth need alternative paths to maturity; America is currently making excessive demands on the adaptability of our schools.

Any book is built on the shoulders of those who have gone on before it. Certainly, this is the case for this handbook. We have freely borrowed from the works of scholars and writers from classical Greece to the present. Much of this work has been drawn from the views of our contemporaries, friends, students, and colleagues. All of these persons have been struggling with the problems of American schooling for many years. And, while we have borrowed from them, we must quickly add that we bear the total responsibility for how these ideas are interpreted and applied. While indebted to many, the blame is ours alone.

We also owe thanks to certain individuals who have read and reacted to various drafts of our manuscript. Specifically, we must acknowledge Thomas Masty, James Grandison, and Judith Wynne for their thoughts and reactions. Marilyn Ryan and Cathleen Kinsella Stutz labored over several drafts of the manuscript and gave us thoughtful and often penetrating criticism. We wish to thank the following academic reviewers for their careful criticism and praise of drafts of our manuscript: Jacques Benninga, California State University–Fresno; R. Lewis Hodge, The University of Tennessee–Knoxville; Mark Holmes, Ontario Institute for Studies in Education; and Robert C. Serow, North Carolina State University. Further, our editor, Linda Sullivan, has been a model of patience and support through this project. Finally, the authors want to acknowledge one another. Whatever the merits or defects of this book, the task of composition has been intellectually and personally satisfying. Surprisingly, we are better friends at the end of the project than we were at the start. It has been a labor of love.

—E. W.

K. R.

Brief Contents

About the Authors

For more than 20 years, Edward A. Wynne has been Professor at the College of Education, The University of Illinois at Chicago. He has published, coauthored, or edited 10 books and more than 100 articles and other writings. He has published in journals ranging from *Phi Delta Kappan, Educational Leadership*, and *Educational Evaluation and Policymaking*, to *The Wall Street Journal*. In addition to his many personal studies of individual public and private schools, his students, under his supervision and training, have conducted more than 300 school studies. He has also written and edited a number of writings dealing with character and founded two successive national periodicals, *Character* and *Character II*. He was also the principal organizer and editor of *Developing Character, Transmitting Knowledge*, a national statement on the issue of character and education. The statement was signed by 27 prominent Americans. His most recent book is *A Year in the Life of an Excellent Elementary School* (Technomics, 1992). He is probably the academic most prominently associated with the revival of intellectual interest in the topic of character as a goal of education.

Kevin Ryan is Professor of Education at Boston University, where he is also Director of the Center for the Advancement of Ethics and Character. A former high school English teacher, Ryan has been associated with higher education for nearly 30 years. He has taught on the faculties of Stanford University, the University of Chicago, Harvard University, the University of Lisbon, and The Ohio State University. Ryan has written or edited 15 books, including *Those Who Can, Teach* and *The Roller Coaster Year: Stories by and for First Year Teachers*, and over 80 articles. His primary academic foci are moral education and teacher education. Ryan has received awards from the University of Helsinki, the Association of Colleges for Teacher Education, the Association of Teacher Educators and, in 1990, he was the recipient of Boston University's Scholar Teacher Award.

Contents

Introduction

This handbook has evolved from the findings from our own research in public and private schools, from the numerous suggestions we have collected from educators, and from our interpretations of the extensive contemporary and antecedent literature and research.

Portions of this handbook will concern both elementary and secondary school educators. Other materials are suitable for particular grade levels. Some of these differences are noted in the text; in other instances, the level of emphasis is evident. Our discussion will say little or nothing about such volatile issues as sex education, AIDS education, or drug education. We are infinitely more concerned with the general prevalence of sound moral instruction in a school or classroom than with systems of problem-oriented instruction in schools that are otherwise moral vacuums. We believe moral schools will comfortably devise ways of handling immediate, topical moral issues. Conversely, schools without sound moral norms may well misapply the most wholesome problem-oriented instruction.

Our subject matter is sometimes controversial. However, the handbook does not aim to inspire grand intellectual conversions among readers.

Instead, its premises are more realistic. It assumes that the values underlying the conduct of most experienced educators, whether they are protradition or not, have already evolved. This assumption even applies to many teachers in training. Much of the moral formation of neophytes has already occurred through their parents, communities and schools, and the motives that caused them to select teaching as a career. As you proceed, we invite you to weigh the innumerable implicit practical questions posed throughout the text. Through such examination, you will be helped to examine yourself in an intellectual mirror. The examination can permit you to better see the connection between certain traditional values and many concrete, common school practices. There will be some readers of this book who are uncertain of the merits of traditional moral education in schools. Such objectors may discover that many school policies they essentially favor are really rooted in moral perspectives.

From such interpretations, you can learn to identify and apply more coherently your own values through this book's mix of analysis and concrete examples; your own personal introspection; and carrying out the exercises provided at the end of each chapter. An able principal once explained the importance of such coherence when asked, "What is the first thing you look for in hiring a teacher?"

He replied, "A well-thought-out philosophy of teaching. It is not crucial that I agree with the applicant's philosophy. However, it is important its different parts cohere—fit together in a predictable fashion. Without coherent personal philosophies, it is difficult for teachers to maintain classroom control. Their practices and expectations for students will be inconsistent and disrupt their classes."

THE SCHOOL ASSESSMENT CHECKLIST

Practicing educators prefer concise, focused professional literature. At the same time, educators concerned with transmitting traditional morals must sometimes engage in refined analysis. They must identify the connections between immediate acts and relatively remote effects. This book bridges these two contrasting themes. Its first section is a checklist focusing on observable acts and policies in and around schools. The form has undergone extensive development and field testing, allowing educators to immediately use the list to estimate the quality of their school's (or classroom's) focus on character, academics, and discipline. This estimation process also generates insights into how to improve their current school or classroom policies. In other words, groups or individuals can use the list, and the inventory it provides, as a stimulator. It can identify policies that must change to increase moral learning in schools and classrooms. Finally, the checklist can provide readers with a good idea of the perspectives underlying the critical concept of traditional values.

The checklist focuses on everyday, nontechnical school and classroom activities: flag salute practices; the amounts of homework regularly completed by pupils; the policies applied in publicizing written discipline codes. Most educators will recognize that such mundane activities are usually ignored in formal school evaluations. However, we believe—and will emphasize throughout this book—that such bread-and-butter topics are critical to sound moral instruction. From experience, we know many practicing educators share this viewpoint.

The checklist was developed to identify schools applying highly effective moral education practices, by a team of 15 practicing educators and three academics, all sympathetic to such concerns.[1] Over several years, it was used in about 300 schools. The educators and schools were public and private, urban and suburban, elementary and secondary schools in a large metropolitan area. They ranged from flagship suburban public high schools to schools in disordered, even dangerous, urban neighborhoods. The checklist has been revised periodically in response to many participants' suggestions.

We do not propose that a school is morally flawed if it fails to satisfy every item in the checklist. Such an approach would be simplistic. Innumerable local and historic factors may ensure that variations in policies prevail even among excellent schools. However, the list's items are not mere speculations. They represent carefully considered and field-tested principles. If notable variations exist between a school's policies and a number of the items, the educators involved owe it to themselves and their pupils to reconsider their policies. Perhaps they should even invite in qualified evaluators to help them engage in probing introspection.

Busy educators are properly concerned with knowing how much time an activity may require. In an elementary school, the checklist can be completed by an informed staff member in about an hour; three or four staff hours might be required for the careful examination of a larger high school. But even skimming the checklist can be instructive.

The checklist, in part, asks users to estimate the frequency of certain in-school activities relevant to moral education. Users will see that such questions imply value judgments about what acts are good or bad. Users will also note the list's emphasis on right conduct, or behavior, and on policies that stimulate correct conduct. Such an emphasis on conduct emphasizes a critical premise of traditional values: words and acts (or refraining from bad acts) are the essence of day-to-day virtue. Good or bad character—the word is derived from the Greek word for "marking"—is visible. It may be that, ultimately, each act of good conduct is inspired from within, founded on a person's internal state of mind. But, as a practical matter, educators must focus on pupils' acts or words; acts are the external measure of invisible internal states. A school or classroom devoid of virtuous acts is not transmitting traditional values, regardless of the refined thoughts that may be passing through pupils' minds.

To derive the benefits from the self-study, educators simply have to consistently ask themselves: Are we now doing as much as we can or should to emphasize the good activities the inventory focuses on? Users will inevitably ask if statistical norms are provided to identify high and low levels of frequency; in other words, what levels are desirable? The answer is that no such norms are available. It is true that our research has disclosed considerable variations among schools in their levels of frequency. Some schools and classrooms are doing better than others. Furthermore, these variations are due in part to deliberate policies adopted by schools. However, the variations are also affected by factors beyond the control of particular educators, e.g., school enrollment, differences among the communities served, age levels of pupils. These factors mean that an extraordinarily large research project would be necessary to collect and analyze enough data to generate broad statistical norms. Such resources have never been available to us. But the checklist can still be of considerable value.

After the checklist, the remainder of this book analyzes the intellectual themes underlying that instrument. The checklist is to the succeeding text as a collection of recipes is to an explication on the theory of cooking. Excellent cooks must know something of both cooking practice and theory. However, we have chosen to put the checklist first. Our experiences have convinced us that adult learners usually proceed from the particular to the general—from examining a list of items to considering its underlying theory.

An analysis is appropriate because our research, as well as the overall literature, shows that teachers and principals have made innumerable profitable adaptations of the list's themes. These adaptations have been related to local circumstances and challenges. For example, some items on the list emphasize the importance of rich communication among faculty and between faculty and administration to foster moral cohesion. This cohesion is important to produce wholesome effects on students. The moral importance (and morale) of such cohesion is later explicated in the analysis. Some educators, already recognizing the value of faculty cohesion, have worked to establish comfortable faculty rooms in their schools for staff socialization and relaxation. Yet the list says nothing about faculty social rooms—or about the hundreds of other adaptations that might be stimulated by considering the premises of the list. Adaptations are discussed only in the following analytical chapters. We encourage other educators to engage in similar imaginative innovations. But innovation, whether in cooking or education, should rest on a sound intellectual framework. Thus, our book examines the themes and traditions underlying the checklist. That analysis will provide educators with the stimulation and tools to assist the re-creation of moral education now underway in many American schools.

The text will also consider some other methods, bypassed in the checklist, of teaching character, academics, and discipline. For example, the checklist deliberately does not discuss using formal curriculum to teach traditional values and stimulate good conduct. It makes no reference to textbooks, readers, or literature. Despite this silence, there is a persisting recognition that curriculum materials are an important resource for teaching values. Again, there is the important matter of helping pupils to acquire the skills and empathy that often underline moral acts: to be helpful because they have learned to see things from the other person's perspective.

It is unsound to settle such subtle matters as curriculum content or the cultivation of empathy by a checklist. But these matters are essential to moral instruction and will be considered in the text.

To emphasize our concern with practical suggestions, each chapter contains a list of questions or proposals. These identify school or classroom issues consistent with the chapter's themes.

The Checklist

The items on the checklist relate to moral education in a variety of important direct and indirect ways. For some readers, the logic of many of these relationships will be speedily evident. Other readers will consider such relationships, even after the explication in the book, as uncertain or problematic. Still, for either type of reader, the list is a good introduction to the opportunities and challenges pervading moral education.

The authors of *Reclaiming Our Schools: A Handbook on Teaching Character, Academics, and Discipline*, Edward A. Wynne and Kevin Ryan, designed the checklist to be used in a variety of different schools, e.g., public or private, elementary or secondary. Readers are encouraged to photocopy the checklist and distribute copies to co-workers informally or at staff, department, or association meetings. Many of its queries are easily adaptable to individual classrooms. However, a few items on the list are only applicable to special categories of schools. Those items are so designated.

The list focuses on what actually happens, rather than what the school's formal policies prescribe. Some items on the inventory can only be answered by making sincere estimates. In some replies, input from teachers and even students can be helpful. Many perspectives can be applied in considering such questions.

I. Interaction Among Staff, Students, and Parents

The following items relate to the nature of the human environment of the school. "Staff members" includes all certified or certifiable personnel.

1. Estimate the average number of hours per year a typical staff member spends in scheduled meetings and conferences with parents, including report card time. _____

2. Estimate the average number of parent contacts (e.g., phone calls, face-to-face, via notes) per week for a typical staff member, apart from scheduled appointments. _____

3. Estimate the percentage of staff members who spend one or more hours per month in out-of-class contacts with students (clubs, chaperoning dances, going to sporting events, tutoring). _____

4. Estimate the number of hours per year a typical staff member spends in scheduled staff, committee, or department meetings conducted for all or part of the staff. _____

5. Estimate the number of hours per year a typical staff member spends informally with other faculty (lunch, parties, coffee break, car pool). _____

6. Does your school have a student council? (Circle)   Yes   No

7. Estimate the percentage of pupils (from all of the grade levels eligible for student council) who participate in student council during the year.   _____

8. Estimate the number of hours per year a typical council member spends on council activities.   _____

9. (For private elementary schools) Estimate what percentage of families provide the school with two or more hours per year of volunteer services.   _____

10. (For private elementary schools) Estimate the average number of hours of volunteer service, if any, rendered annually by the top 5% of volunteering families.   _____

11. Estimate the percentage of pupils who routinely help keep halls, playgrounds, and classrooms neat, without adult supervision.   _____

12. Estimate the number of multiclass school assemblies, ceremonies, or other activities (e.g., viewing athletic competitions) the average pupil attends in a typical month.   _____

13. (Private, church-related schools) Estimate the number of religious assemblies or other multiclass gatherings an average pupil will attend in a typical month.   _____

14. (Typically for elementary schools—also relevant for high schools) Estimate the percentage of pupils in classes who regularly recite the Pledge of Allegiance with the teacher and students standing, hands on hearts, with some degree of seriousness.   _____

15. (For middle, junior high, and high schools) Estimate the percentage of graduating pupils who have spent a considerable time as part of a relatively stable group, under the continuous, immediate direction of one or more adults (e.g., their whole four years as part of the same homeroom or athletic team).   _____

16. Does your school have a school song?   Yes   No

17. If yes, estimate the percentage of pupils who can sing the first verse of that song.   _____

18. Treating the school's annual budget as 100%, estimate, as a percentage of that sum, the value of gifts donated to the school by local persons (excluding parents) or business organizations.   _____

19. Treating this year's graduating class as 100%, estimate, as a percentage of that sum, the percentage of previous graduates who might stop by to responsibly visit the school this year.   _____

II. Character Formation

Good character, or citizenship, is much more than having right or profound ideas. It stresses doing "right" things—engaging in conduct immedi ately helpful to others. Such conduct is comprised of acts, such as being a math team member, serving as an aide or monitor, participating in sports as a good team member, cleaning up a classroom, tutoring others, helping in fund–raising, or providing entertainment for the school. The good citizen is not only an observer or critic, or even just a voter, but also someone who pitches in on a day-to-day basis to make the school or community work.

Proper student conduct is enhanced by a code of conduct that not only prohibits wrongdoing, but also encourages students to do things that immediately help others. Such behavior is fostered by clearly defined policies, in classrooms and throughout the school that (a) invite or require students to practice helping conduct; (b) stimulate praise and recognition for such conduct; (c) surround students with appropriate role models, either adults or students, who engage in such conduct; and (d) present a curriculum that sympathetically portrays real and fictional persons who have displayed helping conduct.

We can analyze a school's (or classroom's) systems for developing student character by counting how many students are involved in positive conduct, how long they stay engaged in such activities, the types of activities they conduct, the forms of recognition for such activities, and the frequency and elaboration of such recognition.

The following list identifies various activities conducted in many elementary and secondary schools. Estimate what percentage of pupils take part in these activities in a typical month in your school.

1. Academic team competitions in or among schools (e.g., math or spelling bees) _____

2. Band or choir _____

3. Cheerleading _____

4. Classroom or building (nondetentional) clean-up _____

5. Class monitors, messengers, hall guards, or office assistants _____

6. Crossing guards, patrol duty _____

7. Community service _____

8. Dramatic presentations (outside of regular classroom) _____

9. Fund-raising in school (e.g., bake sales) _____

10. Fund-raising out of school (e.g., walkathons, selling chances)

_____

11. Clubs or other extracurricular activities not specified elsewhere

_____

12. Interscholastic sports _____

13. Intramural sports _____

14. School newspaper _____

15. Providing deliberate academic help (e.g., peer tutoring) _____

16. Well-organized academic group projects (see discussion on cooperative learning in Chapter 7) _____

17. Library aides _____

18. Other _____

Listed below are types of recognition that may be awarded to individual pupils for positive conduct. Please estimate for each category the percentage of pupils who receive one or more such awards in a typical school year.

1. Athletic or sportsmanship awards _____

2. Certificates _____

3. Mention in school newspaper _____

4. Mention in newsletter or general publication to parents _____

5. Mention over P. A. _____

6. Mention on report card _____

7. Note home to parents _____

8. Pep rally _____

9. Posting name or photo _____

10. Gold star, sticker _____

11. Other _____

Recognition may also be given to *groups of pupils,* as successful teams, classes, clubs, etc. Estimate for each category the percentage of pupils who are members of one or more groups that attain such recognition in a typical school year.

1. Athletic or sportsmanship awards _____

2. Certificates _____

3. Mention in the school newspaper _____

4. Mention in newsletter or general publication to parents _____

6. Mention over P. A. _____

7. Mention on report card _____

8. Note home to parents _____

9. Pep rally _____

10. Posting name or photo _____

11. Special jackets or other garments _____

12. Other _____

III. Academics

The following items assume that academic learning depends on high standards and well-defined expectations of both students and staff, with both groups receiving appropriate support and supervision.

1. Does your school have a written policy of not advancing pupils who are regularly not performing at or above grade or class level? Yes No

2. Estimate how often wall–space coverings (charts, displays of pupil work, notices, materials on bulletin boards) are changed in a typical classroom. _____

3. Estimate the amount of homework per night a typical junior (in high school) or sixth- or seventh-grade pupil (elementary or junior high) would have to do away from the school premises. _____

4. If the average is one hour or more, what percentage of students regularly finish and submit their homework each day? _____

5. (For high school) Does the school have any programs that invite—or require—seniors to stay engaged with academic and other purposeful activities through the end of their final year?   Yes   No

6. Is there an honor roll for academic achievement that is conspicuously displayed, changed at least twice a year, and that lists between 5% and 25% of the pupils in the affected grades?   Yes   No

7. Estimate the number of times per year the principal or other administrator meets with a typical tenured teacher on a one-to-one basis, either formally or informally, to discuss teaching. _____

8. Estimate the number of times per year other professionals (teachers, administrators) enter the typical teacher's classroom while class is in session. _____

9. Are lesson plans for all teachers collected and reviewed on a routine basis with written comments occasionally sent back?   Yes   No

10. Is there a teacher's handbook that is thorough, has been revised within the past two years, and is distributed to all teachers?   Yes   No

11. Do teachers and administrators apply the handbook consistently in dealing with students and other staff?   Yes   No

12. Estimate the percentage of teachers strongly dedicated to stimulating students to attain their maximum potential. _____

IV. Discipline

Preventing pupil misbehavior is part of fostering pupil character development. Codes of conduct that prohibit foreseeable violations, are widely disseminated, and apply appropriate sanctions are important for preventing misconduct.

1. Does your school have a written code of conduct that clearly specifies desirable and undesirable conduct? Yes   No

2. Is there a procedure that ensures that copies of the code are annually put into the hands of at least 90% of the parents (e.g., parent signs a receipt)? Yes   No

3. Do some or all of the school's students ride school busses? Yes   No

   If Yes, is there a code explicitly covering bus conduct? Is it distributed as provided in questions 1 and 2? Yes   No

4. If your district has a districtwide conduct code, does your school also have a "local supplement," in writing and widely distributed, that deals with the problems and opportunities relevant to the school? Yes   No

5. Do prompt, simple consequences, which almost all pupils perceive as unpleasant, routinely result from moderate rule violations? Yes   No

6. Does the code specifically prohibit rudeness and abusive or foul language among students? Yes   No

7. (More appropriate for older pupils) Are cheating and plagiarism clearly defined in the code? Are clear consequences mandated? Yes   No

8. Does the code provide that violations of the criminal law (e.g., possessing drugs in school, bringing in weapons) will automatically be referred to the police? Yes   No

9. If a student is referred to the police, does the school regularly monitor the case and student to assist rehabilitation and ensure the case does not get lost? Yes   No

10. Estimate what percentage of pupils routinely observe the code almost all of the time. _____

11. (For middle, junior high, and high schools) Does the school regularly attempt some systematic assessment of illegal substance use by pupils (e.g., an anonymous survey)? Yes   No

12. Are there effective student organizations that directly promote responsible conduct (e.g., SADD)? Yes   No

RECLAIMING OUR SCHOOLS

A Handbook on Teaching Character,
Academics, and Discipline

CHAPTER 1

Educators and Teaching Values

Speaking of the testimony of early travelers to the good manners found in Ngoni households, a Ngoni elder said: "Such honoring of each other came to the Ngoni because they liked living together without any scattering as was the custom of other Malawi people . . . Such honor was not shown by young people for fear of being beaten, but because all children were well taught that this behavior was right and proper for the upbuilding of the land."

—Margaret Read, *Children of Their Fathers*[1]

This chapter will identify the primary audience for the book and explain why we have written it for them. We will present graphs and other research studies about trends in youth conduct to show why there is dissatisfaction with our moral education policies. We will then interpret these data to demonstrate their relationship to more traditional education approaches. Then we explain the philosophical implications of our analyses, as well as the relevance of formal religion to the practice of moral education. Finally, we will examine the feasibility of providing traditional moral instruction in secular public schools.

This book's primary audience is the numerous—we estimate hundreds of thousands—teachers and administrators who believe that

- ✦ transmitting character, academics, and discipline—essentially, "traditional" moral values—to pupils is a vital educational responsibility.
- ✦ some educational approaches to transmitting morality, such as values clarification or other consensual methods, underestimate the importance of parents and educators in establishing pupils' moral priorities. More effective means of moral education stress goals such as character formation and the importance of day-to-day good conduct in routine situations.
- ✦ schools should generally hold high academic expectations for pupils.
- ✦ maintaining good pupil discipline is a critical and sometimes difficult job, but it can and must be done.
- ✦ teachers must be in charge in their classrooms and provide pupils with positive role models.
- ✦ schools, like other complex institutions, must be led by principals, i.e., managers. These leaders should listen to and consult with teachers and cooperate with parents but must finally make and monitor the key decisions within the institution themselves.
- ✦ students have specific responsibilities that are integral to their education and the effective functioning of the school.
- ✦ all pupils deserve a 100% effort from their teachers. But schools, especially as pupils grow older, are not responsible for attaining 100% success. Insistence on such perfection undermines the coherence of many

education programs. Pupils, as they mature, must assume increasing responsibility for their own accomplishments or deficiencies.

+ many of the "softening-up" changes in education fostered in the recent past have not been helpful for most pupils.

These principles are not novel. In some ways, they represent education themes going as far back as Plato and Aristotle. And, in our own era, they are congruent with many of the demands made on education by protradition reformers. The reformers include academics such as E. J. Hirsch, Diane Ravitch, and Allan Bloom; present and former state and federal officeholders such as Bill Honig, Lamar Alexander, Thomas Kean, and William J. Bennett; and practicing educators such as Jaime Escalante. Despite such congruence, a distressing tension has developed between many reformers and most practicing educators—school teachers and school administrators.

THE TENSION

A special irony colors this tension between educators and reformers. In fact, the two groups have more congruence than meets the eye. The authors, as researchers and teachers of educators, have worked with hundreds of practicing and potential teachers and administrators. Our experience convinces us that a great many educators strongly sympathize with the principles urged by the previously mentioned critics. (We did not say "all" or "almost all," but "a great many.") The first paragraph in this chapter echoes some of their criticisms. For instance, all of the critics have emphasized holding high academic expectations for pupils; educators should assume that most pupils are capable of performing better and working harder than their current levels.

The causes of the problems identified by the critics extend far beyond policies developed and applied by educators. Thoughtful authorities have noted many contributing factors: shifts in popular values; the role of the mass media; the increase in comparative affluence among the young; the growth of single-parent (and two-working-parent) families; and the decline in vigor of many extended families. Still, many educators can do more to moderate the effects of such problems than they are now doing. This book identifies constructive things educators can do and acknowledges the right things some of them are already doing.

Proposals for educational reform have come from a myriad of directions. And many such demands, even some of the responses we propose, cannot be classified along a right/left political continuum. For example, the checklist mentioned the importance of keeping pupils in relatively stable, coherent, adult-monitored groups through high school. This stress on cohesion among high school pupils has been found among protradition groups (favoring smaller, family-based schools), and more liberal reformers, such as Theodore Sizer. But, to our mind, the protradition criticisms generally represent the most coherent and relevant body of reform proposals. Unfortunately, many antitradition academics and educators, to their detriment, have failed to engage seriously such proposals and their underlying premises. Many academics and "education leaders" are too removed from the realities of the typical school and classroom. As a result, they are intellectually trapped in a Rousseauian perspective, and its naive vision of the innocence of childhood and the natural joys of learning. The harmful effects of such misperceptions are notorious. New teachers holding the same visions are regularly subjected to profound culture shock as they enter their first classrooms. The shock is largely due to the neophytes' dysfunctional romantic views. Those views on the incorruptibility of nature and people have been reinforced by their academic training.

True, many educators who value character, academics, and discipline do not actually see themselves as traditionalists. But in practice, they strongly support traditional values and try to apply such values in their work. Furthermore, we have studied policies applied in many successful public and private schools and classrooms. To a large degree, these schools and classrooms are managed on quite traditional principles—to the benefit of pupils and teachers. And in other schools and classrooms, many educators try, with varying competence and success, to apply such principles.

In sum, protradition reformers have many potential allies among practicing educators. However, communication between these two groups has been poor. And too many reformers, on both the pro- and antitradition sides, have displayed more arrogance than appreciation towards the real constraints affecting practicing educators. As a result, too many educators tend to reflexively withdraw from anything with labels like "traditional." It is almost as if only new (and inadequately tested?) ideas and approaches deserve defense. Other educators feel that protradition reformers have made educators into scapegoats for deficiencies not of their making. A considerable antipathy has developed between the two camps.

Bridging the Gap

We are trying to bridge the gap created by this antipathy. Our book also may be informative to many noneducators concerned with education reform. But our first audience is educators.

The distressing reality is that many protradition reformers, like adept agitators, have allowed their contentions to generate considerable polarization. In addition, those reformers, despite their vision and courage, have an imperfect knowledge of the typical patterns in elementary and secondary schools. They lack what the anthropologist Clifford Geertz called a fine-grained approach to the complexities of schools.

Furthermore, many reformers lack an appreciation of education history. Conversely, all mature teachers have had considerable experience with successive waves of widely touted—and relatively transitory—reforms. This knowledge has caused practicing educators to approach many reform proposals with suspicion. The teachers feel they will be left to pick up the pieces when the promoters of some expiring innovation skip off to sell another fad. Such experiences have engendered deep cynicism among many educators.

Finally, some reformers have made unrealistic proposals. We hear reiterated demands about what every child *should* know. What such reformers must mean, if they have ever taught a typical group of pupils for any length of time, is "here is what we would *like* every child to know." Unfortunately, the word *should* is interpreted to mean that practicing educators are at fault if only—let's say—87% of all pupils learn the recommended knowledge. Many reformers have also spoken strongly about students' "right" to an education, their right to be taught this and that, and their right to be treated as responsible individuals. Finally, many political leaders make proposals about the "right" of all students "to attain certain competencies." Where such rights come from, what are the "rights" of such students' teachers, and what responsibilities are attendant on being students are too often washed away by a warm bath of rhetoric.

Teachers understandably object to the idea they must attain a 100% success rate. They especially resent it when such proposals come from college professors who teach carefully screened students, often in elective upper-level or graduate classes. (Or from businessmen, who *choose* whom they employ or keep employed.) And no one dares inform college professors they must attain a 100% passing rate for *their* pupils! Sometimes, educators, too, are told, "Well, the Japanese are able to do this or that." Some Japanese practices *are* ingenious and adaptable in the U.S. But it is one thing to adopt particular practices. It is another to expect American schools to be able to apply an integrated body of norms embedded in a 2,000-year-old insular culture.

In this book, we aim to

- ✦ show many educators how their present concerns and even practices are congruent with the proposals of many reformers.

- ✦ help readers appreciate the profound and ancient roots of such proposals (the proposals are essentially not adaptations of yesterday's fad, but of thousands of years of experience).

- ✦ explain why certain proposed reforms need refinement in the light of school realities and identify ways certain proposed reforms are discordant with vital moral principles.

- ✦ identify a variety of measures, many now applied by educators, that can help schools improve pupil character, academic learning, and discipline.

A Shopping Mall Story

Arthur Powell and his fellow researchers coined the vivid term *shopping mall high school*.[2] The term characterizes high schools with strong patterns of work avoidance by many pupils and teachers. The lack of diligence in schools has emerged as a key complaint of the reform movement. The researchers concluded that such shopping mall schools are relatively common in our era. In these schools, *some* pupils and faculty work hard at constructive learning. Yet many pupils and faculty, as far as education is concerned, only go through the motions. Students and teachers essentially make and carry out mutual pacts to avoid creating trouble for each other. The pupils avoid conspicuous breaches of discipline and don't make trouble for the teachers, and the teachers do not hassle pupils with demanding assignments. The system of elective course selection facilitates the whole pattern. Such systems license disengaged pupils to take gut courses. The courses are often taught by teachers who do not take things too seriously. At the same time, some engaged pupils and their teachers are working diligently in the demanding electives or academic programs they have chosen.

As we will emphasize, many of the problems confronting educators are as much philosophical as tangible. One typical story about a shopping mall high school illustrates common patterns of philosophical confusion.

Several high school teachers complained to one of the authors about their school's lax enforcement of a tardiness policy. Some students did not promptly enter their classrooms immediately after class change. Instead, they hung out in the halls, talking and disturbing other classes and students and obviously wasting their own time.

The teachers said, "We believe the principal should more vigorously suppress such hanging around. The students should be identified, reprimanded and, if necessary, punished."

The author replied, "What about the teachers whose classes these pupils are going to? Shouldn't they identify their own tardy students and punish them?"

The teachers answered, "Well, part of the trouble is that some teachers themselves are regularly late for class. It is their students who most frequently hang out, since their teachers are not in their rooms."

The author remarked, "It seems the problem is more tardy teachers, rather than tardy students. If the principal would simply pressure the teachers to be on time, that would do more good than harassing the students."

The teachers mumbled something. Then they dropped the matter.

The teachers were willing to try to mobilize the principal against the unruly students. However, they were unwilling to complain about their equally erring colleagues. That would be impolitic. So things were left as the principal's "fault" or the pupils' "fault."

Of course, the situation just portrayed could occur at work sites other than a public school. Norms among many workers discourage them from complaining to the boss about their colleagues' lack of diligence. But we are often told teachers want to be seen as professionals, and such "ain't it awful" perspectives erode teachers' professionalism and responsibility. Unfortunately, the story is typical of the philosophic contradictions that too often pervade education.

The pupils who hung out in the halls were breaching the norms of this shopping mall high school. It was acceptable for students in some teachers' classes to kill time. It was also all right for teachers to be frequently late for class. But, according to the tacit school code, students should not kill time so as to disturb others, and the late-to-class teachers had erred in letting their students drift into the hall. However, it was not proper for teachers to complain about one another's tardiness. While they would have liked to see themselves as dedicated professionals, they felt no responsibility for monitoring their peers. It was the principal's job to correct such defects.

Due to the general laxity in the school, the complaining teachers did not have to work extremely hard. But they were frustrated with their situation. They were not pleased to see pupils hanging out in the hall, not just because it disturbed their own classes, but also because it symbolized the triviality of many pupils' school experiences. While the general lassitude in the school excused much teacher malingering, it also undermined the work of many other teachers.

The patterns of toleration (or permissiveness) that have evolved in many schools are too often taken as the way things "should be," or "must be," unchangeable, immutable. At the same time, the patterns make many teachers defensive. They do not feel they receive (or deserve?) respect. Further, much of their time is spent dealing with breaches of school conventions—such as pupils hanging out in the halls—that leave them embarrassed. In their hearts, they know what should be done in many situations, similar to the teachers who really knew the first blame was on the late teachers. But too many tacit compromises have been made to allow a clear attack on the issues. And so faculty muddle on, complain about peripheral questions, feel a degree of shared complicity, and grumble about burnout.

Such Dismal Images Do Not Represent the Only Reality

Fortunately, shopping mall patterns are not inevitable in high schools. We have also observed many vital public schools that have escaped or corrected this disarray. These schools apply policies that stress character, academics, and discipline. The rest of this book will describe and interpret such policies and identify some of the barriers to their implementation. It is our consistent impression that faculty in vital schools are more diligent than educators in more lax schools. But such diligence is tied to purposive patterns of accomplishment. The educators' "work" is not routinely undermined by "trivial" discipline problems, such as pupils not being monitored by their assigned teachers. Instead, the teachers' work is typically related to the predictable challenge of providing demanding teaching to reasonably engaged pupils. Such diligence is often associated with understandable teacher (and pupil and parent) pride and sense of accomplishment.

Teachers in these schools also feel they work in highly supportive environments, instead of being largely on their own. Their colleagues and supervisors provide them with advice, encouragement, and constructive criticism. People work together to plan and put into effect sensible, coordinated schoolwide policies.

In a sense, protradition schools are high-demand/high-payoff environments—for faculties, pupils, and their families. All involved find more asked of them, and they similarly receive more from the others. Conversely, more permissive environments—like shopping malls—do not make such high demands of their "inhabitants." However, their inhabitants often feel more alone and unsupported, due to the very "freedom" from intrusion and coherence their school practices.

The matter of diligence also requires some consideration. This concept has strong moral overtones. It relates to the obligations human beings owe to certain other persons. It connotes trying *hard*, striving to attain a legitimate goal. Teachers are obligated to parents, pupils, and taxpayers to teach diligently. Pupils owe it to themselves, their families, and the taxpayers to work hard at school. Parents should diligently encourage their children to learn and be responsible. In sum, whenever people display nondiligence, it is likely they are simultaneously violating an obligation to others. They are betraying a moral duty.

TRENDS IN YOUTH CONDUCT

All serious discussions about school reform should begin by confronting a body of facts. As Abraham Lincoln said in his House Divided speech, "If we could better know where we have been, and wither we are tending, we could better see how to confront our challenges."

As we will see, a variety of measures shows there has been a substantial, long-term decline in the conduct of young Americans. These shifts in conduct have not been especially related to school attendance or in-school incidents. Instead, the measured acts of misconduct are more general, e.g., increased rates of death due to suicide and homicide. True, there is no explicit tie between these data and school policies. However, it seems reasonable to believe that the widespread and remarkable trends we will examine inevitably affect pupils' in-school conduct and are probably partly due to deficient school policies. After all, the school is the main public institution that absorbs the away-from-home time of these increasingly distressed young people.

As one example of such patterns, consider Figure 1, which portrays changes in the rates of youth homicide, suicide, and out-of-wedlock births for the races designated, up to the most recent year now available.[3] These phenomena are counted by tabulating official documents, i.e., birth certificates and medical determinations of causes of death. The graph displays *rates*. That term means statistical allowances have been made for shifts in the size of the youth population. The years covered by the graph present all of the national data now available. In general, the data presented focus on whites. They represent our most advantaged ethnic group, which would be less affected by the pressures of discrimination and poverty.

Since 1940, out-of-wedlock births for white females ages 15-19 increased 650%. From the "low" year of 1944 to 1988, the suicide rate for white males ages 15-24 increased 277%. From the "low" year of 1951, the equivalent homicide rate increased 219%. Other data indicate that most youth homicides are committed by members of the same age group, sex, and race as the victim. In other words, young Americans have become more prone to kill one another, and (realistically speaking) to act in ways that trigger aggressive responses from their peers.

The data about out-of-wedlock births are especially striking. Strangely enough, during the years of the increase, there have been many innovations in the areas of contraception, sex education, and the availability of abortion. Assume that, in 1950, you were told that such innovations lay ahead and were asked to forecast trends in out-of-wedlock births. Presumably, you would have forecast a decline in the rate. As we see, such a forecast would have been wrong.

Another important source of data are long-term trends in rates of arrest on criminal charges. These are portrayed in Figure 2.[4] The figure shows that, for

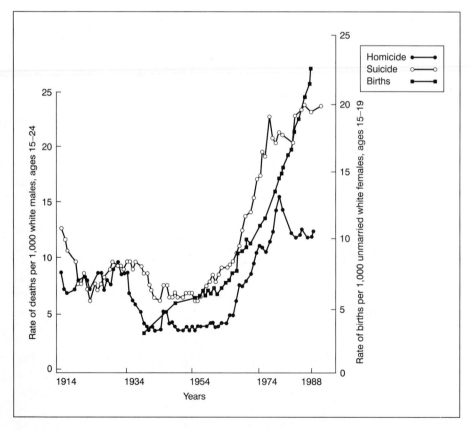

Figure 1
Changes in the National Rates of Youth Homicide, Suicide, and Out-of-wedlock Births

the years covered, 1950–1988, the rates of arrest of youngest age groups increased fastest of all.

All of these distressing figures are at or near the highest points since national record keeping began, and probably at the highest points in U.S. history since 1607.

Another trend we should keep in mind is youth drug use. To identify such trends, since 1975 the University of Michigan Center for Social Research has conducted annual, anonymous surveys of a national sample of each year's graduating high school class. The respondents were asked whether, and how frequently, they used specified illegal substances. The surveys disclose that the peak point of such usage was in 1981 and 1982. At that time, 65% of the respondents said they had used marijuana at least once in their lives, and 45% also had used another illegal drug (e.g., LSD, cocaine, amphetamines). Smaller numbers of respondents used such drugs monthly or daily.

Since 1980–81, youth drug use trends have fortunately moved in a more favorable direction. The center's report for the class of 1990 revealed that marijuana use had gone down to 47%, and the use of other drugs was at 29%. Still, most authorities would agree that contemporary levels of youth drug use are far higher than they were in about 1970. We still have far to go before we reattain the levels prevailing before the youth drug epidemic.

Public perceptions about the spread of youth disorder are congruent with all of these distressing data. The public has routinely rated "pupil discipline" as the major problem facing education in the annual Gallup polls on education.

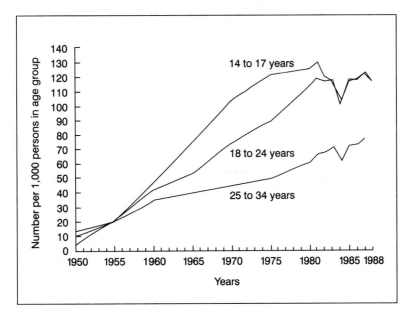

Figure 2
Number of arrests per 1,000 persons, by age: 1950 to 1988

And, if the national data show persisting high levels of all forms of youth delinquency, it is understandable why the public sees schools as troubled with indiscipline.

Despite frequent public complaints about pupil discipline, it is true that some educators regard these concerns as exaggerated. From our own research, we recognize that few schools are affected with conspicuous, gross disorder. It is equally our impression that many schools and teachers tolerate mild, persisting disruptions that would have been prohibited in most earlier eras. The differences in educator/citizen perception may also represent an instance of the phenomenon of denial—the rejection of information disruptive to one's comfortable expectations.

The U.S. Department of Education conducted a series of surveys in 1985–1987. One survey of school administrators found that 65% believed pupil discipline in high schools had improved in the past five years. Unfortunately, a similar survey of teachers actually working in classrooms found that only 34% of them believed there had been improvement. Furthermore, there were also equivalent administrator/teacher differences about the decay in discipline over those same five years: three times as many teachers (37%) as administrators (12%) thought things had actually gotten worse. The question is, Who is correct, the pessimistic teachers in their classrooms or the optimistic administrators (often away in their offices)?

But there is other evidence, even more striking, of the prevalence of denial. A 1988 national survey examined teachers' and pupils' perceptions about in-school discipline.[5] The students reported far more discipline incidents than did their teachers; 16.6% of all students said "physical conflicts among students" were a "serious" problem. The comparable figure for the teachers was 7%. While 15% of the students also saw student drug and alcohol use as a serious school problem, the equivalent figure for the teachers was 7%. From the differences in administrator/teacher perspective already reported, one might also speculate the administrators would have found even fewer disorder problems than the teachers.

Students See the Reality

We believe that students' estimates about disorder are more accurate than the teachers' and administrators'. The students are much closer to the acts of indiscipline and have no particular reasons for exaggerating the problems. Unfortunately, the further the adults are from such matters, the greater the likelihood they will minimize the problems.

This denial makes the administrators' and teachers' lives easier. Many acts of indiscipline—pupils sitting bombed in class or tense about being pushed around after school—do not directly impinge on the adults' lives. Furthermore, assume administrators *do* make an issue of improving discipline. They will need to initiate new policies. For example, assume they initiate a policy of expelling students 16 or older who use schools as places to hang out away from the cold. Inevitably, the changed policies would attract public attention. As a result, there would be community concern about safety and order in schools. This could lead to bad publicity. Furthermore, some community groups might object to such get-tough policies. The contradictory messages about discipline that pervade our society—"get tough, but don't hurt anybody's feelings"—undoubtedly provoke many administrators to try and bury discipline problems. So denial—and the victimization of many young people—goes on.

Disturbing changes in youth conduct have been accompanied by concurrent declines in measured pupil learning. There have been long-term declines in the pupil scores on standardized tests, such as the Scholastic Aptitude Test. From 1955 to 1982, the annual average SAT verbal score declined from 479 to 425. Since 1982, annual test scores have stopped declining, but remain at or near the all-time low in that year. It is true that various technical criticisms have been made about the representativeness of such test data. But researchers serving the Congressional Budget Office have examined not only the SAT, but also a mass of test-score data from different states and school systems.[6] These researchers have concluded that the decline in precollege test scores approximately parallels a similar decline in a variety of test scores. In other words, measured pupil learning in America has declined wherever consistent systems of testing have been applied. And, in view of the youth disorder that has been occurring, these shifts are not surprising. It is true, however, that no existing research shows a clear and definitive relationship between disorder and the learning declines.

Definitive findings would be hard to derive. The methodological problems involved are extraordinary. Still, there is a commonsense assumption that *can* be justified: young people who are more prone than in the past to violate the law, commit suicide, abuse drugs, and indulge in sexual exploration are also likely to do poorly in schoolwork. Furthermore, the prevalence of indiscipline in American schools—despite the equanimity of administrators—must have harmful effects on teacher conduct and pupil learning. When the American researcher Benjamin Bloom visited classrooms in America and Japan, he was impressed with how little energy Japanese teachers had to put into maintaining pupil order. He concluded that, if Japanese classrooms were given a score of 20 (out of 100) regarding teacher time spent keeping order, the average American classroom would rate an 80.[7] Presumably, the ease of maintaining order among Japanese pupils is one reason for their schools' educational excellence.

What the Changes Mean

No one knows definitively why these many unfortunate changes in conduct and learning have occurred in our young. Few thoughtful people suggest it is solely the fault of shifting school policies. There is more general agreement that a vast number of economic and social changes have occurred over many years.

In different ways, these changes have helped generate disorder in schools. Exactly how much weight should be attributed to each influence is highly problematic. How much of the change is due to television? the increased stress confronting two-parent families? the spread of the one-parent family? the general increase of affluence? a variety of shifts in popular values? The list goes on.

Some striking cross-cultural research, summarized by Daniel Goleman, provides a backdrop to such speculations.[8] The research shows that, by a variety of measures, typical contemporary Americans place a higher value on individual fulfillment and personal equality than citizens of any other nation. In one study, Americans working together on group projects were asked to estimate their contribution (in percentages) to their project. When the figures are summed up, they typically total more than 100%. In other words, Americans believe they do more than their share. And, in the U.S., when people feel they are doing more than others, we know the typical response—a sense of exploitation. Conversely, in other societies, the study found, team members underestimate their individual contributions. The sum of estimates is usually less than 100%. Presumably, these respondents do not believe they are doing enough for the group. Again, in many countries, especially traditional societies, studies show that citizens attribute special talents to their leaders, even if they are democratically elected. Conversely, American citizens typically believe they know as much as their leaders. A contrary position would be "elitist," currently a pejorative word.

The research demonstrated that individualistic attitudes were more typical of industrial societies, rather than traditional cultures. Still, Americans consistently displayed the highest levels of such attitudes. The research did not clearly show long-term trends, i.e., whether contemporary Americans are more individualistic than Americans 25 or 50 years ago. But there are undoubtedly popular impressions to that effect.

The research did not study the relationship between these findings and topics such as youth unrest. Still, it is not hard to identify a hypothetical connection between the two phenomena. It is easy to imagine that young people who believe they are as competent as anyone else (objective evidence to the contrary!), or who believe they usually contribute more than their share to joint enterprises, may begin to feel put upon, angry, and impatient with the ordinary circumstances of life. Furthermore, everyday experience demonstrates that, in many situations, there are people with greater ability than their evident peers or subordinates. These people are often designated as experts, leaders, bosses, supervisors, or teachers and principals. Finally, adults who share with the young opinions about their own "exploited" status are likely to prefer immediate over delayed gratification. They will not provide the young with purposeful care or wholesome role models.

Some considerations about the nature of American individualism are analyzed in a pamphlet prepared for foreign students visiting the U.S.[9] The pamphlet made the following remarks about friendship among young Americans:

Historically, many Americans have not been able to enjoy the continuity of long friendships because they have not lived in one community long enough. This mobility is thought to contribute to the open, outwardly friendly style with which Americans meet people. It may also encourage the making of friends quickly, rather than developing complicated relationships with various obligations. . .

In contrast, in many cultures, a family remains in the same city for generations, friendships between families have long histories, and children go to school with the same group of young people throughout primary and secondary school. Circles of friends are stable and provide an important source for the next generation's friends who have strong ties and obligations to each other throughout life.

It is easy to identify the connection between the relatively fragile friendships of many American pupils and the egocentric patterns described by Goleman. "Complicated relationships" are inconsistent with egocentricity. Such relationships require participants to accept frequent imbalances in obligations and to tolerate external, hierarchal structures that define family and community ties. Unfortunately, the policies in many contemporary American school environments, as we will demonstrate later, place many pupils in structures fostering transitory relationships. It is not surprising that adults raised by such a process learn the distressing attitudes portrayed by Goleman.

One Hopeful Sign

There are some signs a cycle of improvement in American education may be under way. In the recent past, many of the measures of disorder and declining learning have slightly moderated.[10] For instance, in 1982, as Figure 2 shows, the rate of youth arrests stopped increasing and later notably declined. In 1981, the SAT scores (and other academic indicators) stopped declining. And, starting in 1983, the levels of reported youth drug use began to decline.

Since these "turnaround" dates, the various measures have followed irregular patterns. Some measures, like rates of out-of-wedlock births, have never stopped increasing. Some, like youth arrests and suicide and homicide, briefly improved and then started going up again. Others, like the SAT scores, moderately improved but then began to decline: the mean SAT verbal score in 1991 was 422, while the previous record low was 424 in 1981, and the high was 476 in 1951. In effect, we have possibly only moderated a 20- to 30-year pattern. We hope pressures towards disorder have moderated. Unfortunately, it is not clear if and when we are returning to the more wholesome conduct patterns of the past.

These data do not augur well for the emotional health or character of the young adults we are now rearing.

Our interpretation of these shifts in test scores and measures of conduct is as follows. During the past 10 to 15 years, the American public has gradually developed more sympathy with traditional values. Perhaps the very spread of youth disorder has been one reason for this shift. Much of the public and many educators concluded that, in practice, the application of relatively permissive values produced bad effects.

This shift has been evident in a number of ways:

- ✦ Many political candidates who are more protradition on social issues than previous officeholders have been elected to office. Some of the candidates have emphasized concepts such as diligence and discipline in education.

- ✦ Demands on public education have changed. For example, criticisms have been made of social promotions, lax discipline, and value-free education.

- ✦ The judges elected or appointed to our courts are more protradition than their predecessors. As a result, courts have reversed or moderated some decisions (made 10 to 20 years ago) hostile to traditional educational practices.

- ✦ Laws passed and proposed in various jurisdictions have placed greater emphasis on prohibitions and punishments of different forms of misconduct.

These changes, most of which have been in protradition directions, have had some effect on the environments around many young Americans. They have even caused some shifts in school policies. On the whole, the changes have been beneficial to the young. Because of them, we have seen some improvements in youth conduct and learning, as reflected in some improved measures. Unfortunately, the shifts in values and policies have not completely remedied the situation. The causes of youth disorder are numerous and deeply embedded in our society. Uplifting speeches and dramatic (and sometimes superficial) reforms can be constructive. However, more deliberate and persisting improvement is still required.

The modest but real improvements in youth conduct that have occurred provide us with precious clues about what to do next. One can interpret such clues in different ways. Such differences are important. They have practical effects.

The evidence shows that better education policies should emphasize the goals of improving pupil character, academics, and discipline. Conversely, the long-term decline in youth conduct, which has recently shown some improvement, offers a telling caution. That decline was associated with innumerable attempts to relax the demands for order in youth environments by

- ✦ lessening the requirements on the young for academic diligence
- ✦ inviting students to make more choices among elective courses
- ✦ shifting the focus in literature studied to materials stressing the antihero and the absurd

✦ presenting history materials that emphasize revisionism—wrong things our predecessors did—and imply that all events are determined by power and self-interest

✦ making literature and social studies more morally relativistic

✦ making schools and classrooms more "democratic," which means more authority for pupils and less for teachers

✦ deemphasizing the importance of character as a goal of education

✦ encouraging teachers to recruit pupils into various problematic value systems, e.g., making one's own decisions about sex and drugs

✦ lessening the emphasis on traditional patriotism

✦ restricting the application of discipline

✦ tempering the influence of the criminal law

✦ applying measures popularly characterized as "permissive"

True, no one can demonstrate a cause-and-effect connection between such shifts and the increased youth disorder. Still, it is remarkable to see that disorder has moderated, just as permissive measures have declined in popularity. All of this is rich food for thought.

THE RELEVANCE OF PHILOSOPHY

Many current education-reform proposals are fraught with controversy. An important intellectual principle underlies many of the controversies: the rights and wrongs of the proposals cannot be clearly settled by some body of facts or research. Facts are not irrelevant. For instance, the data about youth disorder and test-score decline provide an important foundation for any discussion about school policies. But, once the data are recognized, one is still left to derive practical principles from them. And that is not simple. The problem is that many of the basic issues are essentially philosophical, not pragmatic. Let us consider an example of such philosophical roots.

Suppose one contends that a reason for the disorder was a softening of school policies; schools became too permissive. Assume one also contends that a reason for the moderate improvement was a concomitant tightening-up. Then, suppose one went to great length to identify and measure instances of such permissiveness and tightening-up. We can even imagine that, during the period of tightening-up, measured levels of youth conduct and learning improved. That pattern of events would still not prove tightening-up was generally better for pupils than permissiveness. After all, perhaps the improvements were due to other forces than the tightening-up. Indeed, maybe pupil conduct and learning would have improved even more if the tightening-up had not occurred. Someone might contend that, but for the tightening-up, the rate of improvement would have been greater.

Furthermore, assume we could prove that tightening-up caused the improvement. In other words, we can only now show that tightening-up and improvement apparently happened at the same time. But that is only correlation. That could be due to coincidence. But suppose we show that the tightening-up made certain things get better—that it was a cause of good things happening. Even that would not necessarily settle matters. Someone then might say that the long-term repressive effects of tightening-up would eventually become generally deleterious. The democratic quality of our way of life might be undermined. In five or 10 years, we might see those bad effects.

Finally, despite any improvement caused by tightening-up, some pupils would still be doing poorly. Indeed, perhaps some pupils—who had previously done satisfactorily—would find themselves doing worse during the tightening-up. In other words, the tightening-up generally raised average performance, but some pupils' performances (among the thousands of pupils who benefited) actually declined. Perhaps the costs of some new policy to a particular group of pupils is so high that it is not worth its benefits for most pupils. Weighing such conflicting and unmeasurable alternatives is the province of philosophy.

To Be Concrete

All of this may sound hypothetical. But the underlying issues are critical to school and classroom management. Imagine a relatively rigorous academic high school, where teachers are distressed about high levels of pupil cheating. This is a problem in many high schools. Some adults might propose the school should develop a detailed list of cheating infractions. That list would identify and define the kinds of cheating the faculty believes are practiced by some students. It might cover matters such as plagiarism, letting other students observe one's exam, passing notes around during exams, and a variety of other acts. The list would be publicized to pupils, and significant consequences could also be announced. Some schools now do apply such a formal practice.

It is certain that some adults will say that such an approach is a bad idea, since it will

+ remind some students of ideas for cheating they had not yet considered
+ serve as a challenge and provoke aggravating adolescent bravado
+ overemphasize distrust of the pupils by adults

Such objections are similar in spirit to many of the complexities we have recited in the preceding hypothetical analysis. For example, it might be possible by sophisticated and relatively costly research to prove rates of pupil cheating declined after the promulgation of the prohibition and consequences. Even then, suppose the punished pupils include disproportionate numbers of males, children from poor families, or other identifiable groups. Then the policy, though it inhibits cheating, may still be labelled discriminatory. Some accused cheaters (who really are innocent) may be mistakenly punished. Some cheaters will not get caught, and learn contempt for rules.

The preceding discussion may seem strained. However, it is not irrelevant that a small proportion of high schools promulgate well-organized and comprehensive rules against cheating. Furthermore, our own college pupils regularly report that cheating was widespread—and the prohibitions weak or poorly enforced—during their high school experience.

The nub of the matter is simple. A major component of one's evaluation of an anticheating rule is one's basic philosophic disposition. How important is it that high school-age pupils be held individually accountable, regardless of family circumstances or ethnic factors; faced with significant consequences if they fail to observe published rules; and allotted grades that are serious measures of personal learning?

The themes underlying the topic of cheating also affect many other important school practices such as amounts of homework assigned; policies regarding pupil tracking (or class assignment), promotion, enrollment, examinations, and testing; the place of honor rolls and other forms of pupil recognition in school life; a variety of discipline issues; and many other matters. In all such areas, when difficulties arise, important questions of fact must be considered. What are the ages of the pupils involved? What are the school's previous practices? What parent responses to any changed policies are likely? Still, in the end, issues of personal philosophy—and even wisdom—are important elements of any sound policy decision.

Learning About Philosophy

Eminent philosophers have often focused on education: Plato, Aristotle, John Locke, Confucius, Buddha, John Dewey, and others. These thinkers have articulated educational insights of enduring value. Generally, until quite recently, the major philosophers concerned with education have stressed the critical role of moral education. They were nearly unanimous in assuming that adults, as either teachers or parents, should bear the central authority and responsibility for shaping youth character. They also emphasized that such activities should be carried out with love and diligence. Plato, through his whole adult life, expressed his gratitude for the attention he received from Socrates, his mentor. But there was little or no sympathy for teachers surrendering authority to the young until they had attained a relatively late stage of development.

The important insights of these philosophers were usually articulated long before the creation of our present education structures. These authorities typically envisioned situations where parents were their children's principal educators, or where external teachers were family slaves or paid employees of individual families. Furthermore, the philosophers' concerns were often really directed at the education of young adult members of elite classes. *male*

These concerns seem far afield from our typical current public education institutions: individual schools and colleges enrolling hundreds and even thousands of pupils from all social classes and ability levels, for periods of from 12 to 16 years. Each institution is staffed by tenured, paid government employees. Each employee may relate to numerous pupils for often brief periods of time. Even Dewey's basic educational writings were composed during the early 20th century—over 75 years ago. (At that time, perhaps 5–10% of the youth population completed high school. The current figure is 80%.)

Despite such shifts, many insights of earlier philosophers are still relevant. Ironically, their philosophical comments are often pervaded with a practical wisdom, a realism sometimes unusual in our era. Plato made trenchant remarks about the important role of the arts, and music in particular, in shaping the moral life of the young. He proposed that young people should be supervised by responsible adults, who would monitor their artistic exposure. Otherwise, the children would be exploited by irresponsible artists. This insight is surely relevant in our own era of MTV and sexually explicit songs. Today many adults are urgently concerned—just like Plato—about the effects of popular music on youth values.

Aristotle recommended that intensive training in philosophy be withheld until pupils were over the age of 30—until they had acquired the wisdom of experience. Otherwise, immature pupils might apply their learned skills at argumentation to unsound ends. This caution is pertinent to some modern education practices. For example, in 1991 the New York State Department of Education appointed a Social Studies Syllabus Review Committee. The committee recommended that elementary and secondary school pupils "must be taught social criticism" and to "promote economic fairness and social justice" and "bring about changes in their communities, the nation, and the world." The historian Arthur Schlesinger, Jr. was a member of the committee and one of the dissenters from the report. He was unsympathetic to the idea that the public schools should strive to inspire a new children's crusade. He observed that he would be "satisfied if we can teach children how to read, write, and calculate." Undoubtedly, Aristotle would have agreed with Professor Schlesinger.

Many earlier philosophic perspectives cannot be mechanically applied to contemporary education without considerable intellectual adaptation. Thus, much of our philosophical discussion will involve interpreting traditional perspectives in the light of our immediate, and historically novel, situation. Our efforts at adaptation are congruent with the contributions of several contemporary philosophers, such as Alasdair MacIntyre and Russell Kirk. This discussion may be of special help to some protradition educators, who may be heartened to discover their experiential perspectives about education have far more intellectual legitimacy than they realize.

It is also relevant that many currently popular psychological principles used to justify contemporary educational practices are founded on philosophical premises. For example, the Harvard psychologist Lawrence Kohlberg wrote a lengthy volume on the philosophy of moral education. Such an interdisciplinary approach is quite legitimate, even traditional. But many philosophical approaches to psychology actually fail to appropriately confront the philosophical issues involved. They apply a form of pseudoempiricism to justify what are really philosophical arguments. For example, the prominent psychologist B. F. Skinner was a vigorous opponent of punishment as a means of maintaining order, although the experimental data he cited to prove his point were very limited in scope. Skinner's proposals would have been much more direct if he had simply said, "Let us logically think about the nature and effects of punishment," rather than reflexively reciting "Research shows . . ." However, such deliberate appeals to logic would probably have undermined his problematic contentions.

Finally, we recognize that most adults' personal philosophies are not due largely to reading books. Instead, they are based on some amalgam of their previous experiences, including their religious commitments, if any. Such personal learnings, quite properly, are deeply rooted. They are not likely to be changed by professional books. But we will be more directly philosophical than many education books in one important way.

We will tacitly and persistently raise the question, "Do you think such-and-such a school or classroom policy is good or bad? Why? Why not?" In particular, our questions will confront important elements of prevailing intellectual norms, such as

✦ the sanctity of the doctrine of the classroom as a democracy, rather than a learning environment managed by a responsible and authoritative adult

✦ the hostility towards the unapologetic use of appropriate punishment as one tool to maintain order

✦ the tendency to emphasize relatively limited goals for education, such as pupil test scores or an almost exclusive focus on emotional development

We will stress the practical implications of particular beliefs. We aim to stimulate readers to clarify the ramifications of their own beliefs.

There is little doubt that beliefs about education can have important effects. For instance, take a philosophical belief that it's not worth the trouble to vigorously suppress adolescent cheating because they may simply respond with counterchallenges. The major effect may only be a sterile confrontation. It is true that adolescents sometimes respond in such a way to mandates. It is also true that many adolescents simply do what persons in authority tell them to do. Furthermore, some adolescents do try in different ways to test authority; if they finally perceive the authority means business, they yield and get down to work. There are surely other variants of this hypothetical situation.

In the end, most commentators recognize that almost all adolescents have points at which they will discontinue resistance. Rebellion—or, at least, successful, persisting adolescent rebellion—is not very typical. Successful rebellions, indeed, are probably more a sign of adult weakness rather than of adolescent determination. In the cheating example, the basic philosophical issue is, How important is it for adults to enforce anticheating rules, or comparable institutional norms in general?

Some readers may find it beneficial to see the topic of adolescent rebellion, or testing, in such a light. The answers to the issues are not self-evident. Still, the issues invite readers to manipulate or reexamine their principles and test them in alternative perspectives. Helpful practical insights may evolve from such an examination.

Philosophy is also important because it relates to the issue of consistency. Consistency is an element of the virtue of fairness. We all know how pupils, and parents too, stress the importance of fairness in school.

Fairness means treating equally situated persons and equivalent acts of virtue or offense alike. It means being predictable. For instance, consider some general principle we believe is right, e.g., pupils should obey faculty. Teachers should make that principle a classroom goal and regularly apply it in different situations. Or they can vary the application of the principle, e.g., distinctions should be made among pupils of different ages. Mature pupils who have displayed considerable responsibility might have more freedom to question certain teacher directions. However, such variations should be internally logical. The exceptions must be plausible, not arbitrary. Neither fairness nor consistency can occur without the analysis of existing or proposed principles. We must consider the ramifications of these principles in diverse real and hypothetical situations. Such an analysis touches on the fields of ethics and philosophy, as well as on the realities of teaching and administration. It is our aim to help readers acquire this valuable intellectual discipline.

To conclude the matter, let's examine one other specific instance of practical philosophy and consistency. Some educators and many psychologists believe pupils should learn altruistic motivations for actions. These authorities deprecate school policies that provide pupils with recognition (e.g., gold stars, certificates, conspicuous good-conduct awards) to honor virtuous acts. To these authorities, altruism means good deeds done without expectation of reward. The idea is akin to John Dewey's concept of intrinsic motivation: pupils should learn because of the innate appeal of the subject matter, rather than from a desire to earn grades, please adults, or otherwise respond to adult pressures. These authorities label as consequentialism the contrasting doctrine that proposes pupils should be encouraged to do good or avoid the bad through the application of rewards and punishments.

However, almost all such no-reward prescriptions for encouraging altruism tacitly approve of the innumerable reward structures now typically existing in schools. For example, intrinsic policies regarding good conduct assume each school's academic programs will continue as currently instituted. This means that successful academic learners will still receive their typical awards: good grades, certificates, excellent papers posted, names listed on the honor roll, being considered for scholarships, and so on. This generates an anomaly. Should educators conspicuously praise competence in academics and fail to praise notable helping conduct? Furthermore, do we really mean that teachers should not praise virtuous conduct? Should teachers refrain from sending appreciative notes home to parents, or otherwise expressing gratitude for good conduct? In practice, such reliance on intrinsic rewards and no-reward proposals seems incredible. To propose a pun, inconsequential.

The questions just posed about intrinsic motivation may stimulate readers to reconsider their own views about recognizing pupil good conduct. There are not necessarily right or wrong answers to the questions. But assume we hold consistency as a virtue we want to cultivate. Then, tensions will be generated by policies that propose to ignore good conduct and only reward academic learning. Again, assume that realism is an important element of an effective philosophy. Then, it seems unlikely most teachers will, in practice, ignore pupils' good acts that occur in their classrooms. Teachers, we hope, will reflexively say "Thank you" or "Isn't that nice." Anyone concerned with promulgating a no-reward policy should anticipate the inconsistencies between the abstract principles of that policy and the day-to-day practices of teachers.

Now, it may be that some administrators who believe in ignoring pupil virtue (while some teachers informally praise it) deliberately intend such ambiguous policies to be applied. They intend for teachers to do one thing and for administrators to follow contrary policies. We have seen many schools where little or no official recognition was provided for pupil virtue, though many teachers still tried hard to encourage such conduct. As one might expect, such muddled policies generate mixed effects. In such schools, there were at best only moderate levels of pupil good conduct. Many teachers and parents felt frustrated. The administration did not support the efforts of teachers and parents to encourage such conduct. Even so, some of the administrators involved seemed self-satisfied. They believed they were carrying out the intrinsic-altruism theory, just as certain authorities had recommended. Furthermore, developing schoolwide policies for encouraging pupil virtue requires administrative diligence. The administrator could also enjoy the satisfaction of applying a philosophy that made her job easier.

Of course, in the adult world some citizens pursue serious learning or do good deeds without formal stimulation. But, despite such occurrences, few adults advocate abolishing report cards or honor rolls in schools. Perhaps similar realism should be applied in teaching pupils to practice virtue. This discussion offers guidance to readers who believe that virtue in children should not be regularly and systematically rewarded; perhaps such adults should consider the ramifications of their beliefs.

Teacher Diligence

Diligence is another important topic that often arises in discussions of protradition reform. The reality is that many protradition reforms, various sorts of tightening-up, often require educator diligence.

Take pupil cheating, for example. Precise restrictive rules against cheating may or may not be a good idea. We may not even be sure they diminish cheating if they are enforced. But we *can* be sure that it is more work in the short run for teachers to enforce clear anticheating rules than casually to apply vague prohibitions. Diligent enforcement requires teachers to design a system of prohibition; carefully monitor exams; maintain the security of exam questions; issue clear warnings to students; probably detect and punish some violations; and often deal with the angry parents of violators, with all the tensions of such incidents. Conversely, imagine a more lax school environment. Teachers do not need to work as hard monitoring student conduct, maintaining the security of their exams, or confronting students or parents. They can afford to be less diligent.

There is one essential point underlying most tightening-up reforms: the changes require teachers and administrators to be more diligent in monitoring pupil conduct. That is what tightening-up means. And this requires work. Some of the work is physical—actually expending more time and labor—and much of it is emotional: talking to pupils and parents (and teachers) who may be angry and defensive. There is a basic human disposition to avoid unpleasant activities. Some people seek entirely to escape diligence. Others resist new work demands, since such demands will conflict with their existing network of obligations. More dedicated professionals recognize that diligence is a critical element of commitment.

It is also relevant to recognize that the greatest work demands occur at the shift from indifference to greater rigor. At that moment, educators are under the twin stresses of abandoning an old habit, which is usually a frustrating experience, and applying a new mode to their resistant pupils and other persons. It may be that, when the new mode is firmly in place, things work better than ever. But the process of transition can be arduous and prolonged.

One of the authors recently faced a simple example of the ramifications of diligence, cheating, and teaching. He volunteered to proctor an exam for a colleague who had to be out of town. When he arrived at class with the sheets of objective questions, he discovered that the classroom was filled with 50 or so closely pressed desks. All the desks were occupied. Obviously, even good-intentioned students might be tempted to cheat. He was peeved at his colleague for drifting into such a situation. Then he recalled that classroom space was at a premium in the college. And, due to the large class, there were legitimate reasons for favoring an objective exam—it made grading more manageable. But it made cheating more tempting. Trying to make the exam more cheating-proof would have been difficult. Furthermore, the administration had given faculty no signal that preventing cheating was an important consideration, or that in difficult situations extra resources (such as a second proctor or temporary assignment to a larger room for the exam) would be provided. Indeed, a professor who handled such a vexatious situation without asking for extra resources would be viewed as a good soldier, one who knew how to get along.

The matter of increased adult diligence is quite important in considering teaching morality to pupils. We often see situations where conflicting claims are made for protradition and more permissive approaches. Arguments can be offered for either side. It seems the protradition approach, whatever its ultimate merits, also requires adults to be more diligent. One need not be a cynic to imagine that, for many people, the less-work factor may be the clinching argument for permissive approaches.

Consider, once again, the shopping mall high school. Much philosophy and education research can be amassed to justify such shopping mall patterns, e.g., teaching to pupils' interests, making learning fun, teachers and pupils should have open and relaxed relations. But, beneath such rationales lies a profound reality—a shopping mall school also makes some teachers' work easier. Teachers' lives would be harder if they had to diligently assign and insist on homework, give and grade serious exams, fail pupils who did not apply themselves, and justify their rigorous policies to distressed parents.

In sum, tradition and diligence usually mean pupils are subject to more demands than in the typical shopping mall school. And maintaining such demands means more work for faculty: more energy dedicated to class planning, monitoring and counseling students, and grading papers. But this prospect is not entirely bleak. Today a great many educators, while they work relatively hard, are frustrated by the disjointed schools they operate. Shopping mall high schools are a mixed benefit for teachers. Some forms of work *are* avoided. However, the schools are pervaded by indifference, and often the moderate disorder goes over the edge into turmoil. Furthermore, most teachers went into education partly for moral reasons: to help better the human race. They are often properly offended and discouraged by the moral indifference and mediocrity affecting their schools.

Of course, not all pupil options, like shopping malls, are entirely unpromising. Some students and teachers may use their new flexibility to design or learn approaches that require extreme ingenuity and intense pedagogical work. It may be that more permissive classrooms actually stimulate *more* work for teachers than do traditional approaches. But Ann Swidler, Jonathan Kozol, and others have looked at the realities of many such experimental schools.[11] They concluded that, despite individual exceptions, the expansion of options for teachers in the recent past did not unleash a vast increase in pupil and teacher creativity. In too many instances, they found that freedom from restraint meant freedom to be slovenly. Diane Ravitch supported these conclusions in *The Troubled Crusade*. Interestingly enough, the historian Lawrence Cremin, describing the progressive education movement of the first half of the 20th century, made similar observations about the patterns of open pedagogy during that era.[12]

THE ROLE OF RELIGION

Transmitting character, academics, and discipline is critically intermeshed with teaching morality. And many persons consider morality closely related to formal religion. Indeed, most religions have much to say about childrearing. For example, the Old Testament says "Honor thy father and mother," and

"Train up a child in the ways he should go; and when he is old . . . "
Undoubtedly, many educators working in public schools consider precepts like
these important parts of their own values base.

We have a few remarks to make about the role of formal religion in teaching values in public or private schools. Some private schools are religiously
affiliated. In these schools, the curriculum can be organized to teach fidelity to
that religion and to advance its moral values. The methods of achieving such
ends vary widely. They depend on the particular religion, the communities
involved, and the judgments of individual educators. The methods may include

- hiring teachers strongly committed to the expression and transmission of
  a particular faith. One evangelical Christian school principal told us his
  first concern is whether teachers acknowledge Jesus Christ as their Lord
  and Savior. The employment application asked potential teachers to
  detail this discovery. Theoretically, it was possible for applicants to try to
  deceive the principal. But the school was small, with comparatively low
  salaries. It would be difficult and unrewarding for teachers to conduct
  such an arduous deception. Obviously, teachers satisfying such criteria
  and employed in a religious school might approach their work with a
  special perspective.
- asking pupils to witness their faith in daily conduct, e.g., praying publicly, attending religious rites, displaying appropriate virtues
- using faith doctrines to justify certain policies, e.g., a discipline code
  based on the Ten Commandments
- teaching the doctrines of the faith as if they were true, rather than simply
  saying "this is what we believe"
- expecting parents to support the school's religiously oriented endeavors,
  e.g., observing religious holidays in their families
- being willing to reject or expel students who do not support the values of
  the religion or school
- asking families to express their belief by contributing not only money,
  but also time and energy to the school

Through much of U.S. history, public schools, depending on the communities they served, acted in congruence with many of the preceding themes.
Even today, Constitutional prohibitions to the contrary, some public schools
probably have both Bible readings and teachers who assume a common body
of religious values among their pupils—and appeal to those values in their
teaching. When the space shuttle Challenger exploded before television cam-
eras, with millions of horrified school children watching during class, we know
a number of public school teachers who suggested to their students that they
might wish to pray.

Actually, current interpretations of the prohibition in the Constitution against religion in state schools are relatively new. They were identified in decisions by a divided U.S. Supreme Court in about 1960. And, since that time, those prohibitions have been undergoing continuing redefinition. The decisions have created a wider gap between religion and state-supported schools than exists in any industrial democracy in the world.

For a century and a half before those decisions, such matters were at the discretion of the individual states, where practices and policies varied widely. Technically speaking, the prohibitions do not transform educators who violate them, through choice or mistake, into criminals. If a complainant objects to some allegedly religious practice in a public school, he must bring a civil suit. In the suit, he must persuade a court to issue an injunction—a prohibition— against the objectionable practice. The court may agree with the complainant or with the school and its educators. If it agrees with the complainant, it will then enjoin, or prohibit, the continuation of the practice. Only if a school (or educator) then disobeys the injunction can it (or he) be punished—for contempt of court.

Most educators do not want to violate the law. Nor do they want to be subject to a court injunction, with the loss of face that entails. Thus, many public educators eschew significant contacts between school activities and expressions of religious belief. Others take mild risks. They have religious invocations recited at graduations or encourage pupils to sing religious Christmas carols and/or Hannukah songs. The courts have emphasized that schools may teach about religion. It is a notable historic force, like major political movements, and the Bible is a literary resource. Such a license, however, is unlikely to satisfy many religious believers. The license places their religion and sacred book on the same plane as other secular academic subjects, e.g., Nazism, the Democratic or Republican party, or *War and Peace* or *Gone With the Wind*.

Questions about the appropriate role of religion in public schools must finally be considered in light of certain statistics. These data emphasize the role of religion in contemporary American life. American citizens place a higher value on religion than citizens in any other modern industrial country. For instance, one survey asked citizens in a number of countries to characterize the importance of God in their lives. On a 1 to 10 scale, with 10 the highest, the average answer for Americans was 8.2. The only higher rating was given by citizens of Malta.[13] But not only are Americans quite religious, but also their beliefs are relatively congruent. A 1991 nationwide phone survey found that 86.5% of respondents characterized themselves as Christians.[14] Only 3.7% were religious but non-Christian (Jewish, Buddhist, Muslim). Characterizing themselves as nonreligious were 7.3%, and 2.3% gave no response. The data make our current patterns of disaffiliation of religion from public education seem anomalous. Moreover, most textbooks lack any references to God and religion. It is one thing to protect the young from sectarian evangelizing; it is another for a government agency to tacitly ignore the profound beliefs of most of its citizens. It seems almost intolerant to so thoroughly disassociate children's schools from such an important force in many of their lives.

The matter of teaching or enforcing abstract nonreligious values (e.g., pupils should not lie, or pupils should be kind) must be considered. Is such teaching legally permissible in schools? Here, public schools can go as far as their communities and school boards will support them—as long as they do not use religious rationales for their assertions. Undoubtedly, it may be easier to teach some values if they can be founded on religious premises. But many nonreligious persons, and their children, lead morally wholesome lives. It would be defeatist to assume that wholesome nonreligious schools cannot hope to transmit moral values.

PRACTICES AND POLICIES

1. Identify some actual elementary or secondary school or classroom you know. List some ways the school or classroom either (a) holds pupils personally accountable for their good or inadequate conduct; or (b) does not maintain such accountability. Do you believe that the level of accountability applied by the school or classroom is appropriate or not?

2. Do you know of any school where the faculty seem to accept second-rate pupil performance partly to avoid the work of insisting on academic learning and appropriate discipline? What examples of such conduct can you cite? Do you believe the faculty would be better off showing more diligence to attain better pupil learning and conduct?

3. An effective policy against pupil cheating requires the school (and/or teacher) to identify all foreseeable forms of cheating; specify significant punishments; publicize the forms and punishments; and strongly encourage teachers to transmit and enforce such procedures. Does your school have such a policy (appropriate to the ages of the pupils involved)? Cite evidence to support your conclusion.

4. Generally classify the ways a school or classroom you are familiar with formally recognizes individual pupils or groups of pupils who succeed in academic learning, e.g., honor rolls, posting good papers, transmitting report cards, mention in school newsletter, certificates, recognition at awards assembly, oral praise from teachers, etc. Then, similarly classify the systems for recognizing pupil-helping conduct in and around the school or classroom. Finally, compare the intensity of the two systems. Are they equivalent? If not, which is stronger? How great is the disparity? What does such disparity imply about the goals of the school or classroom?

CHAPTER 2

The Multiple Goals of Education

. . . [my children] at this moment my love for you has increased so much that it seems to me I used not to love you at all. This feeling of mine is produced by your adult manners, adult despite your tender years; by your instincts, trained in noble principles which must be learned; by your pleasant way of speaking, fashioned for clarity; and by your careful weighing of every word. . . Therefore, most dearly beloved children all, continue to endear yourselves to your father and, by those same accomplishments which make me think I had not loved you before, make me think hereafter (for you can do it) that I do not love you now.

—Letter from Thomas More to his four children, 1517[1]

For most of history, educators have directed their energies towards three related goals: teaching pupils character, academics, and discipline. Pupil academic learning has been only one of several critical learning goals. To our mind, these integrated priorities constitute an important measure of any educator's personal values: is the educator dedicated to following that tradition of multiple goals? Educators who see their roles in such a light are, by definition, sympathetic to traditional values and will be interested in seeing how traditional institutions, or modern schools dedicated to tradition, pursued such diverse learning outcomes. In this chapter we will focus on character and academics, turning to discipline in Chapter 4.

It is instructive to look back on the classic writers on education, such as Plato, Aristotle, and Plutarch. These writers "invented" tradition. In their works, one sees a persistent concern with moral learning, as well as technical skill. The Roman author Quintilian (c.35 A.D.–c.95) said in his *Institutes on Oratory*, "No man will ever be thoroughly accomplished in eloquence, who has not gained a deep insight into the impulses of human nature, and formed his moral character on the precepts of others and on his own reflections."[2]

The matter of attaining multiple learning goals even antedates the evolution of historical societies, with their reliance on written records. Many anthropologists study surviving preliterate societies. Their studies provide some idea of how humans lived for the tens of thousands of years preceding urbanization and literacy. It seems that such societies also gave a higher priority to moral instruction than to technical training. Of course, the word *moral* should be construed in a broad light; it signified the sense of propriety or values prevailing in a society. And almost all such values relate to social relationships: how members of a society should treat one another (one of the Ten Commandments articulates children's obligations to their parents). Or, as the anthropologist Yehudi Cohen put it, "No society allows for the random or promiscuous expression of emotions to just anyone. Rather, one may communicate those feelings, either verbally, physically, or materially, to certain people."[3]

THE GREAT TRADITION

The long-term perspectives that have governed education and the conduct of educators can be characterized as the Great Tradition. That phrase was first applied by the literary critic F. R. Leavis to identify a body of writings that supported traditional moral values. But the phrase is equally applicable to classical approaches to education.

In education, the Great Tradition emphasized the transmission of good moral values to students, although skills and information were also taught. However, no one imagined these matters were more important than teaching good character. In many earlier societies, the institutions we now call schools and families were more intimately intermixed than in our time. Teachers or tutors were often relatives or family friends. And teaching was not so much a matter of formal discourse, but of role modeling, emphasizing politeness, good habits, and other appropriate conduct. Furthermore, family members, especially in rural environments, were usually involved in teaching children significant work skills. It was natural due to such intermixture for these teachers to stress the relationship between formal knowledge and the right conduct appropriate to different situations. In our own era, distancing has frequently occurred between homes and schools; teachers find it difficult to reinforce the moral values of pupils' parents, whom they may not even know.

As David Tyack and Elizabeth Hansot have observed, the tradition of multiple educational goals prevailed in American public education from our founding in the early 17th century until well into the 20th century.[4] However, beginning in the mid–19th century, applying the tradition became complicated. Efforts were made to separate public education from explicitly religious influences.

The shifts occurred partly because of the spread of secular values among intellectuals and opinion-formers. Previously, moral teaching in schools had usually been intertwined with Christian beliefs and doctrine. Up until the mid-19th century, this policy was respected by most public figures. Gradually, public figures became more secular, and demands for church/state separation intensified. Another cause of the shift was the rising rates of Catholic immigration. These immigrants believed the schools' religious perspectives were too Protestant. Eventually, many schools adopted secular (nonreligious) moral education. These efforts were later described by Yulish as the "Character Education" movement.[5] Although the movement had a nonreligious thrust, it included a strong moral focus. The movement enlisted many public educators and persisted from about 1900 into the mid-1930s. Finally, the movement's intellectual support declined; it lost its appeal—often for poor reasons—to academics and education intellectuals. (Some causes for its decline will be considered later in this chapter.)

Due to this shift, many education leaders abandoned the teaching of traditional values, especially character, in public schools. But this does not mean that all practicing educators ignore traditional values. Different public schools and teachers

✦ still, to varying degrees, communicate moral values by way of explicitly religious themes.

✦ try to transmit moral values tied to traditional, but secular, themes.

✦ make no deliberate efforts to transmit moral values.

✦ transmit antitradition values to pupils against the objections of many parents, e.g., provide pupils with free contraceptives without informing individual parents; conduct highly relativistic discussions about values-laden issues such as obedience, sexual experimentation, or drug use, or the limits of loyalty to one's country; or make low or no academic demands on pupils.

The Great Tradition is still important for many educators in our era, despite the frequent tendency to appraise schools largely or solely on academic outcomes, including pupil test scores. The vitality of the Great Tradition is evident to anyone who listens to discussions among teachers about particular pupils. The reader will quickly recognize that much of these discussions focuses on pupils' moral traits: their kindness, honesty, diligence, and obedience, or their laziness, dishonesty, or unkindness. Most teachers, for a myriad of reasons, are profoundly interested in pupils' characters. One important reason is that teachers spend long periods of time with their pupils; they are inevitably concerned about their conduct and other indices of their moral lives.

Old-Fashioned

Our book's sympathy with some past practices may upset some readers. After all, in a literal sense, past practices are old-fashioned. But does this mean they are automatically out-of-date, obsolete, or invalid? Some things that prevailed in the past are gone and probably will never return. For instance, over the past several centuries, the average human life span throughout the entire world has lengthened by about 30 years—an increase of from 50% to 100%, depending on the nation involved. We assume there will continue to be variations in that average. However, we do not imagine the average life spans of several centuries ago, 20 to 30 years, will return. Similarly, some other long-term developments are probably immutable, e.g., increases in rates of literacy and the increased speed of communications.

On the other hand, certain changes have been—and will be—mutable. During the Great Depression of the 1930s, the average unemployment rate in the United States approached 25%. Eventually, the Depression ended, and the employment rate since that time has ranged from 6% to 12%. Apparently, our country returned to employment patterns that had prevailed before the Depression. Again, during the 1970s, our average rate of inflation was over

10% per year. This was perhaps the highest long-term rate in our history. Circumstances changed, policies shifted and, at this moment, our inflation rate is less than 6%. Finally, the historian Ted Gurr has carefully measured, over several centuries, long-term shifts in crime rates in the United States.[6] He has concluded that, at this time, our crime rates are abnormally high. Presumably, Gurr believes that those rates may decline, as they have from previous high points. The concept of historical cyclicity is ancient. The theme is stressed in Ecclesiastes in the Old Testament: "To every thing there is a season, and a time for every purpose under Heaven."

Again, in our own era, the concept of cyclicity has been rearticulated by the historian Arthur Schlesinger, Jr.[7] He has written extensively about liberal/conservative cycles in American politics. Evidently, some practices or patterns common in the past have perished and will never return, and some practices that have declined or expired will revive, sometimes with even greater vitality. It would be nice if one could identify which changes are permanent and which transitory. But such forecasting is beyond the aims of this book. We only emphasize a simple point: the criticism that certain proposals are old-fashioned, in the sense that they are obsolete and impractical, tells more about the critic's lack of imagination than the virtues of any proposal. Perhaps diligence, honesty, and kindness are also old-fashioned; however, we cannot assume they are extinct and will never be revitalized.

The Intellectual Rationale for the Great Tradition

The emphasis on pupil's right conduct, that is, the moral elements of education, has been undervalued by many observers of contemporary education. In our era, questions about the appropriate goals of education are asked in an ambivalent intellectual environment. Educators adhering to tradition often feel uneasy about publicly declaring their values. Therefore, it is especially important that the roots of education's moral traditions be carefully identified. As John Dewey observed in *Democracy and Education*, education, broadly speaking, is the process through which society renews and maintains itself. Any particular human being is born with the capability of adjusting—or learning—to live in any one of innumerable forms of societies. All of us, depending on when and where we were born, could have been reared as 10th-century Italians, contemporary Japanese citizens, or Aztecs. As we mature, our almost infinite panoply of human potential is refined and narrowed. Finally, we emerge with the limited and focused learnings and dispositions relevant to our society and our roles in it.

Most of us do not precisely remember how we were taught our current roles. Similarly, most of us do not remember exactly how we learned to read or write. Indeed, even while reading this text, we are unconscious of applying the specific learned skill we call reading. Yet, if we are reminded we recognize that an elaborate process of formal and informal instruction underlay our learning to read. Similarly, in learning our roles in society, there has been an elaborate process of formal and informal instruction. Often the instruction worked just because we saw our choices as self-evident: is there any other possible way of doing things?

The most important components of belonging in any society are moral: knowing and accepting the society's standards of right and wrong, what is expected and what is disapproved. There are certain inevitable differences in such standards: Muslims believe polygamy is moral and Christians do not; the Aztecs believed in publicly sacrificing thousands of war captives by cutting out their hearts while they were alive, but many cultures despise such practices. Some societies may even explicitly regard one society's morality as their own immorality. Still, if a people strongly disagree with what their society calls moral, they are aliens in their own country. This is why the Pilgrims left England and Holland to found a colony in New England. They wanted to leave a land whose morality they found deeply objectionable.

The centrality of teaching morality is evident when we recognize that all societies apply the most severe sanctions against people who violate their moral codes. All societies want people to be formally competent, to possess appropriate skills. But the greatest opprobrium is directed at *morally* incompetent people. It is bad to be stupid, but worse to be evil. Societies also generally recognize that a technically skilled person who is seriously immoral poses a special danger to society. Skills minus morality enable immoralists to commit more consequential acts of immorality than unskilled people. Moral teaching is also given the highest priority because right morality is harder to transmit than formal, or technical, skills such as reading or mathematics.

Conceptually, it is easy to motivate people to learn most technical skills. One can usually demonstrate that such skills often bring benefits: because people recognize they are better off knowing how to read, literacy is considered a valuable individual good. It is not equally evident that people are better off being moral, even though many philosophers and thoughtful people have made that contention. It may even be that the contention is objectively correct. However, it takes considerable ratiocination to make that point stick.

Conversely, the arguments that selfishness pays, or that being polite is often a waste of time, contain powerful primitive logic. In the Christian tradition, they are the arguments attributed to Satan, an eloquent advocate. Societies only endure if their citizens learn the morality appropriate to their status. And morality is a very difficult subject to teach. As Freud observed in *Civilization and Its Discontents*, learning morality requires learners to inhibit and redirect many powerful emotions, emotions that drive us to pursue raw power, untrammeled self-expression, and reflexive erotic gratification.[8] Perhaps in the long run people are happier because they repress such drives. They have learned to be unselfish, or to redirect their gross emotions. However, it is unrealistic to rely solely on such long-range considerations to persuade pupils to be altruistic. That was Freud's basic point: only through pervasive, indirect, artful, and imaginative tactics do societies succeed in teaching altruistic values.

Each such socialization system must be so strong that most successful learners never realize that they have had tacit options; they never consider they might have chosen to be polygamous or drug users, to survive by being hunter-gatherers, or to live solely on meat and fish. This foreclosure of options has some implications for the word *pluralism,* a current education catchword. Like many other educational catchwords, there is no clear definition of the term. However, pluralism connotes a sympathy with licensing, or even encouraging, divergent values and traditions within particular schools. Sometimes, such divergencies relate to matters of race, religion, or social class. Some degree of tolerance and diversity is essential to a wholesome community. But, whatever the virtues of pluralism, there are some patterns, typically associated with social class, that we hope most supporters of diversity would want to suppress. For instance, drug and alcohol abuse are more typical of lower-class (compared to middle- or upper-class) life. Some children are reared in environments where such options are vividly placed before them. But we refer to such children as *at risk,* and we surely do not rejoice about their access to pluralism. Supporters of pluralism are clearly obligated to define what they believe is acceptable and unacceptable diversity.

Protradition educators recognize that American schools and colleges are important components of our country's elaborate, pervasive, and powerful system of teaching morality. Indeed, without the support of our schools, the system cannot meet its essential ends. It will not be sufficiently elaborate, pervasive, and powerful. Furthermore, American education, including schools and colleges, uses 9.3% of our gross national product and enrolls our youth population for long periods of time. If such an enormous institution is not clearly in favor of our basic moral norms, its effects are not merely neutral.

The statistics about youth disorder in Chapter 1 bear a special relevance to the topic of moral instruction. Those statistics suggest that the moral instruction young Americans have been receiving is less adequate than previously. It seems plausible that one serious deficiency in our current system for moral instruction is the relative disengagement of public education from its traditional promorality role.

UNDERSTANDING LEARNING

All educators have had extensive practice in trying to analyze and apply learning theories. Despite such rich experience and courses in psychology, many educators do not recognize exactly how pupils learn important moral values. Indeed, the bulk of psychological materials taught to education students focuses on cognitive, or academic, learning. Yet we have emphasized that moral instruction is an important function of schools. We will directly consider some psychological propositions about learning important and complex values and beliefs, such as personal morality. We will present an intellectual model. Our model is not attributable to one particular authority, but is derived from a variety of sources. This model of how we learn morality will be the foundation for many practical proposals made in later chapters.

Before we describe our model, we need a definition. By the word *learned*, we mean that the person has used the information learned, to the extent possible, to change her conduct. If a person has learned to cook, she not only knows the elements of certain recipes, but also is able to prepare attractive and tasty food. If she has learned arithmetic, she can add, subtract, and so on with relative accuracy. Conversely, a person has *not* learned to swim if she can write a clear description of swimming but cannot keep herself afloat or move about in deep water alone.

Let's begin by examining a series of levels of learning of increasing profundity and complexity.

First, consider the variety of things an adult might learn in a day: the weather forecast, the day's television news, a daughter's good grade in school, or the manipulation of algebraic equations. All constitute learnings.

Then, we can identify things we have learned in the past month: our new coworker is not too competent; in the future, some foods will be fortified with anticancer agents; I am learning to be an adequate bowler; our last stock investment is not turning out well; or my husband sprained his ankle.

Then, we can list things we have learned in the last six months: I have decided to enroll in graduate school; in the future, knowledge of genetic background will reveal much about our current physical and mental make-up; my married sister is pregnant for the first time; my wife is going back to work; and one of my brothers had a heart attack.

Finally, if we make an equivalent list for over the past five years, we will inevitably touch on profound learnings: deciding to get married to a particular person (or deciding to get divorced); learning to live separated from particular people we love; choosing a career (or leaving one career and going to another); or newly affiliating with a religion.

All of such things are *learnings*—changes in our values, dispositions, and conduct. And learning is only completed if the acquired information is integrated into our life. Thus, we do not say someone has "learned to be married" until she regularly conducts herself as if she were actually married to a particular person. This definition of learning is consonant with the ancient concept of *habituation*, an important theme in the writings of Aristotle and others. Habituation stresses that learning must generate desirable habits—routine, reflexive ways of acting. There is a large body of traditional psychological principles about how to foster habituation.

Our varied list of learnings reminds us of a number of truths; for one, many important learnings in our lives have little to do with formal education. And, by *formal education*, we mean learning focusing on lectures, routine written examinations, classroom recitals, typical homework assignments, and periods of deliberate study and reading—in other words, everyday school instruction. Even if students were invited to develop a broad list of their learnings, their in-school academics would only be a fraction of that list. Furthermore, a great many of our learnings occur as by-products of the incidents of life. We do not learn most important things (e.g., habits) from going to classes, hearing lectures, or reading texts.

Another truth about learning is that many of the important things we learn are unpleasant, even destructive, such as to accept the death of loved ones, to adjust to a divorce, or to practice destructive habits like cigarette smoking or drug addiction. People also "learn" to be criminals, sadists, and the like.

Let us now see how the preceding list of trivial and profound learnings helps us understand the principles of learning moral conduct, particularly in schools.

Incentives for Learning

It is easy to derive principles of learning from the list. The more profound— the more important and difficult—a thing is to learn, the more profound the learning pressures that must be applied. As we have noted, learning to prefer right to wrong is perhaps the hardest thing for humans to learn. Obviously, strong learning pressures must be applied to transmit such knowledge. We learn easy things—tomorrow's weather, who won the ballgame—simply by casual listening and reading. But the greater effect a particular learning has on our lives, the more substantial the relevant pressures or incentives must be. Some of these principles have been recognized by the researchers Krathwohl, Bloom, and Masia.[9] In their taxonomy, or outline, of affective learning objectives, they said,

> . . . we should point out the high cost in energy, time and commitment in achieving complex objectives in either the cognitive or the affective domain. Such objectives are not to be attained simply by someone expressing the desire that they be attained or by a few sessions of class devoted to the attainment of the objectives . . . educators who wish to achieve these more complex goals *must be willing to pay the rather great price involved.*" [emphasis added]

The model of learning we have presented is homeostatic. Because profound learning is difficult and uncomfortable, people will try to avoid it. This makes for stability. People try to avoid learning, i.e., change, since stability is usually desirable. It is "good" that profound learning is difficult. As we will explain, such difficulty makes for better mental health. After all, profound learnings bring about important changes in our conduct or way of looking at things. And changes in our perspectives, if they are really important, eventually lead to major conduct shifts. Important changes in conduct disrupt our relationships with persons or institutions we are close to. If we pursue a dramatic new career, shifting from being a social worker to a CIA agent or a rock band drummer, it may seriously damage our social and family relationships. We may be occasionally amused at someone who moves about from one novel pattern of belief to another—today Buddhism, tomorrow New Age crystals, next day, . . . ? However, we usually do not become good friends with such people.

As an example, assume you must adapt to the death of a loved one. You may witness her slow physical decline, stand outside her hospital room, touch her as she is dying, see her in the coffin, go through the wake or other services, and perhaps be present at the burial. Now assume a dear one dies suddenly, or while you are away, or the mourning process is otherwise truncated. Then, your adaptation may be disordered. You may continue the habits you applied while the deceased person was alive.

Or you can turn to literature to interpret the meaning of *profound*. In Shakespeare's *Hamlet*, a ghost tells Hamlet that his uncle, with his mother's help, has murdered Hamlet's father. Much of the play is concerned with whether Hamlet should believe this disturbing message. In effect, *Hamlet* is about profound learning and the ramifications of such learning. The hero tries to decide if this new information is true and, if so, how it should change his values and conduct. Such learning drives Hamlet into deep depression and leads him to contemplate committing suicide or killing his mother and stepfather. It is not surprising that the being who bears this disruptive message to Hamlet is his father's ghost. Information from such a remarkable messenger would not be lightly cast aside.

It is finally obvious that many forms of profound learning are objectively bad. Thus, it is good that people are careful about adopting dramatic new habits. In sum, all emotionally healthy people have basic and wholesome patterns of resistance to important learning. They approach such potential occasions with suspicion, just as Hamlet suspected the ghost's plausibility. It is understandable why great pressures or incentives are needed to bring about morally profound learning.

Intensifying Learning

Several factors should increase the intensity of the learning situations proposed in the model. Such factors are applicable to all subject areas. If the designers of learning systems are imaginative, they will find ways to apply these factors towards a variety of ends.

1. Time—The longer the learner is exposed to certain influences, the more likely the subject will be learned.

2. Status—The greater the power or prestige (in the eyes of the learner) of the instructor or the institution of learning, the more likely it is the topic will be learned. We know from modeling studies that people tend to want to imitate or satisfy attractive people.

3. Rewards and punishments—The more powerful the rewards and punishments involved, the greater the likelihood of learning. For many effective people, the most significant reward is conspicuous praise and attention (or criticism) from large numbers of people. When such attention is favorable, it is called fame.

4. Insight—The greater the insight and imagination of the instructor or the agency of instruction, the greater the likelihood of learning. The insight may be into a particular person or topic, or some general psychological insight about how effectively to conduct an institution set up for a particular end. For instance, one might propose that U.S. Marine Corps boot camp is designed with considerable insight. Most "graduates" have learned to be Marines and they are proud of what they have overcome to attain that status. Conversely, many modern prison systems do not have insightful designs. It is notorious that they rarely succeed in improving convicts, i.e., teaching most prisoners to become honest. (Part of such insight involves the institution's intake system; it may be easier to teach Marine volunteers than seasoned criminals. However, the Marines' message is harder to teach. Their recruits are taught to fight and die; all prisons want to do is teach unsuccessful criminals the plausible proposition that honesty pays.)

5. Proximity and Intensity—The more intense the physical closeness between the instructor and the learner (e.g., a mother hugging a child, a lover caressing a mate, or a bully beating a victim), the more powerful the learnings transmitted.

6. Consistency—The greater the consistency in the environment around the learner during most of the teaching process, the more powerful the learning.

7. Body Management—The more the teaching process requires learners to change the way they manage their bodies, the more powerful the process. Such changes include the imposition of a particular diet, the prescription of particular garments (e.g., uniforms, wedding gowns) or hair styles, requirements that learners assume particular postures, often during public ceremonies or rites (e.g., publicly stand as a group, hold their hands over their hearts, and salute the flag), or, in some cultures, the acceptance of scars or other conspicuous marks on their bodies.

8. Volition—As learners mature, learning environments will have important elements of discretion or choice. When learners voluntarily and publicly commit themselves to a course, they lose dignity when they fail. Conversely, when they have been forced or drafted in, they maintain dignity by resisting compulsory learning. Boot camp partly works better than prison because people enlist in the Marines ("We're looking for a few good men."). In contrast, prisoners are sentenced to prison. It is often better for learning if adult learners can choose whether to commit themselves to particular patterns of demands, e.g., marrying, joining the Baptist Church, or pursuing a specific career.

Reconsidering "Learning Is Fun"

The preceding discussion implicitly questions the popular educational aphorism, "learning is fun." It is indisputable that many forms of learning—adjusting to death, falling out of love or facing the rejection of a lover, adopting an important and different moral doctrine—are not fun by any definition. *Hamlet* is a tragedy about an intelligent, sympathetic person who could not handle the enormous learning demands thrust on him. Everyone can recall academic materials they are happy to have learned, even though they did not enjoy the process. We all have different lists of difficult subjects we learned, and we all recall situations where we had to struggle (often successfully) to learn particular subjects. Someone might contend that truly brilliant teachers might organize things so all academic learnings are enjoyable for all students. Maybe. But the prospect seems utopian.

When we consider the evident implausibility of the learning-is-fun doctrine, its intellectual vitality is remarkable. Because of such vitality, we must understand more deeply the history and meaning of this mischievous and seriously flawed doctrine. Fundamentally, the doctrine traces its roots to the French philosopher Jean-Jacques Rousseau (1712-1778). Rousseau, in influential works like *Émile,* argued for letting learning be a by-product of natural development, or the routine incidents of life. He echoed Shakespeare's "Ripeness is all" and urged teachers to adopt noninterventionist postures.[10]

A little more than a century later, John Dewey articulated similar themes in his praise of intrinsic motivation. Popular statements of such ideas were more explicit. In 1905, the principal of the University of Chicago Laboratory School (founded less than 10 years earlier by Dewey), in a bulletin to parents, remarked, "The School realizes the utter futility of trying to teach anyone anything when he is not in a happy frame of mind."[11] It is not clear that Dewey would have stated this obviously incorrect proposition so baldly. It is evident, though, that the principal believed his proposition was derived from the concept of intrinsic motivation for learning. Furthermore, the bulletin's statement articulates a point of view that has appealed to many 20th-century educators and education theorists. For instance, we can see elements of such themes in recommendations that children should develop or freely choose their own moral values—rather than adults "imposing" values on them. After all, pupils will obviously be happier learning values they freely choose instead of being directed to learn more demanding values. Such educational approaches are logically rooted in the concept, "learning is fun."

Another flaw is the difficulty of developing a clear, operational definition of fun or happiness. Is someone happy when they are drunk? High on drugs? Then there is the matter of the time frame applied in testing for happiness. The Greek historian Herodotus contended that no one should call himself happy until he had reached the point of his death. He buttressed his point with tales of prominent persons who died lonely and dishonored and contrasted such disappointments with stories of persons of relatively low status who died surrounded with praise and honor.

The anthropologists Robert Le Vine and Merry White vividly characterized many of the theories and practices about the enjoyability of children's learning. The key word in their discussion was "sentimentality." Their remarks focus on the 19th century. However, we could extend their vision backwards a century to include Rousseau. We believe he is one of the foundations of the sentimentality they identify. The two authors said

> In the nineteenth century, literary and artistic romanticism established an emotional climate on which the struggle for children's rights as a form of political liberation could draw. . . the sentimental idealization of childhood combined with the liberal notion that children had rights to be politically enforced, in such cultural phenomena as the novels of Charles Dickens and the legislative struggles against child labor. Much of the complexity of this history derives from the fact that the debate over freedom versus constraint in childhood has not led to a final revolution, but continues even today, in issues specific to contemporary contexts.[12]

Sentimentalism aside, the fact is that most learning is not fun, but work. Ironically, some of the things we truly enjoy learning to use, e.g., drugs, alcohol, and do, e.g., commit certain crimes, are bad for us. When wholesome learning is fun, it is at about the level of a hobby—something we do not have to do, which has no vital effect on our lives or our relationships with others, and where we can enter or withdraw at will. It is like learning bird watching, fishing, or amateur photography. Conversely, if we had to do any of these things for a living, and our income or children's security depended on our success, the process of learning would probably be both accelerated and require more diligence. And it would be less fun.

This does not mean the diligent pursuit of learning is never enjoyable. We all recall situations where we finally were gratified at the outcomes of certain demanding learning activities. Still, in spite of such gratifications, it is misleading to portray such activities as fun. That word does not characterize the efforts, discipline, and stress that often underlie such activities.

The doctrine that says learning is fun condemns educators to trivial activities. Why, then, has it gotten so far? There are two attractive arguments for the doctrine.

The *pragmatic argument* contends that if teachers only teach what keeps students happy, they need not be diligent. It is also true that students do not learn many important good things in such permissive environments. As long as fidelity to the doctrine of keeping them happy persists, teachers have a relatively easy time. They are teaching motivated pupils because they keep presenting subjects that win pupil approval. Of course, when in-school learning is designed to be fun, sometimes parents, and even some students and teachers, discover that serious learning is being avoided. Then they get upset. Even many students occasionally become bored with the triviality of the whole process. Even though the approach is not without practical difficulties, it still has a powerful superficial appeal.

The other argument for "learning is fun" is the *philosophical argument*. Unlike the matter of pragmatics, which appeals to adult irresponsibility, the philosophical argument has honorable substance. Assume teachers reject the doctrine that learning is fun. Then they are obligated to apply their power in an interventionist mode, to strongly encourage and even coerce pupils to learn things that often do not immediately please them. What should such adults decide to teach, and what forms of significant incentives (and punishments) should they apply to learners? For, after all, putting strong pressure on people to learn (partly against their will) is a severe constraint on their liberty. There is no doubt that teachers—especially when compulsion is involved (as it often must be since our society makes education mandatory)—may abuse their necessary power. This danger has been recognized for many centuries. Dramatic examples from folklore and literature easily come to mind, e.g., the Pied Piper or Fagin in *Oliver Twist*. These evildoers led children astray by teaching them bad things.

Despite such potential for abuse, the reality is that adult determination is essential to form good morals in children. Human beings must receive significant and powerful instruction. Otherwise, they cannot acquire sufficiently stable moral identities to meet the identity challenges of adult life. How will they learn to resist the temptations to cheat or abuse drugs, how will they remain loyal to their spouses and children, apply themselves when confronted with legitimate arduous demands, and so on? It is impossible to form strong personalities without a profound molding system. This system must have considerable authority (and potential for abuse). In most societies, the systems that teach young people their identities—and identities largely involve moral matters—are principally under the control of their parents. Due to the nature of typical parent/child relations, the conditions for fostering profound learning are generally present in families. Coincidentally, the potential for abuse is also at hand. In our own era, we are familiar with contentions about rising rates of child abuse by parents.

It is hard to say whether such abuse has become more prevalent, or merely more visible or aggressively investigated. But the potential for such abuse, whether by parents or other authority figures, is surely an essential, but tragic, concomitant of the power to transmit significant instruction. A world in which the potential for child abuse was eliminated would be a world in which parents were surrounded with enormous constraints. They would be subject to frequent and intrusive inspection and external reviews about problematic and subtle issues. Such pervasive monitoring, if it were ever possible, would necessarily undermine the intensity of parent/child relations. Relations would become more legalistic and formalistic, less spontaneous and intimate. Families characterized by such relationships would still teach children important things, but most of these learnings would probably be undesirable. None of this is to deny the appalling reality of child abuse or to discourage efforts to moderate abuses. But we are engaged in a balancing process. We may be pressing our antiabuse efforts too hard if we undermine the power of legitimate adults to subject children to strong learning. For instance, the word *punishment* is almost nonexistent in professional literature for educators. The word *consequences* is usually used as a substitute. But the two words have notably different connotations. *Punishment* has a more profound moral tone. We believe the delegitimization of punishment is related to the same perceptions that underlie the rising oratory against child abuse. Unfortunately, when the moral framework of parenting is eroded, many harmful effects occur.

Although the family is a child's first and most important source of profound instruction, many other agencies have always been involved. As long as schools have existed, they have been important allies in this process. The recent partial break with the Great Tradition represents a notable historic shift. The shift may not persist. We should also say something about school/family conflicts around the values taught to children. This issue, too, has a long history.

WHO DECIDES WHAT VALUES?

We will later consider various theories to decide what should be taught to children. However, there is a related, but separate question: regardless of the rationale applied, what persons or institutions should have the power to make such choices?

There have often been shifts in the location of such authority. In the early Roman Republic, in about the third century B.C., families had life or death power over their children. The family completely decided what values their children should learn. Gradually, however, the institutions of the Roman Republic obtained power to intervene in cases of aggravated abuse by parents of children. Since that era, public institutions, in limited instances, have tried to supplement "teaching deficiencies" in some families. For instance, if children are learning "delinquency" in some families, or otherwise being severely abused, some right of public intervention is recognized. While acknowledging that intervention, it still is extremely difficult for societies to invent sound substitutes for families. Therefore, intervention, or what some consider undermining of parental values, has generally been attempted by schools very circumspectly. This is a sound and realistic principle.

We have not finally stated what persons or institutions should decide what morals children should learn and what forms of incentives or pressures can be applied. We have implied that parents and educators should play important roles, with the parents' concerns receiving top priority. However, beyond that general remark, we have not definitively answered that question. The broader answer to "Who should decide?" is essentially a political issue. In all societies, individual families play a vital role. But, beyond the family, external agencies, e.g., extended families, formal religion, schools, and local and national institutions, also play a part in shaping such policies. The precise roles assumed by these institutions depend on a medley of factors: the political structure of a society; the nature of its economy; its technology; and the like. In totalitarian countries, such as Germany in 1935, the Nazi party was an important factor in deciding how German children should be formed. In the former Soviet Union, the policies of the Communist party carried heavy weight. Conversely, in the highly decentralized and pluralistic United States, such decision-making power is widely diffused. Significant authority is possessed by local and national legislatures and local school boards. However, this formal authority is also shared with many informal agencies, such as the creators of television cartoons, sit-coms, and soap operas, rock musicians and their promoters, and various religious entities.

Said in another way, America is a complex, multilayered democratic society. In our country, deciding what values should be taught to children is not largely a matter of some group debating and passing a definitive law, although particular laws are not irrelevant. It would be ridiculous to propose that the Supreme Court be given the authority and responsibility for deciding what values should be taught in our public schools, or that some nationwide convention with real authority be created for this purpose, and so on. Possessing the power to decree national homogeneity, except at the most abstract levels, in such an intimate matter as education would be tyranny.

Instead of national decrees, here is what we envisage. At this time, a variety of patterns of child-rearing values exist (though some communities and some parts of society have more coherent values than others). Additionally, as circumstances change, child-rearing values also shift. Changing circumstances can include matters such as changing public and intellectual perceptions, different technologies, the development of new or different evidence (such as the statistics about youth disorder we outlined in Chapter 1), and the formation of new organizations and the decline of existing ones. Such shifts may move in a good or bad direction.

These diffuse networks of authority are implicit in the U.S. Constitution. That document implicitly grants states and other local entities control of critical education policies. However, in the recent past, more control over moral education policy has shifted towards more remote authorities. Some of these authorities are governmental—the federal courts, Congress. And other authorities are nongovernmental—our national media and national professional and labor organizations. The shift has diminished the authority of local entities, which are more sensitive to the priorities of parents and other protradition forces. What are some examples of the policies stimulated by the shifts? Greater emphasis on simplistic in-school egalitarianism. Lessening ability of educators to apply vital discipline due to actual and potential court decisions. Increased youth interest in immediate gratification and freedom from constraints.

The locus of authority in the system for governing American moral education should shift. The shift should bring about more decentralized, deliberate, discrete, and altruistic adult authority over young persons and youth-serving institutions. The particular names and affiliations of such agencies will vary in different communities. However, we are not concerned with explicit designations, but with a clear statement of a changed policy. Conversely, some current decision-makers should have their influence lessened: popular musicians; youth marketeers; highly individualistic intellectuals and popular figures; and certain national private associations concerned with education and strongly dedicated to advancing particular adult self-interests. This shift to more local authority will encourage the development of policies that will help the young learn more traditional values. Such a shift will not extinguish all the moral deficiencies in our current situation; this would be utopian. However, our current youth morality situation is perhaps at its worst point in history. In this light, a change that cuts current disorder levels in half would be a notable improvement. Exactly how such a complex change can occur is beyond the scope of our book, except to say that this book, by presenting data and arguments, may provide ammunition to assist that change.

PROFOUND LEARNING IN SCHOOLS

Let us now compare the list of intense learning incentives with typical patterns of learning that occur in most schools. One element becomes immediately apparent: most day-to-day learning in schools is of rather low profundity. Likewise, many of the instructional devices used—lectures, exams, film strips, recitations—are means of comparatively low power. To some degree, these perceptions are correct. We tend to overestimate the significance of most schools' academic curricula. But we should not underestimate the actual and potential power of in-school instruction—if we consider things in a broad light.

Schools usually do meet the criterion of absorbing pupils' time; students typically stay enrolled in formal education (often through college) from 12 to 16 years. It is true that the subject matter at different levels varies, and the formal lessons are often forgotten. How many readers recall how to do trigonometry, or what genetic mixes determine which hereditary patterns? Still, certain school-taught dispositions usually linger: learning how to keep quiet and at least appear to pay attention; learning impulse control and some patience; and learning that adults believe schools are important. Furthermore, if pupils are required to work diligently at schoolwork (e.g., do considerable homework, be subjected to demanding grading), they will also learn diligence, even if they forget the particular subjects of their work. If the school has a rigorous dress code or uniform requirement, it can also heighten the students' learning about their group identities. They will learn that life is more enjoyable for members of purposeful, well-managed groups. Learning the values of group identity are important for learning morality; to keep our affiliation, we will strive to learn the morality that will ensure our continuing membership.

There are other powerful forms of in-school learning that may be skipped in our classification. In particular, we should particularly study the learning that occurs for members of school athletic teams. Through such study, we can obtain an appreciation of the other learning means sometimes available to schools.

Competitive Athletics

Membership in athletic teams is voluntary. Coaches can expel players who will not conform, and players who cannot "take it" can quit. This licenses coaches to make more severe demands on learners. Through such choice, learners learn about commitment and loyalty. Team practices are often very intense and make little pretense of being fun. Team members wear special uniforms. Teams sometimes perform before audiences and occasionally even are encouraged by cheerleaders. Sometimes, the audience pays to see them perform—pretty heady stuff for an adolescent! Team members see that their activities are similar to the much-publicized feats of adult professional athletic heroes. The team's record is often displayed in various ways, including in the community newspapers. The achievements and deficiencies of individual players are carefully and publicly enumerated by elaborate tabulation systems, e.g., times at bat, hits, strikeouts, walks, batting average, runs batted in, runs scored, home runs. The school may hold pep rallies. Coaches are often selected for their ability to motivate team members to make intense efforts and usually have considerable prestige in players' eyes. There is great emphasis on improving team performance. Coaches are licensed to make contact with players' bodies. They often pat players on the back, use their hands to set players' bodies or hands in correct positions, and otherwise engage in legitimate touches. Finally, students on teams are usually in vital social systems, and their competitive commitment is supplemented by horseplay, easy give-and-take, and the assurance of continuing lively social relations.

Athletic teams constitute very powerful learning systems. It is well known that many pupils work infinitely harder to learn athletic skills—to tolerate exhaustion and ignore pain, hold their temper in the face of provocation, control their weight, and do other difficult things—than they do at academics. The learning systems surrounding athletics are very intense.

The discussion about competitive athletics suggests a variety of ways the principles of profound learning can be, and are, employed in many school programs. Particularly with high school students, such principles can deal with diverse learning goals, including character, academics, or good discipline. Without specifying the particulars of such programs, which will be considered later, let us generally sketch some examples. We can:

1. intensify rewards for successful learning: public attention and praise; publicity; conspicuous symbols to be worn by or given to successful learners (similar to athletic letters and trophies); public audiences watching contests among learners.

2. increase the opportunities for voluntary enrollment: pupils and their families can be invited to enroll in high-pressure, prestigious programs or schools, where they choose to accept strong learning demands.

3. increase the status and power of teachers: give them prestige and simultaneously ask them to hold to high standards, e.g., work very hard like dedicated coaches; be rated by the success or failure of their pupils; permit them to expel pupils from their classes to lower-status classes.

4. increase the punishments for poor performance, lack of effort, and indiscipline: more or less conspicuous public humiliation; being sent to various

forms of "exile"; being kept out of enjoyable activities; being sent to lower-status "reform schools" where highly repressive policies are applied to students; being required to display their inadequate learning before some audience by looking bad in a public competition.

5. increase the role of ritual, art, and ceremony in emphasizing incentives for learning: the articulation and attainment of learning goals can be ceremonially demarcated; colorful posters and other artwork can emphasize the importance of particular goals; and assemblies, pledges, musical performances, and speeches can intensify commitment to learning.

6. increase students' learning obligations to particular groups (their "teams"): use uniforms and other identity-creating symbols and forms of group grading and grouping to heighten collective identity; provide students with occasions for friendly but work-centered socialization; publicize the successful and unsuccessful groups, as well as the names of group members.

7. increase the learning demands on pupils: teachers should show them they know pupils usually can do much more than they have been doing, just as coaches make rigorous demands on athletes.

8. clearly identify learning goals related to character, academics, and discipline and provide students with precise and dramatic feedback about their progress: students will know what is expected and can tell when they are nearing success, like participants in an athletic contest.

9. encourage whole schools or whole programs consistently to press towards common learning aims: pupils will receive uniform reinforcement in pursuing difficult goals.

10. increase the diversity of learning demands on pupils, just as different athletic teams use different forms of talent, from beefy weight lifters to slender long-distance runners: more pupils will have some activity where they can shine.

11. provide incentives for pupils to graduate from programs more quickly: pupils who do not like school do not have to be "kept in jail their full term." They can earn "early release" if they learn to work hard. It is better they apply themselves than become resigned.

12. emphasize pride, rather than novelty and fun, as the objective: pride suggests effort and accomplishment.

It is well known that interscholastic athletics is sometimes affected with many dishonorable acts.[13] Sometimes the players engage in such practices, but more often they are done by coaches. Such practices are much more frequent in college than in high school athletics because much greater temptations are involved at the college level. Some coaches receive large salaries, and television contracts and similar activities also involve large amounts of money. However, to a lesser degree, some misconduct spills over into high school athletics. Readers may naturally ask, "Shouldn't such misconduct serve to sharply moderate any praise of high school athletics?"

To our mind, a major cause for such misconduct is the high-stakes nature of interscholastic competitive athletics. The moment the desire for some team to win is shared by both the athletes and other community members—their in-school peers, their families—pressures inevitably arise to increase the likelihood of team success. Most of these pressures are healthy and even natural, e.g., people want the school to employ an able coach, athletes are urged to work hard at practice and play, and more attention is paid to their victories and defeats. Of course, sometimes these pressures become unwisely intense, or particular players or coaches succumb to temptations the pressure generates. Such acts of misconduct must be prohibited, monitored, and punished. However, it would be unwise, except in the most aggravated situations, to simply suppress interscholastic athletics. Part of its learning value is precisely the strong emotions it engenders in players, coaches, and the audience. Such emotions can greatly increase the constructive power of the learning experiences involved. Pupils are learning how to control their emotions under considerable pressure, which is a notable act of learning. Furthermore, as far as the pressures on players goes, the pupils have volunteered to enlist in such environments and have the right to leave at any time. Most of us are familiar with pupils who have begun to play sports and later dropped out, even when they possess the necessary skills. Such volition is a valuable characteristic of team sports. It licenses the sports system to subject players to somewhat greater stress than would be appropriate for regular students, who are often drafted into and "imprisoned" in their academic activities.

None of this is to say that dishonorable conduct in athletics should be ignored or licensed. Rigorous attention is quite appropriate. However, the monitors should also understand the special virtues of athletic competition.

Transformational Education

Our discussion should conclude with some harsh words about the "transformational" aspirations some authorities have for education: the idea that certain unique forms of education, almost on their own, can transform significant segments of society into human beings possessing novel virtues and talents. Such aspirations are often a dangerous fallacy. Educators who apply diligence and imagination and are supported by informed and insightful parents *can* form many pupils into persons who are relatively unusual compared to typical Americans. Our research has identified various institutions that have attained such effects. Typically, such institutions have served traditional ethnic and religious groups, e.g., Lithuanian-American Catholics, Orthodox Jews. A few of the institutions have been secular and served highly literate, liberal, individualistic families. But to call the goals of all of these schools *novel* is problematic. The schools have only succeeded to the extent their novel values are strongly supported by the pupils' families.

One Lithuanian Saturday school we studied succeeded in forming second- and probably third-generation bilingual Lithuanian-American adults, who saw themselves as Americans deeply identified with traditional Lithuanian values. Students attended the school every Saturday all day from the ages of 6 to 16 and learned Lithuanian language and traditions. The school required its pupils' parents to speak only Lithuanian in their homes, while they and their children spoke English at work, during regular school and college attendance, etc.; send their children to a Lithuanian-American summer camp; participate in the life of Lithuanian-American Catholic churches; and otherwise evince a deep commitment to supporting Lithuanian traditions. While recognizing the success of such a school, we must also keep in mind that many other Lithuanian-Americans chose not to accept such significant constraints on themselves and their children, or began their children in this program but found it too rigorous and withdrew them. Our study provided no estimate of the proportion of such refusers and dropouts. All of these powerful schools expect their graduates to marry persons from the same group. Orthodox Jews will marry Orthodox Jews or very liberal people will marry other liberal people. Without such in-group marriages, the unique values the schools aspire to transmit will be dissipated by the exigencies of adult life. Furthermore, one measure of a school's strength is its pupils' determination to carry forward its peculiar values focus, or if one chooses, its parochialism. Students choosing to marry someone who shares values learned in the school is simply another example of the school's shaping power.

It is also theoretically possible for schools to form new or unusual personalities without the support of pupils' families. But such unsupported schools will not work effectively unless:

1. the pupils are completely separated from immediate community and family values, e.g., set off in the country. Then, the schools can deliver a simple, clear message. The political scientist James Q. Wilson has proposed such systems of separation for the education of seriously delinquent urban children and adolescents.[14]

2. the school and community are closely aligned, and the child's parents are evident deviants. Then, as the children mature, they may prefer school and community values to those of their parents. Such a shift might occur through a child abandoning delinquent parents in favor of an ordered school and community, or abandoning moral parents for the attractions of an immoral school and community, like German or Russian children in the 1930s growing up pro-state while their parents were not. (Schools in the communist Soviet Union taught pupils to honor a 13-year-old student "martyr" who informed on his parents' antistate conduct. Students were told that the parents were sent to jail and the hero/student was killed by a local antigovernment mob.)

3. the "schools" are powerful institutions that informed adults deliberately choose to join to shape their personalities into different forms, e.g., Marine

Corps boot camp, Catholic religious orders. Much of the power of such institutions depends on the learners' voluntary enlistments. Volition provides the institution with a deliberately selected group of learners and licenses the institution to apply powerful techniques inappropriate for "drafted" pupils. In general, transformational powers are inappropriate for institutions that draft their members. However, even typical public schools should *somewhat* increase their power.

Schools with transformational powers *can* be created. However, such schools are like a potent medicine. Their powerful effects are often unpredictable, and the risks of abuse and error and costs involved are often unjustified. The general school norm should be to reinforce parents' values. Of all the complex values surrounding children, those of parents are usually the most realistic and helpful. However, suppose circumstances compel us to conduct schools that must conflict with many parents' values in certain communities. Then, we must recognize the complexities involved and proceed only with realism, caution, and determination.

About Education Research

The relationship between the findings of education research, particularly psychology, and moral education must be particularly considered. The topic is complex, and the existing research far from definitive. Still, a general survey is justified.

Mankind has a long history of reflecting about moral growth, of puzzling over what helps an individual live a good life and acquire the habits that enable him to live in harmony with neighbors. We have evidence of the centrality of these questions for many ancient peoples even before the Greeks, who were deeply concerned with these issues. The cardinal question for ancient Greeks about education, "What is most worth knowing?" was, in turn, driven by the question, "What type of mind and character are worth possessing, and how can they be acquired?" Central to our education at all levels, then, is a probing of what leads to—and away from—ethical development and character.

In the recent past, the discipline of psychology has been most prominent in trying to answer such questions. Psychologists from Sigmund Freud to Jean Piaget to Lawrence Kohlberg have offered theories to explain how we develop moral consciousness and the stages our ethical thinking is capable of passing through. But antedating even the formal development of psychology, other thinkers, such as Plato, Aristotle, and Rousseau, have contributed to the "science of the mind." Modern psychology has made substantial contributions to education. However, its supply of practical classroom aid to teachers struggling with how to promote moral development and character formation is yet to come. Less prominent among the sciences aiding educators are anthropology and sociology. Their concerns focus on people in community. This emphasis makes them ideally suited to address the moral realm. In fact, though, much contemporary sociology and anthropology are relatively critical of traditional values. Too often, such disciplines display the sentimental and romantic focus decried by Le Vine and White.

One major exception is the French scholar Émile Durkheim, considered by many the father of sociology.[15] During much of his life, Durkheim was a rector of a teachers college, conducting classes for aspiring teachers. He gave serious attention to the role of school in aiding the child to acquire the community's best values. In particular, Durkheim advocated the development of a strong school spirit and ethos; the necessity for forging self-discipline; and the school's commitment to moving children toward moral maturity. Indeed, much of what we have written in this book has been strongly influenced by Durkheim's views. We have also been influenced by the sociologist Orrin Klapp, who has written extensively about the role of institutions in shaping individual identity and values.[16]

Some contemporary research on education has demonstrated that different public schools apply different teaching priorities to learning objectives such as character, academics, and discipline. Not every public, or private, school gives the same emphasis as other schools to each of these different goals. Other research has indicated that schools that deliberately define such goals and pursue them as serious priorities are more likely to attain them than more "indifferent" institutions. Furthermore, some research has indicated that the three goals are not inherently contradictory or competitive. A school that makes pupil character a priority (as well as academics) may do better in academics than a school that supposedly emphasizes only academics. The more problematic research is about the connection between good pupil conduct in and around schools and its effects on each pupil's general character formation. If pupils display good character in and around school, will this make them better adults, or better youths while they are away from school?

For most of Western history, the development of proper habits, "habituation," was the basic mode of teaching good conduct. That approach was founded on what came to be called "trait," or faculty, psychology. Aristotle was one of the early promoters of this doctrine, which assumed that each person was a bundle of latent traits (e.g., honesty, diligence, good humor). Education's task was to encourage the shaping of those traits in the right direction. Eventually an adult would develop with a collection of good dispositions. To give a commonsense example, believers in trait psychology were not surprised when a disproportionately high number of early American astronauts turned out to be ex-Eagle Scouts. Dedicated Boy Scouts were likely to display the traits required in adult astronauts, e.g., discipline, determination, independence, and high capability for learning.

The doctrines of trait psychology provided a ready foundation for the practices of the Great Tradition. But in the late 1920s, a series of elaborate studies by the psychologists Hartschorne, May, and Shuttleworth questioned the rationale for trait psychology.[17] Their research concluded that the relationship between students being "taught" any trait and their later good conduct in a somewhat different moral situation was quite slight. The generalizability of moral learning was not great. If a pupil was honest in the classroom, he still might steal from the cash register as a store employee. These research findings had a considerable negative impact on intellectual sympathy for the Great Tradition in general and the Character Education movement (discussed earlier), in particular. As the psychologist Lawrence Kohlberg later derisively remarked, the tradition was merely a "bag of virtues" approach.[18]

To a great degree, in education the concepts of trait psychology were replaced by concepts allied with developmental psychology. Those new concepts were relatively congruent with the values identified by Rousseau. They gave heavy emphasis to letting the "natural virtues" of the child emerge. At best, the teacher would act as a facilitator. More intrusive intervention would be ineffectual, immoral, and distorting.

Despite the rise of the new concepts, it remains evident many practicing educators still apply the doctrines of trait psychology. Presumably, these teachers cannot condone cheating or other misconduct, even if research allegedly shows that teaching a child to be honest in exams has little generalizability. In other words, responsible educators are inevitably concerned with their pupils' moral formation.

Furthermore, regardless of the research, any observer can see that much teaching throughout education, including the offering of graduate degrees, relies on tacit forms of the discredited trait psychology. The major purpose of most doctorate programs is to teach modes of thought. These programs assume that one can be taught to think like a researcher, just as one can be taught to be honest or diligent. In sum, many of the diverse attitudes that educators at all levels try to impart to students are still founded implicitly on trait psychology. Trait psychology is the "underground psychology" of most education and is probably applied to graduate students by the very researchers who decry any school emphasis on trait psychology.

Since the 60-year-old studies of Hartschorne and May, innumerable other studies have affected the significance of their findings, refining some of the original calculations. The corrections undermined their anti-trait psychology findings. Later studies, summarized by Philip Rushton, have gone even further.[19] They have generally found higher correlations than did Hartschorne and May between the teaching of virtues and subjects' later virtuous conduct. Actually, such muddled findings about the ways of teaching virtue were consistent with the important themes of the Great Tradition. All earlier authorities recognized there was no perfect system for teaching virtue. Even the best approaches would occasionally produce imperfect products. Indeed, in the area of cognitive instruction, imperfect success is also the norm in teaching complex subjects to randomly chosen audiences. Human beings are just too complex to be stamped out like widgets.

Some systems of moral instruction work better than others, and the issues involved require persistent intellectual analysis. In practice, even elaborate programs of transmitting virtue do not ensure later virtuous conduct by all participants. The generalizability of such efforts is moderate. Yet this applies to many types of instruction, e.g., the factual knowledge or skills we learn in one environment often do not transfer to other situations. All such efforts are only probabilistic: it is more probable that we will display particular conduct or values if we have received earlier instruction. Perhaps the correct way to interpret Hartschorne and May's findings, and the later research, is that Americans had exaggerated expectations for their prevailing systems of moral instruction—not that the approaches were bad, but the expectations were unrealistic. But Americans usually have unrealistic expectations for education innovations, regardless of whether the basic ideas are good or bad. It is likely that, whatever the flaws of trait psychology, this approach to moral instruction is more efficacious than all other alternatives we have tried. Indeed, trait psychology is the actual psychological theory applied by anti-trait psychologists when they train their own students. It seems protradition educators who choose to stick with trait psychology make a sound decision.

PRACTICES AND POLICIES

1. Does your school have a written statement of philosophy? Can teachers easily derive coherent operating policies from its text? In conducting your examination, pay special attention to concepts such as "learning is fun," or any references to ideas such as diligence, voluntary commitment to learning, the importance of the school as a social institution, and the recognition of different sorts of excellence.

2. If no such statement exists, or the statement is obscure or ambiguous, does this lack signify (a) there is coherence among the views of the school's professional staff, but the statement fails to reflect it; or (b) the views of the staff are too disparate to permit drafting a coherent statement?

3. Have a school philosophy statement (either real or hypothetical) drafted or updated, reflecting the issues posed in this chapter. It might stress concepts such as diligence, commitment, institutional pride, and high aspirations. If possible enlist other faculty members in the process. In drafting or revising the statement, try to ensure the prose is precise enough so readers can identify practices congruent with the statement. Compare the statement to the practices that prevail in the school.

4. Classroom teachers can draft a written statement of the philosophy of their particular classes.

5. Does your school (or classroom) have a pledge or other brief eloquent statement of principles that students can memorize and recite periodically? The following is an example of a daily school pledge publicly recited by students in one Chicago public elementary school.

I pledge, as a student of Schiller School, to strive toward excellence in my scholastic performance, my school attendance, and my behavior. I will work diligently each day toward reaching my goals. I deserve and will only accept from myself and others the very best education possible. Excellence is my goal.

CHAPTER 3

How To Teach Character and Academics

. . . the implication of the most recent concept [of equality] is that the responsibility to create achievement lies with the educational institution, not the child . . . This is a notable shift, and one which should have strong consequences for the practice of education in future years.

—James S. Coleman[1]

Certain traditional principles of instruction apply to teaching morality, or, more particularly, teaching of character and academics (the topic of discipline will be addressed in another chapter). The principles are:

1. Decide the information, values, and skills you want pupils to learn.
2. Provide pupils with occasions to absorb and apply the information, values, and skills.
3. Make the learning demands consonant with the pupils' developmental limitations. As pupils mature, give them increasing elements of choice about such learning situations. Compulsion is not always appropriate.
4. Establish strong incentives for pupils to learn.
5. Measure, by informal and formal techniques, pupils' levels of learning.
6. Examine the results of such measurements to see who has done better or worse.
7. Reward success and rebuke failure.
8. Analyze the overall instructional proess (steps 1-7), make appropriate changes, and resume instructing the learner.

Educators should carry out these activities in a framework stressing the necessity of aiming at objective, identifiable goals, e.g., acts of good conduct, higher levels of pupil diligence, and measured academic learning. We will separately structure our recommendations on teaching character and academics. This approach, unlike some contemporary systems of moral education, does not give top priority to changing pupils' states of mind or reasoning abilities about moral issues. Approaches that claim such results may sometimes be justified. However, the key issue is improving pupil conduct, their words and acts in social situations.

TEACHING CHARACTER

Character centers on conduct. It focuses on the regular display of desirable traits by pupils. The good traits we want pupils to learn must be identified. For example, take the secular components of the traditional Scout Law: A scout is trustworthy, loyal, helpful, friendly, courteous, kind, obedient, cheerful, thrifty, brave, and clean.

This listing makes two points: any list is relatively arbitrary (what about diligence, patriotism, or charity?); and there is some overlap among any list of more than six or eight virtues, e.g., are not *helpful, friendly, courteous,* and *kind* about the same thing?

Listing can be useful. However, one should not be preoccupied with developing a perfect list. The Maryland State Commission on Values Education proposed a list of 23 values to be taught in that state's schools.[2] Most of them are quite admirable. Still, one cannot imagine a teacher keeping all 23 in mind during curriculum planning or any pupil remembering the whole list. On the other hand, the Scout list was designed to be memorized. That process of memorization is a traditional mode of teaching character. And, apparently, adults who previously taught traditional values consciously created lists that were easy to memorize.

Listing virtues brings to mind the issue of competing priorities. Is kindness more important than bravery? What about diligence versus loyalty? Such concern about comparing virtues has sometimes led moral education down the slippery path of relativism and ambivalence, or of tendentious attempts to compare different virtues. After all, we are focusing on people between ages 6 and 17. Weighing comparative virtues is not, and should not be, a vital activity for most people in that age group. Everyday experience shows that the typical moral problems for young people do not arise from subtle moral conflicts. Instead, the problems occur because many young people fail to observe even rudimentary rules. They fail to obey legitimate authority, satisfy appropriate responsibilities, or even practice simple politeness. These are among the reasons a disproportionate number of auto accidents involve young drivers, many of whom have been drinking.

Many literary works about moral topics focus on more problematic and novel conflicts than ones such as young people deciding whether to drive drunk. To return to the instance of Hamlet, should Hamlet kill his uncle and perhaps his mother to avenge his father? The complexity and novelty are touched with glamour. The works engage reader interest. However, educators with moral concerns should not let such precedents mask the typical situation. The first moral need of the young is to learn to avoid ratiocination. Instead, they must accept the centrality of doing the hard thing without thinking about it; they must delay their gratification.

Understandably, as pupils mature, or consistently display wholesome conduct, their ability to handle more complex issues increases. More problematic topics can be discussed in literature classes, or practical-values conflicts can be considered in small group or one-to-one teacher/pupil meetings. But all of such explorations must be grounded on obedience and diligence. The formal priorities among traditional virtues that schools transmit are far less important than the depth of their pupils' commitment to these demanding ends.

In practice, the virtues educators teach are not so much determined by the refined analysis of competing values. Instead, such priorities are shaped by the practical exigencies of school life. This is precisely why authorities like Durkheim and even Dewey have regularly characterized schools as microcosms of society. Both healthy schools and societies should be shaped by important moral norms. Pupils and teachers live and work in the community of the school. They learn character by carrying out planned and incidental activities in that environment. The activities invite pupils to absorb and practice virtues. Part of that process involves the ordinary curriculum presented to students in literature, reading, and social studies. Those materials traditionally have provided pupils with historic and fictional role models. Such models stimulate pupils to healthy emulation and also identify cautionary instances of heinous misconduct, e.g., Benedict Arnold, Adolf Hitler, or Jack in *Lord of the Flies*. The matter of using these materials to teach character is important and will be separately considered later. But virtues should be applied, as well as studied, in schools.

They can be applied in activities in individual classrooms, typically in elementary or preschools, or in schoolwide activities, which can occur in schools at all levels through high school. Some intraclass activities can be under the direction of an individual teacher on his own initiative. Most schoolwide activities require administrative support. Essentially, all such activities involve pupils engaging in prosocial conduct: words or actions of immediate, evident help to others or to the common good of a larger group, which cause the pupils some trouble. The formal term *prosocial* is helpful. It emphasizes the distinction between "being good," which sometimes simply means being quiet, and taking affirmative steps to do good. To our mind, the important but passive process of not making trouble is better encompassed under the topic of discipline.

Prosocial Conduct

The emphasis on prosocial conduct as part of good character is ancient. In the first century B.C., the Roman moralist Cicero wrote that people should be generous by giving personal help, rather than donating money. Providing such help "is nobler, more impressive, and worthier of a strong and generous man . . . generosity that consists of service and hard work is more honest, has wider application, and can be useful to more people."[3]

From our research we know a vast number of prosocial activities are carried out by pupils in schools at all levels. Educators encourage such conduct so pupils can practice virtues and learn character.

School service organizations are one form of activities. Such organizations are formed to allow students to provide service to the school itself or to its surrounding community. Service organizations and individual volunteers have had an important place in American life for many generations. Recently, however, a number of social forces have eroded this important aspect of our community life. For one thing, we have institutionalized a number of functions formerly performed by individuals or local groups. Care for the elderly and infirm has been assumed by institutions for the elderly and nursing homes. The needs of our poor neighbors have been assumed in large part by welfare. The family's care for the retarded or physically disabled has been augmented substantially by state agencies. As a result, many states, having taken on responsibilities previously handled by the family, are staggering with the costs and are being forced to cut back on such services. At a more profound level, many persons have asked whether the quality of our lives has been undermined by transferring these responsibilities to paid employees, rather than keeping them with our relatives, friends, neighbors, and fellow students.

It is in the nature of being human that we both give and receive. We are all born into the world helpless and dependent on others. If we live until old age, we will end our lives helpless and dependent on others. Most of us will experience other moments in our lives when we will be vulnerable and need to rely on others. It is imperative, therefore, that people learn how to come to the aid of others; to take the responsibility that others cannot, or should not, assume. We must learn to help, to serve others.

Some recognize in this need for effective helpers a sociological and biological fact of life, while others see it as a religious fact of fulfillment. The saints and holy men found themselves in helping others. Albert Schweitzer, the great doctor, churchman, and musician, once said, "There is no higher religion than human service. To work for the common good is the greatest creed." Whatever the motivation, secular concern for the common good, spiritual fulfillment or both, people need to be taught how to be of service. Caring attitudes and skills do not just happen.

Schools can and should teach students how to serve others. Ideally, a school's service program should have a number of characteristics:

1. Training. Students may fail when they first try to provide service. Many students, with little experience helping others, lack the skills to be effective helpers. Before a student is put in a helping situation, he should be trained in the necessary skills, often by a more seasoned student.

2. Supervision. Students normally find performing service very satisfying. However, initially they often experience conflicted reactions. They present themselves to help another and can be met with ambivalence or tension. For example, a high school volunteer may read to a blind person, who peevishly complains about the student's performance. Service programs do not always work out the way they were planned on paper. Therefore, it is critical that the school provide some overall supervision for service volunteers, especially in the beginning phases. Helping the student adjust to the situation and develop new skills, as well as providing feedback and encouragement, are necessary components of a service program.

3. Ongoing support. Once service-givers are settled into their work, they should not be abandoned. Students should regularly come together to dis-

cuss their work. The focus of these sessions is primarily to solve problems the students are having in their work and to receive additional training. However, the sessions should also encourage reflection. Teachers should help pupils recognize the value of what they are doing. They should be continually reminded that they are both doing important work and forging important habits.

In addition to formal, schoolwide service programs, many other forms of prosocial conduct can be encouraged, either in individual classrooms or on a schoolwide basis. In individual classrooms, the activities include:

1. Directly helping teachers as aides, messengers, monitors, and during clean-up.
2. Directly helping other pupils as tutors, homework contacts, participants in well-conceived cooperative learning projects, or in team games, dramatic performances, or singing (where the pupil's engagement assists the group activity).

School-wide activities can include:

1. competitive sports, interscholastic or intramural, especially those involving teamwork.
2. membership in performing groups—band, choir, dramatics, forensics. When students perform as group members, they inevitably accept certain demands and make sacrifices on behalf of the whole. Thus, they are engaged in a prosocial activity.
3. student service groups serving either the school or the community.
4. fundraising for worthy causes.
5. miscellaneous extracurricular activities, e.g., clubs, school newspaper, tutoring students in other grades, student council. (Some educators have objected that student-council type activities often involve mere popularity contests, compared to legitimate service activities. From our research, we conclude that well-managed schools can shape such activities to ensure that character, and not mere conviviality, is the measure of council officership.)
6. representing the school, class, or team in academic competitions.

Such activities are common. However, our research discloses there are important variations in the frequency and quality of the activities. Schools with high levels of activities, almost by definition, are doing a better job in developing student character. Of course, individual students participate in these activities for a wide mix of motives, sometimes including deliberate character development. As for the adults in "activist" schools, from our studies we believe most of them are quite conscious of the connection between such activities and the formation of pupil character. For example, consider the following quote from a student handbook, similar to many found in high schools with an elaborate variety of activities:

> Clubs, teams, and other such activities are an important part of a student's life. They not only provide each member with a lot of fun and friends, but help members to learn the necessary skills of working together with others in an organization. Organizing ideas, making decisions, learning to compromise, and working towards a common goal are all part of every activity.

It is also significant that there have been a number of long-term studies measuring the effects of college and high school activities on pupils.[4] The studies asked: if pupils received the same number of years of education, was it better to get good grades or be heavily involved in activities? The studies have found that involvement in extracurricular activities is a better predictor of later-life success than good grades. "Later-life success" was measured by a variety of means, including levels of income, expressed self-gratification, and a stable marriage. In retrospect, the findings are not too remarkable. Very few adult roles require subjects to spend most of their time doing reading assignments, or homework, or listening to lectures. Many adult roles require people to work closely with and get along with others, compromise, and display both initiative and obedience—the sorts of behaviors involved in prosocial conduct.

The checklist in the beginning of this book can help educators estimate the richness of their prosocial learning programs. You may want to apply its questions to your own classroom or school.

Supervising students engaged in prosocial conduct is a challenging and rewarding responsibility for many educators. The supervision often requires a subtle mix of inspiration, direction, and even moral counseling. Some educators became teachers precisely because they wanted to carry out such responsibilities. Organizing prosocial activities requires imagination, commitment, planning, and insight. Adult monitors must recognize the developmental limitations of their charges and tread the fine line between unrealistic delegation and stifling intrusion. The monitors can increase pupil learning if they identify the parallels between student services and the conduct of many adults. Like the students, many adults contribute time and energy to community activities. Furthermore, most paid employment involves assuming various helping roles with coworkers, customers, clients, or subordinates. Students practicing prosocial conduct are partly being trained for such later roles in everyday work.

Something should also be said about courage as an outcome of prosocial conduct. Courage reveals itself in a variety of situations. Among children, it often is tested in the child's willingness to carry out unpleasant duties, to resist the tyranny of the peer group, to dare to seek adult counsel, or to confront wrongdoers. As pupils approach adulthood, it can be displayed in the willingness to admit error and accept difficult responsibilities. Finally, in adulthood, courage may even be displayed when a reflective adult resists the wrongful imposition of authority. But assume that such adult resistors never had the courage, when students, to support the rightful assertion of authority against peer-group abuses. Then, one can wonder whether their adult "courage" is little more than persisting adolescent rebellion. Courage without obedience and discipline can lead to acts of willful malfeasance.

Incentives

We have already emphasized the worth of explicit incentives to stimulate pupils to develop good character. Undoubtedly, as adults, these same pupils may (and probably should) often display good conduct for altruistic reasons, without concern for evident rewards. But similar principles apply to cognitive learning; we expect adults to read without receiving praise or formal rewards. However, whatever our adult reading expectations are, we usually are willing to reward reading competency among students. We assume that children need special support, or incentives, to learn literacy. It seems reasonable to apply similar principles to stimulate moral learning.

What incentive structures should educators establish to foster learning? How profound should incentives be? Profundity is especially important since we are trying to teach values that we hope will last a lifetime. Very powerful incentive systems sometimes surround athletic activities. We can look for similar incentives to encourage nonathletic prosocial conduct:

1. Conspicuous praise: notes or phone calls to parents; mention over the school public-address system; names listed on blackboard or the class or school bulletin board; photographs prominently displayed; mention in school paper; notations on report cards; certificates on award occasions; bumper stickers for parents ("My child is an award winner at the _____ school."); being invited to a special party; and names on a plaque or poster placed on the school wall.
2. Symbolic recognition (like athletic letters): pins, ribbons, badges, jackets, medals, trophies.
3. Publicly recognized titles: school president, team captain, member of the honor society (where character is one element of deservingness).
4. Contacts with prominent people: breakfast with the principal.

Most of these forms of praise may be awarded to either individuals or groups. Both types of recognition are important, especially for fostering prosocial conduct. Such conduct almost always occurs in a social context and usually must be encouraged by other group members. When groups win awards for displaying prosocial excellence in a particular endeavor, solidarity is enhanced.

If vital awards are offered, criteria for excellence in various activities must be established. Once again, athletics are a useful model. Team members who meet certain basic criteria—"make the team"—receive uniforms, are entitled to wear team jackets, go to games, and are listed on the program. If a member's play is good, he will play regularly. He can then earn an athletic letter to wear on a team jacket. If the team plays well and wins games, the whole team is recognized as successful. Individual players then enjoy the prestige earned by the whole team. If the team wins a championship, everyone gets a special jacket. There are also specific awards, for Most Valuable Player, and so on.

Criteria of successful performance are very important. They tell students what they should try to achieve. Sometimes, even in nonathletic activities, quantitative criteria can be applied: the group raising the most in the fundraising campaign, the student who won the election for class officer. In other activities, the matter of defining what deserves recognition is more subtle. Similar challenges in framing criteria face teachers in academic areas. Teachers have to grade both math exams and prose compositions. We all realize learning is better when we use grading systems more refined than Pass/Fail. It is also good to list criteria so students who are not "stars," but who do improve, can, with a little introspection, identify their areas of success.

After-School Paid Employment

The prosocial activities we endorse, if aggressively fostered, may cause some high school pupils to feel tensions between their school responsibilities and the part-time after-school jobs students often hold. Such patterns of youth employment are common in America. For instance, in one high school in a better-off neighborhood where we conducted a survey, 25% of the pupils worked 20 hours a week or more during the school year. Such notable away-from-school commitments can undermine in-school efforts to encourage prosocial activities. This matter deserves direct consideration.

A school should have several levels of prosocial activities:

1. Certain activities that are required for all students e.g., all students must help in clean-up.
2. All students must choose among certain options, e.g., pupils may select from among certain chores.
3. Some options are only available to students who pursue them and are admitted, e.g., membership on an athletic team.
4. Some activities are open only to invited students.

This arrangement permits many students to opt for less than full involvement and even to hold somewhat demanding paid jobs while attending school. It somewhat moderates the tensions on certain pupils with other commitments. But, at the same time, it establishes minimum criteria for all student-citizens. These requirements are based on an important proposition: a student attending a publicly supported school should be expected to work hard at education. Otherwise, taxpayers' money is not well spent, and the student is learning a bad lesson in civics. Probably some few pupils are working part-time to earn money to support their families or to meet other desperate needs. But many working students are earning pocket money to buy audio equipment, run their cars, and participate in the youth consumer culture. Such participation is their right, but it does not license them to avoid education demands. Furthermore, from the data about youth television watching, which will be presented shortly, it is evident that most youths, despite their paid work, usually manage to find ample time for amusement. When students would rather hold paid work than become invested in school, schools should say to such youths: either up your investment or face certain consequences, e.g., be dropped, or receive a lower status diploma, a certificate of attendance.

Rites of Passage

One separate incentive for moral learning is the "rite of passage." Such occasions are ceremonies that publicly demarcate moments when the subject of the ceremony moves to a new status, e.g., from being single to being married, or graduation from studenthood to the status of alumnus. The rites are a form of instruction and incentive. They stimulate and license the participants to learn and carry out new roles, which usually have important moral elements. The rites also instruct observers how they should act towards the participants, e.g., cry, laugh, offer congratulations, display deference.

Vital in-school ceremonies in general, and rites of passage in particular, are complex activities. The organization of these occasions is discussed in Chapter 9. Many school activities provide natural occasions for more or less elaborate rites of passage: graduations, end-of-year promotions, enrollment of new students, the beginning of the school year, retirements (or other leave-takings) of employees. Different schools handle such activities with varying degrees of style. Well-designed rites can notably increase pupil learning of important values.

TEACHING ACADEMICS

This discussion of academic learning will be solely on the themes of academic diligence (or "press"), schoolwide learning incentives, and pupil grouping. Other elements of academic learning are covered elsewhere in this book.

The data show that, in general, American pupils do not work very hard at learning. Academically, they are not pressed. For instance, the U.S. Department of Education reported that a 1988 survey of twelfth-graders by the National Assessment of Educational Progress found that on a single night, 18% of the respondents had no assignment or did not do it, and 53% had less than an hour's assigned work.[5] The department also reported that another survey of eleventh-graders in 1983-84 found nearly equivalent data: 33% of the respondents either had no homework assigned or did not do it, and 26% had less than an hour's work assigned. Meanwhile, 43% of the sample spent three or more hours each day watching television.[5] School simply is not very rigorous.

The data about homework simply reiterate the point made earlier about shopping mall high schools: faculty members and students at many schools (at all levels) have entered into implicit compacts to keep down stress on learning and teaching. It is fine to talk about well-planned curriculums and imaginative teaching. However, none of such desiderata can replace student and teacher diligence. Protradition educators favor a strong academic press for two reasons: it fosters academic learning and it also teaches pupils to persevere at hard tasks—a precious virtue.

There are a number of measures educators can apply to increase pupils' diligence in learning. They can organize schools and classrooms so students receive significant assignments, which are promptly monitored, graded, and returned to students. They can establish incentives so students are encouraged to work hard. They should take all possible steps to stimulate parent cooperation with such activities, e.g., having parents sign completed homework, promptly calling parents to inform them of their child's significant successes and insufficiencies, inviting parents to sign explicit pledges of support.

We heard of one elementary school teacher's imaginative approach to win such cooperation. The second day of school, her fifth-graders were to bring in their first homework. As might be expected, there were a number of incompletes. The teacher had arranged for an aide to cover the class. She went to the office with some of the offending pupils. With the pupils beside her, she immediately called their parents (often at their work sites). She said she was sure the parents wanted to cooperate with school policy, that homework was very important, and asked their help in correcting the situation. Then she returned the first group to class and went to the office with the next group. It was hard for the parents to object to her direct approach, and the students speedily got the word.

The subject of levels of homework leads to a basic issue affecting instruction: the legitimacy of setting learning demands and rewards that inherently divide students on the basis of innate talent, commitment, or levels of family support. In other words, assume we recognize, "honor", students who diligently do homework, earn good grades, or otherwise demonstrate academic excellence. It is likely that students from certain situations, e.g., nonsupportive homes, will do more poorly than others. If certain patterns appear among the groups of pupils who do and do not earn recognition, the school may be charged with engaging in some form of invidious discrimination. It is against "equality", a sacred American principle. All efforts to establish and maintain public incentives for learning are closely tied to the topic of equality. Therefore, a careful analysis of the implications of equality is critical to examining academic learning.

EQUALITY: A CRITICAL ISSUE

The almost unqualified pursuit of egalitarianism is a root cause for the recent declines in pupil learning. From our own research, we know many educators are reluctant to require pupils to work hard. They are reluctant because they observe that pupils' willingness to work at academics is not an equally distributed characteristic. The educators believe, quite logically, that if they establish strong demands for pupils to work, an identified group of poorer learners will gradually appear.

Furthermore, to some degree, such willingness indirectly reflects the skills and priorities transmitted by pupils' parents. Assume that educators are asked or required to produce learning results unrelated to pupils' home background. This is often the case. Many educators, in self-defense, tend to simply lower demands on all pupils. Everyone receives good grades, measured learning slacks off some, and no pupil's feelings are especially hurt. In such situations, the only pupils who work very hard are those who actually want to. And they only feel moderate pressure, since they are doing what they (and their parents) want.

Most Americans believe in equality. But to most of us, equality does not mean everyone learning the same amount of facts and skills or attaining the same level of education, or having equally happy marriages, equal incomes, equal athletic talents, equal wisdom, or equal levels of diligence. We believe equality largely relates to formal political matters: everyone has one vote, can serve on juries, is equal before the law, and so on. Furthermore, for religious believers, it is common to hold that all persons are equal in the eyes of God. Moral virtue is not measured by external factors. However, it is simply utopian and chimerical to extend the principle of equality further into political and economic life. Such an extension denies the everyday realities that confront us. It is true that certain contemporary Americans favor more expanded definitions of the term. But their propositions are shallowly rooted and have never been applied anywhere for any length of time.

Jefferson's Position

Thomas Jefferson crafted the phrase "created equal" in the Declaration of Independence. He strongly supported the principle through his long and active life. He was also a proponent of public education to foster equality. We know precisely what educational equality meant to Jefferson. He drafted a plan to establish public education in Virginia.[6] In his plan, he proposed that three or four years of grade-school education, at public expense, should be made available to all children. Then, a test would be administered. The pupils who excelled (perhaps 5%) would go to the next education level at public expense. After several years, the second level pupils would take another rigorous test. The survivors would go to the University of Virginia, again at public expense. Students who failed the test at any level would have to pay the full costs if they decided to pursue further education.

To Jefferson, equality meant that all people who demonstrated equal achievements—regardless of their "defects" of birth—should be treated equally. He never conceived of lowering standards to ensure that certain patterns of results were attained.

The Jeffersonian definition of equality is not historically novel. It has been applied by other societies determined to encourage excellence. In France immediately after the French Revolution, an era dramatically committed to equality, an elaborate and "open" system of higher education was created. According to the historian James Bowen, the "main theoretical foundation for the new system was the interpretation of equality as equality of opportunity."[7] Higher education should be open to persons of all social classes who demonstrated academic aptitude.

Earlier, in the Turkish Empire during the 16th century, highly egalitarian approaches were applied in recruiting and selecting the members of the state's upper-level bureaucracy. As very young children, these leaders, the Janisaries, had been drafted from the families of the Empire's Christian slaves. Essentially, the state kidnapped them. They were raised under state guardianship apart from their families and provided with elaborate training. As it were, the Turks applied the proposals in Plato's *Republic*.

Finally, the most able trainees were assigned important positions in the state bureaucracy and army. The Janisaries were selected leaders who were unconstrained by family or regional loyalties. The sultan was the only person holding hereditary power, and most of such power was delegated to agencies managed by Janisaries. A foreign observer, after witnessing one Turkish state meeting, remarked:

> There was not in all that great assembly a single man who owed his position to aught save his valor and merit. No distinction is attached to birth among the Turks; the deference paid a man is measured by the position he holds in the public service. There is no fighting for precedence; a man's place is marked by the duties he discharges. On making his assignments, the Sultan pays no regard to any pretensions on the score of wealth or rank; he considers each case solely on its own merits, and examines carefully into the character, ability and disposition of the man whose promotion is in question. It is on merit that men rise in the service. . . .[8]

We can identify many historic efforts throughout the world to encourage equality through creating opportunities for persons from all classes and groups who show notable competence. These efforts have often been successful. In thousands of years of history, we cannot identify any successful efforts to foster equality by insisting that educators routinely disregard the traditional tests of ability—diligence, acuity, and prudence.

Incentives for Academic Learning

Schools and teachers must establish strong incentives to encourage pupils' academic learning. We have already presented extended lists of such devices.

Regarding recognition of academic excellence, we recall a conversation with one educator about the effects of the Buckley amendment on recognition efforts. The conversation nicely illustrates the complex forces that sometimes inhibit efforts to improve schools. The amendment is a federal law passed to protect pupils' privacy. The educator said the law might prohibit schools from displaying the excellent papers of identified students. The display might violate the pupils' right to privacy. We confess we did not take the trouble to research this arguable interpretation. However, the educator's objections are a sensitive index of the climate of opinion in which academic excellence is pursued. Still, as we all know, many schools do ignore this potential interpretation of the law and post pupils' excellent papers. However, other schools that do not post such papers may be partly motivated by such inhibiting interpretations or by the equally erroneous view that political equality precludes academic excellence. But beyond the matter of legal interpretations, we have to look at the reality of the situation.

How many parents would complain because their children's teachers post their excellent papers in school? Indeed, if a school ever smelled such difficulties arising, it could easily settle the matter. Administrators could invite all parents, on enrolling their children in school, to voluntarily sign a simple legal waiver. This waiver would permit the school to post such papers. If the parents choose not to sign, their wishes would be respected. Any future excellent work by their child would be kept secret. Does anyone doubt that the school would get 99% or more signatures? The point is, too many educators are not strongly in favor of pupil recognition. So when moderate barriers to recognition arise, such as arguable interpretations of laws, the barriers are treated as insurmountable. Where there is not much will, there is often not a way.

Wherever possible, the relevance of academic learning to pupils' adult life success should be stressed. Elsewhere, we will discuss the importance of cooperative learning to pupil character development. We see nothing inconsistent with a school or classroom providing students with a well-planned mix of individual and cooperative academic assignments. As our later discussion notes, the grades provided in appropriate cooperative assignments can be integrated into each pupil's individual academic grades.

The allocation of praise or other forms of recognition has always been a critical issue in education. This sensitivity applies to recognition for either academics or prosocial conduct, and to individuals or groups. One 19th-century study on education made the following enlightening comparison between two different recognition systems:

> As for recognition, no educators have used it so elaborately as the Jesuits. On the other hand, in most English schools the prizes for academics have no effect whatever except on the first three or four boys, and marking is so arranged by teachers that those who take the lead in the first few lessons can keep their position without much effort. This clumsy system would not suit the Jesuits. They often, for prize giving, divide a class into a number of small groups, the boys in each group being approximately equal, and a prize is offered for each group. The contests between competing classes, too, stimulate the weak students even more than the strong.[9]

We should also mention the form of grading, e.g., letter grades versus percentage. The different forms provide different incentives. Two-digit, or percentage grades, mean that even moderate improvement in a pupil's performance can lead to higher grades, and a little slacking off can cause a decline. Thus, two-digit grades encourage consistent, or even moderately improved, performance. Almost every student can raise his two-digit grade to some extent. Conversely, letter grades recognize neither moderate increases in performance nor declines in effort.

Students will try harder to improve or stay in place with two-digit grades. Of course, two-digit grades also make demands on teachers to justify fine distinctions in grading: "Why did he get 78%, and I get 75%?" But making and explaining such distinctions is part of excellent teaching. When one succeeds in teaching a pupil the difference between 75% and 78%, one has really taught. Admittedly, not all subject areas lend themselves to such precise evaluation; two-digit grading systems are not always appropriate. However, we must still keep in mind that deliberate and precise grading, where feasible, is an important component of stimulating excellence.

One other caution should be mentioned about the application of rigorous grading. Some allowance should be made for the developmental level of the pupils involved. In particular, younger pupils probably should be subjected to less academic pressure. Exactly how and where to draw the line is a subtle question, but the concept of such a line is widely recognized in American education. Still, it is interesting to note that some evidently successful foreign education systems operate on different premises. An American who taught Chinese public school pupils in Taiwan reported that, according to school policy, her first-grade pupils received two-digit grades, and all individual pupils' names and grades were posted outside the classroom. Our reporter was distressed at the academic press in her school, as well as enthralled at her pupils' application to learning. True, there were a variety of modes used to sustain academic press on the students (for example, the parents applied strong pressures on children to stimulate their application). But many of the modes, like the two-digit grades, assumed the students could and should be subject to demanding pressures.

What do we think about the Taiwan story? Are such pressures justified? Frankly, we do not feel comfortable judging, in a vacuum, one such practice that is woven into the fabric of a complex, long-persisting, and relatively vigorous culture. The only clear point is that children, without being absolutely destroyed, are apparently capable of far greater learning efforts than American schools ask of them.

Another comparison is also relevant. Researchers report that Japanese elementary schools maintain stronger, uniform academic pressures than is the case in America. The Japanese see learning as more the outcome of work, compared to natural endowment or luck. And it is assumed that all pupils are capable of hard work. This egalitarian assumption is relatively successful, at least at the elementary-school level. But fractured families and two-parent working families with children in elementary schools are far more common in America than in Japan. Furthermore, the order pervading Japanese society makes pupils and parents more disposed to carry out the school's directives. Japanese children are surrounded with more powerful learning support systems at home than are most American pupils. And schools get pupils to work hard.

Social Promotion

Social promotion is a policy of moving pupils to the next grade (or graduating them) even when they have not learned the appropriate material. The policy has important implications for the organization of academic learning. Social promotion is a poor idea. Because the topic is complex, and our general premises have already been made clear, our discussion will be somewhat summary.

First, as to rationale. There is a body of research critical of retention, as well as relevant research of another perspective. In addition to the research, we should also recognize that many observers see the problem from understandably different perspectives. Oftentimes, many opponents of retention emphasize the immediate situation of the retained child. And, undoubtedly, many children are unhappy at being retained. Many supporters of retention, on the other hand, look beyond the individual child at a particular moment and focus on the overall policies involved.

For example, the most supportive research on retention is not directly about that topic, but about an analogous issue. In the early 1980s, several states adopted minimum competency tests as criteria for high school graduation. Charges were made that such tests would discriminate against students from low-income backgrounds, especially blacks. A considerable controversy arose, involving several federal court cases. Barbara Lerner, one researcher on this topic, reported that, when some of the programs were put into operation, high proportions of African-American students actually did fail. They were provided with appropriate instruction and a chance to retake the test.[10] Eventually, about 95% of the first wave of flunkers passed. Today, in the states involved, the proportion of students who pass the test before their scheduled graduation date is almost 100%. Putting it simply, the process of pretest instruction has improved. Pupils now graduate knowing more, as well as more relevant information and skills.

The reality is that the adoption of the minimum standards test, and the demonstration that the schools meant business, eventually achieved the desired effect. The adult opponents of the tests, many with undoubtedly good intentions, were actually fostering an unsound policy.

The tests were not extremely difficult. Many able students were able to pass them in ninth or tenth grade. Thus, the high proportion of passers did not signify that the students concerned had attained notable competency. However, before the test was initiated, about 10% of graduates received diplomas without possessing even minimal skills. Lerner proposed that gradually enlarging the reach and rigor of such minimum requirements was very desirable. The enlargement would continue the process of improvement that had begun.

Other interesting data also emphasize the evident connection between social promotion and general student inefficacy.[11] Across America, social promotion was apparently at its zenith in 1977. In that year, in eighth grade, 23.5% of all male pupils were one year or less behind their age group. This was the smallest percentage of eighth-grade boys behind their group between 1970 to 1988. Presumably, in 1977, the slogan was "pass them along." At the same time, this was a period of relatively poor national test scores. Conversely, since this low year for behind-schedule pupils, the percentage of eighth-grade boys out of phase steadily increased to 33.4% in 1988. Evidently, things have been tightened up. And, perhaps not coincidentally, the turnaround in national test scores began in about 1983—just as tightening-up got under way.

Of course, there is a time gap between pupils being in eighth grade and taking their national college exams several years later. But the more basic point is that stringency is an across-the-board principle. If schools pass inept pupils on at lower grades, we should not expect them to suddenly demand academic competence of older (high-school) pupils. The slogan "pass them along" helps create and sustain an environment that is generally subversive to academic excellence.

Important benefits would flow from the adoption, in individual schools and districts, of uniform, carefully monitored, written prohibitions against social promotions or graduation for students with evidently normal intellectual abilities. The prohibitions could be enforced in the following manner:

1. Schools should have written policies, instructing teachers how to handle pupils achieving significantly below their peers, i.e., who may be candidates for social promotion.

2. The policies should provide for the (a) identification of such at-risk pupils early during the academic year; (b) written notification of the problem to parents and the principal or other appropriate supervisor; and (c) the development and implementation of a remedial plan for the student.

3. Every effort should be made to obtain the support of affected parents for their child's remediation under the plan, e.g., the parent should enforce the school's homework and study procedure.

4. If, despite the plan, the student fails to significantly improve, efforts should be made to solicit parental support for grade retention or make-up summer work.

5. Unless a special case can be made for an exception, the retention should be carried out.

6. If a student regularly falls behind, a careful special education staffing should be carried out. Perhaps a different school or program placement is needed.

A moderate number of schools and districts already have such programs in operation. Generally, the reports are satisfactory.

Pupil Grouping

The topic of grouping, or tracking academic learners by apparent ability, is an important and sensitive subject. The issue has strong implications for the management of academic learning. Diverse concepts can be applied to implement such grouping. Pupils can be grouped on evident ability, demonstrated commitment, completion of appropriate academic prerequisites, or parental support for a particular program. Such techniques have always been widespread in education; they permit teachers to focus their instruction on certain defined classes of learners. The techniques were implicit in Jefferson's education proposal for Virginia: before the pupils advanced to the next level, they passed a rigorous test. The teachers at the next level undoubtedly planned their instruction on the assumption that the students had acquired certain knowledge. Today, such selective practices are applied by many public and private colleges and universities, and by most independent private and some public high schools. Diverse adaptations are applied in many elementary schools, especially at higher grades.

Even in nonselective, or open-enrollment schools, there are often selective programs that require students who want to be enrolled to show notable levels of commitment or competence: Great Books, accelerated math, advanced placement courses, honors programs, gifted programs, and innumerable other forms of tracking and academic groupings. Frequently, scores on objective tests are used to determine eligibility for these activities. Such selective programs are often criticized because they foster inequality. Of course, legitimate criticisms can sometimes be made about particular selective criteria. Not all tests are fair. And pupils assigned to one program, typically a less desirable one, should be shifted up (or even down) if their capabilities change. The root criticisms of such programs are not really about flaws in their mechanics. Instead, they are about the truisms the meritocratic programs emphasize: human abilities are not evenly distributed. Pupils from supportive homes tend to especially benefit from such selectivity. Many forms of learning can be more efficiently transmitted if learners have uniform levels of ability or knowledge.

Definitions of Equality. It is poor policy to apply definitions of equality (or inequality) that discourage schools from making special demands on able pupils or pupils from supportive families. Nondemanding schools prevent pupils from learning critical truths: human attributes, such as mathematics ability or hand-eye coordination, are not equally distributed among individuals; attributes can often be dramatically improved through learning and diligence; and one of the great challenges of life is to optimize the mix of attributes and limitations we possess.

Schools can only provide pupils with differentiated demands if some system of pupil grouping is applied. And this is what happens at Harvard College, the Bronx High School of Science, and in the fifth-grade math honors class in your local public elementary school. In the learning area of character, an equivalent system is applied by educators who manage competitive athletic teams or the elementary school student council.

It is sometimes argued that pupil ability grouping is bad because it undermines academic learning, or, at least, does not help it. But the research findings are not especially hostile to grouping. One recent exhaustive review of elementary school grouping by Robert Slavin covered only up to the sixth grade.[12] Slavin said his findings only applied to small and medium-sized schools with relatively homogeneous student bodies. He concluded that strict grouping was not effective in such schools. However, he found that something called the Joplin Plan was useful. Under this plan, pupils were kept in the same homeroom, but moved in ability groups to separate classrooms for reading and math. Incidentally, the tone of his findings implied that grouping might well be appropriate above the sixth grade. Another recent review by Robert Dreeben and Rebecca Barr concluded that grouping is unnecessary if the school enrolls a relatively homogeneous population.[13]

It seems from such research that tracking and grouping, even at lower grade levels, are usually justified to permit demanding instruction when pupils' abilities vary widely. The real challenge to grouping and tracking lies in its implementation:

1. The curriculum presented to such grouped students must be appropriate to their alleged competencies.
2. Assignments to groups must be based on sound criteria and a variety of observations, e.g., test scores, grades, and teacher recommendations.
3. Educators should be prepared to shift pupils up or down if their performance changes or the initial assignment seems in error.
4. Parents should be informed about the nature of the assignment process, and consulted often about their child's assignment.
5. The aim of grouping, to maximize the opportunities for all students, should drive the application of this policy.

PRACTICES AND POLICIES

1. Complete the sections of the checklist in the beginning of this book that deal with learning academics and good character. See if you can persuade any other schools (or teachers in individual classrooms) in approximately similar situations to also complete the checklist. Share your data.

2. Ask an appropriate faculty committee to come up with suggestions for how the school can improve its showing on the checklist. What new policies or practices should be developed?

3. Ask a faculty committee (perhaps with student input) to come up with ways to enrich the school's extracurricular program.

4. Solicit expert help (from an academic or district staff member) on how to improve the school's use of test scores to monitor pupil progress.

5. Ask the school's PTA or equivalent organization to help raise funds to increase the school's ability to provide prizes and other incentives for individual and group pupil excellence in character and academics.

6. Teachers can carry out the counterparts of each of these activities for their individual classrooms.

CHAPTER 4

Teaching Discipline

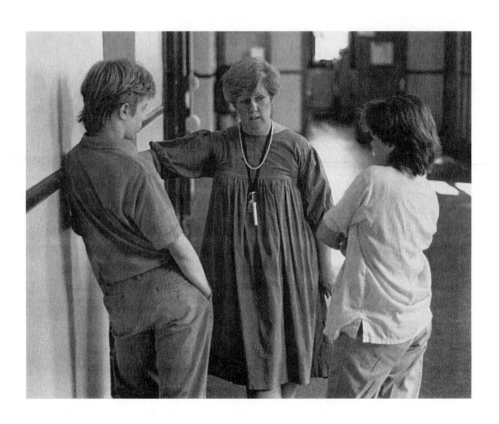

A boy's spirit is increased by freedom and depressed by slavery: it rises when praised, and is led to conceive great expectations of itself; yet this same treatment produces arrogance and quickness of temper. We must, therefore, guide him between these two extremes, using the curb at one time and the spur at another. He must undergo no servile or degrading treatment; he never must beg abjectly for anything, nor must he gain anything by begging. Let him receive it for his own sake, for his past good behavior, or for his promises of future good conduct.

—Seneca (c. 4 B.C.–65 A.D.), On the Education of Children

Education would be a good deal easier if it were not for human nature. If students were all intellect and desire to know, teaching would be a snap. We all know this is not true. Students, even with well-organized teaching, sometimes get bored and restless. They can become jealous and resentful of other students. Some resist the authority of the teacher. Some have little self-control. Some are lazy and self-indulgent. Some do not know how to cooperate. Some are deceitful. The list can go on. Furthermore, as children and adolescents, students are highly changeable. Their habits and attitudes fluctuate, occasionally changing from day to day or hour to hour.

These tendencies lead to behaviors that interfere enormously with students' learning and the teacher's efforts to conduct a productive classroom. Students must be taught discipline.

ARE RULES AND PUNISHMENTS NECESSARY?

One of the most famous American quotes is Thomas Jefferson's "That government is best which governs the least." In fact, though, the quote is incomplete and its essence distorted. Jefferson said, "That government is best which governs the least, because its people discipline themselves." Jefferson knew what was needed if the social experiment on which he and his co-conspirators were embarking were to succeed. The people, most of whom were uneducated and many of whom were unruly and undisciplined, would need to be educated to the responsibilities of citizenship. This is why Jefferson was such a strong advocate for education. He assumed education would teach pupils how to display discipline.

Discipline is different from prosocial conduct, which means doing good things. Discipline means not doing wrong things. To teach discipline is to have students learn to obey adult directions not to do wrong things: not to strike another child in school, or ruin the environment of the classroom through disruptive behavior.

Discipline problems are a major concern for most teachers. They are particularly vexing for beginning teachers. As mentioned earlier, for the last 20 years, the annual Gallup Poll of the public's views on public education, sponsored by Phi Delta Kappa, has shown the public's belief that this is the core problem confronting our schools. Poor discipline in our schools not only interferes with student learning, but it also erodes teachers' morale and undercuts the public's confidence in our schools. In addition, poor school and classroom discipline subvert the proper moral growth and development of students.

While not often acknowledged by educational theorists and writers, students are quite human; they have vices and failures just as adults do. In other words, it is impossible to imagine any large society without some system, formal or informal, of prohibition, adjudication, and punishment. Rules exist because people are tempted to harm others. Anyone skimming a daily paper will see it is replete with examples of such misconduct. For instance, one of the authors resides in a relatively tranquil suburban village. The village has a weekly paper. The paper has a regular column describing the village's reported crimes and arrests. There are usually 20 to 30 items in each issue. That's 1,000 to 1,500 incidents a year. While it is true there are only two or three murders a year in the town, most of the regularly reported misconduct—petty theft, burglary, assault, car theft—would be extremely disruptive in any school or classroom. Similar principles about victims and victimization apply to pupils enrolled in schools.

In classrooms, some students find manifold ways to disobey their teachers. Some pupils, disengaged from academics, focus their intellectual energies on antisocial activities. In some schools, groups of students gang up on pupils who are likely victims, ones who are unprotected and vulnerable. They drive good teachers out of teaching either purposefully or as a by-product of their bad behavior. Some do very evil things that emotionally, and even physically, scar their fellow students. Recently, one student in a disordered Chicago public high school became the first of the school's students to win a National Merit scholarship. The newspaper report mentioned that, in his final year in the school, the student had to eat lunch in the teachers' lunchroom. The faculty let him in to shield him from the jealous ragging he received in the pupils' lunchroom for his success with academics.

Undoubtedly, some of such disorder can be moderated by improved instruction techniques. There may even come a day when all disorder is extinguished by a different and dynamic pedagogy. Meanwhile, adults have a solemn responsibility to ensure rules and laws are promulgated and enforced on behalf of pupils trying to pursue knowledge.

After all, we should recognize that children display some patterns common to adult taxpayers and automobile drivers. They often adopt lawful behavior for fear of punishment. Some students do their homework, not always because they find the workbooks intrinsically fascinating, but because they fear the consequences of not doing homework. Again, there are students who would rather curl up and go to sleep in a corner of the classroom than attend to the lesson. Fear of punishment, and in some circumstances, fear of minor physical punishment, often works. It keeps many students on track. As a result, these students do things that in the future will be to their benefit, such as learning to do percentages and gaining some control over aggressive tendencies. Even if such threats do not permanently change some students, and they resume their misconduct as soon as the threat is removed, temporary order is valuable. It allows teachers to focus the whole class's energy on instruction and suppresses the distractions caused by pupils conspicuously and successfully modeling disorder.

Readers will recall that the previous chapter focused on pupils learning character and academics in classrooms or in the whole school. These activities have tremendous implications for the suppression of pupil indiscipline. The activities strongly encourage pupils to direct their energies and emotions into constructive affairs, instead of drifting towards disorder. Still, even in the best organized of schools, teachers and administrators will have to continue suppressing misconduct.

Policies that Cause Misconduct

Besides our flawed human nature, the causes of discipline problems are many:

- ✦ classroom work that is too easy or too difficult
- ✦ boring instruction
- ✦ confusing instruction
- ✦ unclear pupil expectations (not knowing how to do what the teacher expects)
- ✦ poor school- or classroom-management techniques (e.g., uneven enforcement of lateness rules or chaos every time something has to be passed out to students in class)
- ✦ ineffectual or unenforced punishments

Many of these problems are caused by the teacher not knowing enough content or having poor instructional skills. Such important deficiencies are beyond the scope of this book. Other deficiencies, though, are quite germane to our focus.

One cause of discipline breakdowns is the problem of perception. Students often behave in ways they fail to perceive as problems. Or they perceive the impact of their misconduct as a very marginal problem. Or they may be reluctant to admit the harmful effects of their misbehavior, to talk themselves out of punishment. Being tardy to class or continually talking in class may seem minor to some students, and even to their parents ("That school with their middle-class hang-ups is driving me crazy!"). However, tardiness or talking in class means children coming in after instruction has begun or students chattering about unrelated social concerns. These behaviors are clearly problems to a teacher trying to create an environment where real learning occurs. A core challenge facing the teacher, then, is the students' real or feigned failure to see why their behavior is inappropriate.

A second cause of discipline problems is a lack of incentives (or rewards and punishments) to encourage pupils to behave correctly. Here we are referring to students who know what they should do, but see no strong reason to do it. This is a widespread problem, occurring in varying degrees throughout the grades. Some examples: the student who doesn't do her homework assignments because there is no apparent consequence; the student who cheats because the benefits of cheating outweigh the risk of negative consequences; the students who gang up on another student, perceiving that teachers don't notice; the student who quietly drifts along during the school day, consciously not making the effort required to engage the work at hand, because she knows her teacher and her parents expect little from her.

In all instances of indiscipline, there are two sets of potential incentives and consequences. One set is immediate and relates to the here-and-now world of the teacher and the student. "If I do (or don't do) X, the teacher will do (or not do) Y to me." This is the immediate world of school, involving detentions, praise, and notes home to parents.

The other set of potential consequences and incentives involves the long range. It concerns pupils developing habits of study and self-control. It has to do with a pupil's sense of what she can accomplish in life. It has to do with what others—friends, teachers, college admissions officers, and potential employers—think of us and how they evaluate us as individuals. For some students, these long-range incentives are firmly in focus and affect their daily decisions. For others, they are part of a hazy, disconnected world of the future and have little meaning or power in their lives. Psychologists describe children like this as lacking a vision of the future. Many of the most self-destructive members of urban youth gangs fall into this category.

An awareness of incentives for action and the consequences of our actions, then, are major ingredients in becoming an educated and civilized person. This awareness goes to the heart of the school's intellectual and moral goals. For a small percentage of young students, a simple discussion of incentives and consequences, and short-term goals versus long-term goals, is the best way to incorporate these concepts into their daily lives at home and in school. However, most young people need that most vivid and immediate source of learning, rules.

Rules as Teachers

Rules are guides to behavior. They tell the individual what is acceptable behavior and what is unacceptable. *We don't run in the halls. In our classroom, we don't allow students to use rude words. At our school, our fans don't boo the referees no matter how bad the call.* Rules teach.

Rules, by the very fact of their existence, help children learn the skills and attitudes needed to live in harmony with others. The aim of civility that underlies a good set of rules affects not only the behavior of students, but also the social expectations and attitudes of the child. Much of what is written about the hidden curriculum is about the unseen rule structure and expectations below the surface of school life. On the other hand, much of what teachers actually do is explain the rules, instructing students about the "why" behind the rules: "The reason we don't allow running in the hall is because someone might get hurt. A child could get pushed at the drinking fountain and break a tooth. So, out of consideration for others, we want you to walk." Many teachers find it enervating to constantly explain rules. But explaining is an essential task of schooling. We should also recognize that tasks of explanation are moderated if rules are empathetically announced at the beginning of the year, clearly drafted, and consistently enforced.

ESTABLISHING RULES

Rules exist on two levels in schools. There are schoolwide rules and classroom rules. This duality is an obvious parallel to our system of federal and state or local laws. Ideally, the schoolwide and classroom systems should work together, each addressing different arenas and activities. Here we will consider both.

Schoolwide Rules

The first operating step in developing a set of rules or a schoolwide disciplinary policy is to list the kinds of misconduct that might occur at the particular school. For example, we probably do not need to worry about pupil alcohol use in a K-6 school in a stable neighborhood. But after recognizing such considerations, there will still be a number of problematic issues. Let us be explicit. Should a school prohibit

+ different forms of cheating, defined with some precision?
+ overt acts of affection, such as kissing, holding hands, hugging?
+ getting in fights in or near the school, even defensively?
+ any particular kind of clothing? Should there be a dress code, and should it be defined with considerable precision, e.g., no torn jeans, no miniskirts?
+ tardiness? How many cuts or tardies should be allowed per semester or year? And how should such incidents be defined?
+ bringing gum or cigarettes to school?
+ male pupils wearing earrings or female pupils wearing nose rings in school?
+ loud talking in the lunchroom?

+ disobedience or disrespect to any adult in the school?
+ vulgar language or gestures addressed to other students?
+ wearing t-shirts or other clothes with vulgar or provocative remarks written on them?
+ pupil misconduct at school-related activities away from school, e.g., while attending away athletic meets?
+ failing to report to school authorities serious breaches of school discipline by other students (with the understanding that adults will try to keep the sources of information confidential), such as bringing weapons or drugs into school, thefts, or threats to commit suicide or run away from home?

A clear, comprehensive set of schoolwide written rules or code of student discipline must be developed, aimed at acts of misconduct that can be reasonably foreseen around the school. Conversely, if certain undesirable acts are nonexistent or rare (such as the example of elementary students bringing alcohol into school), prohibition may be unnecessary.

As a general principle, elaborate codes of discipline are less necessary in smaller schools, schools with high levels of staff and pupil stability, schools with younger pupils, schools serving specially selected or recruited pupils and families, and schools serving more orderly communities. But, in deciding what to prohibit, educators should recognize the danger of self-deception. That danger was evinced by the data, referred to earlier, showing that students perceive more serious discipline breaches than do teachers or administrators. Often the school's adults are among the last ones to become aware of serious new troubles.

Still, almost every school should have a set of schoolwide written prohibitions. Obviously, developing and drafting a list of schoolwide prohibitions takes reflection. It is a classic committee responsibility. As one high school principal told us, he solicits faculty, student, and parent advice in developing the list and drafting the text. But the principal recognizes that the buck stops with him. If he strongly disagrees with some faculty recommendations and can't change things by persuasion, he finally decides what's in or out. After all, the public cannot fire or reprimand a teacher committee for failure to draft an obvious rule. Student input can be an important contribution, but it should be identified for what it is—advisory.

The code of discipline must be published and distributed to students and parents. Parents should be asked to pledge to cooperate with the code and discuss it with their child. The parent and child should sign a receipt to that effect and return the receipt to the school, to be kept with the student's records. Classroom teachers should also explain the schoolwide code, and a general assembly early in the school year should go over special points.

In addition, the code should be annually reviewed and updated, and the whole process of publication, distribution, and discussion repeated on a regular basis. One principal we know throws away the student code of discipline every year. She is convinced that having everyone rethink and rediscuss the rules is of fundamental importance to the goals of helping her students to moral maturity.

Unenforced, or unevenly enforced, codes are worse than nothing. They breed resentments among teachers and cynicism among students and present to all a condition of social confusion and paralysis. It is imperative, then, for teachers to uniformly and justly enforce the school's rules. Teachers should not simply leave it up to administrators to sanction other teachers who do not enforce the code. As professionals, teachers must take the responsibility of compliance with agreed-upon rules and, in effect, police their own ranks.

Exactly what should or should not be prohibited? We have not said what rules to establish. In some other parts of this book, we will identify and analyze certain value-laden issues, but not provide definitive answers as to what we believe is right or wrong.

It is evident we believe that, in many schools, discipline codes are not sufficiently restrictive. However, for several reasons, we will not make specific recommendations about exactly what should be prohibited. As we have noted, there are some causes for legitimate differences among prohibitions, e.g., the varying ages of pupils; contrasts in levels of disorder that make certain prohibitions superfluous in some communities and essential in others. But, beyond such matters, there are surely differences in values regarding discipline among thoughtful persons of goodwill. Exactly how severe should the restrictions be on pupils' clothes, e.g., torn jeans, greasy shirts, see-through blouses and short skirts, wearing hats or sunglasses in school, stencilled slogans on clothing?

It would unduly prolong this book to articulate and justify restrictions or licenses regarding these matters. We simply stress that discipline code prohibitions should be carefully drafted; unapologetically reflect mainstream adult values; enable teachers and pupils to concentrate on the business of learning academics and self-discipline; and give maximum weight to the recommendations of educators, pupils' families, and responsible pupils. If these recommendations are followed and the prohibitions enforced, we expect 90% of the controversy about what to restrict will expire.

Classroom Rules

By any standards, classrooms are crowded places. They are crowded with children and adolescents full of energy and vitality. For young people, spending six or seven hours of the day sitting and working quietly with symbolic material (reading, writing, manipulating) is not their first choice of how to spend their time. In fact, for many young people, spending long hours in classrooms is a real strain. So, in addition to the individual student's need for rules to provide structure and guidance to her activities, rules are needed to channel the pent-up student energy that exists in a classroom. Classroom teachers, especially in elementary schools, must supplement the school's rules and discipline code with their own classroom rules and procedures. In secondary schools, such procedures may relate more to academic expectations than in-class conduct, e.g., penalties for late homework. The classroom rules, however, should take into account the circumstances of the particular class and the pupils' developmental level.

Few teachers decide to become teachers because they want to impose rules and regulations on children. Few teachers enjoy being disciplinarians. Many teachers did not give rules and discipline much thought until their first real teaching experience. As a result, one common mistake of new teachers is to fail to establish a clear set of classroom rules.[1]

For many reasons, inexperienced teachers tend to ignore setting rules and making sure the students really understand them for many reasons. Some beginners are very anxious to get started teaching. In their haste, they neglect to give attention to the rules. Or they forget them altogether. Some new teachers are uncomfortable being an authority figure and disciplinarian. They hope either that the class will know how to behave or that going over the rules once will suffice. A few new teachers ideologically oppose "oppressive" rules. However, most beginning teachers change their attitudes towards rules during their first year. Some change dramatically. Often, they change too dramatically.

The practices of effective teachers differ considerably from typical beginner patterns.[2] Research shows that effective teachers spend a significant amount of time during the first two weeks of school establishing rules and procedures. They also carefully monitor students' adherence to the rules. Such veterans seemingly sacrifice a great deal of time on drilling or "grooving" students on classroom procedures in the early weeks. Indeed, they are quite fussy and insistent that the students obey the rules. Clearly, though, this pays off in less disruptive classrooms, both in the short run and in the long run.

Many students struggle against rules, testing teachers to see if they are really serious. We know a first year teacher who patiently explained to his fifth-grade students that they were not to talk in the hall on their way to gym. He soon discovered that the message did not get through. Instead of letting it go on or displaying aimless anger, he had them come back. He explained again and gave them another chance. They talked. He called them back again. Having missed 20 minutes of precious gym time, his fifth-graders made it on the fifth try. There was no more talking in the halls, and many later messages got through with greater speed and accuracy.

Rules for Establishing Rules

It is important that the teacher not simply issue the rules, but that she teach and model the rules. The following are some suggestions for using rules to teach values.

1. Do not confuse preparing children for their future roles as citizens of a democracy and the teacher's responsibilities for rule-making and enforcing in the classroom. Never allow students to think that they are responsible for monitoring and maintaining classroom order. This is the teacher's job. Students should learn about democracy and practice democratic living, but schools and classrooms are not democracies.

2. Nevertheless, depending on the age and sophistication of the students, they should be involved in the formation of their classroom rules. They should come to appreciate that rules are important and they have a role in developing rules. Their sincere input should be considered. Again, though, allowing children's input should not compromise the teacher's authority.

3. Rules must be seen as contributing to moral stability by encouraging prosocial conduct. Therefore, the teacher needs to point out or demonstrate the positive contribution rules make to the classroom environment.

4. Once established, rules should be written down and kept visible in the classroom. In some situations, it is helpful to have students take home copies of the rules for parents to read, sign, and return.

5. Rules need to be applied. Teachers must be ready to stand behind their rules and be willing to go to the trouble of enforcing them.

Rules, Rights, and Responsibilities: A Current Confusion

We will have more to say about the consequences of violating a code of behavior. However, before returning to that topic, let us address briefly something that in many schools has replaced the code of discipline—the student handbook. Many student handbooks are undoubtedly positive documents that contribute to the growth and development of students. Still, some handbooks written in recent years are more part of the problem than part of the solution. This issue is best captured by an account reported by sociologist Gerald Grant.[3]

In the early 1980s, he was studying a particularly troubled and disordered high school in Brooklyn. One day in the school hall he encountered a young teacher in tears. Eventually, she got herself under control and told how she had just been sexually fondled by three high school boys. Grant urged her to go to the principal's office and report the boys, but the teacher despairingly claimed that that wouldn't do any good. She reported bitterly that there were no witnesses. The testimony on the incident would be three pupils against one teacher, and a teacher's word had no special meaning in that school.

Grant was puzzled how such a flagrant situation could go unpunished. Then he came across the school's student handbook, a booklet 26 pages long. All but one page wase devoted to a detailed account of students' rights (e.g., when and under what circumstances their lockers could be searched; under what conditions teachers could give exams and quizzes; and what were a student's rights if accused of cheating). The remaining page was devoted to the students' responsibilities.

This is a particularly egregious case. Still, it demonstrates one of the worst legacies of the recent past: a massive shift of emphasis away from a student's responsibilities to be a good student and good member of the school community to a heightened sense of the student as a consumer of educational services and an institutionalized underling with legal rights. It also indicates a loss of nerve on the part of too many educators, an excessive willingness to yield in the face of actual or potential legal demands instead of vigorously striving to protect important educational concerns.

Other considerations also affect policies regarding rules, rights, and responsibilities. Schools are under great pressures from parents and social agencies to keep troubled children in their classrooms. On the other hand, society is reluctant to establish alternative institutions for disorderly students, whose behavior clearly demonstrates that they cannot handle a typical school environment. The result of such inconsistent policies is evident: the unprecedented high levels of disruption that exist in our schools today. Teachers are asked to tolerate habitual conduct that, in an earlier period, would mean swift separation of the offending student from the school or severe punishment. Policymakers and opinion-shapers responsible for this condition—legislators, judges, academics—have changed fundamentally the American classroom. They have forced classroom teachers to tolerate unequaled levels of offensive behavior, ranging from incivility and intimidation to physical abuse. A major premise of this book is that educators must resist the tendency of some schools, particularly our high schools, to become warehouses for surly, academically disengaged youth. This is an unreasonable extension of the school's responsibility.

Today, all students, not just the offending students, realize that they have to work quite hard to be removed from school. All students know that school is something the adult community compels them to attend. Many see school as continually placing intellectual demands, sometimes arduous ones, on them. It is clear to many students that there is nothing noteworthy about being part of most school communities. Many might say, "There is nothing special about being a student in this school." Belonging makes only limited affective demands on them, e.g., they need not show loyalty or practice courtesy. There is an old Groucho Marx gag, that he would not join any club that would have him as a member. The gag captures the attitudes of many students today.

Too many students think 12 or 13 years of education is a natural right. They fail to treat it as a privilege or, to use an archaic word, a blessing. They have this perception because schooling is forced on them. They know they have to go out of their way (through severe misbehavior) to lose the right. Adults must change this destructive student attitude. The authority of educators to apply sanctions in the name of the community and to separate offending students from the classroom—from brief (15 minutes) to prolonged (days or even expulsion) periods—must be conveniently available. Adult speculations to the contrary, separation from school is typically quite painful for many students. It means not being able to see their friends. It means having to explain why they are being separated from the school to adults, most notably their parents. It means facing up to their own sense of failing at their most important task—getting an education.

On the positive side, the entire school community should transmit the message that education is a privilege and an opportunity. Most important, it is something for which the community must have a sense of responsibility. One clear way for the community to send this message is to emphasize that the privilege can be lost and that the consequences of not going to school are unpleasant.

PUNISHMENT

The themes of prohibition and punishment are closely related. Certain conduct is prohibited in schools and classrooms precisely because it is attractive to some students. If it were not attractive, prohibition would be unnecessary. But prohibition must be coupled with appropriate and significant punishments. Otherwise, the prohibitions will be ineffectual. We will not be able to overcome the inherent attractiveness of the misconduct. Once prohibitions are developed, a system of consequences, or punishments, must be devised. This can be complicated. Obviously, punishment is a two-edged sword. A sword can be used to protect hearth and home, as well as to commit barbarous acts against the weak. There is occasional misuse of punishment in classrooms. Sometimes it is the weapon of a weak or ineffectual teacher, her expression of frustration at her failure to cause students to perform academic tasks. Not knowing how to find appropriate lessons to engage pupils, the teacher begins a regime of punishment ("If I hear one complaint about this assignment, or see anyone's eyes roll, it's detention for the whole class. And I'm not kidding!").

Sometimes, too, punishment is overemphasized when both punishment and treatment are necessary. A student finds himself unable to do the work or keep up with the others. He becomes embarrassed and angry and acts up—fakes sleeping at his desk, swears aloud at the teacher, throws paper on the floor. He has earned some punishment; he has violated the code of conduct. But he needs both academic help and punishment to encourage self-control. In some cases, students are suspended from school. Such punishments can be excessive and may make the student's getting back on track much more difficult. In effect, then, punishment can be an easy out for the teacher, a quick fix for much deeper instructional problems. Still, in the end, punishment, or at least the realistic threat of it, is essential. The reason is simple: the human nature of children has not suddenly in this generation changed.

Effective punishments, or consequences, share certain characteristics:

1. They must be clearly disliked by students—they must deter.

2. They must not absorb large amounts of school resources, e.g., schools cannot afford to assign a full-time paid adult monitor for each disobedient pupil.

3. They must be capable of being applied in "doses" of increasing severity.

4. They must not be perceived as cruel.

5. In public schools, they often must be applicable without strong cooperation from the parent of the pupil involved.

6. They must be able to be applied quickly—the same day, or even within one minute of the infraction, instead of next week.

Very little is written in educators' textbooks about prohibition and punishment. What does exist is surrounded with warnings about the dangers of punishment. Teachers are cautioned about the ill effects of even mild sarcasm towards students, raising their voices in anger, and even pointing at a misbehaving student. They are admonished that publicly embarrassing students is not to be tolerated under any circumstances.

Given such common counsel, it is understandable why many teachers, especially beginners, find the matter of prohibition and punishment extremely complex. It seems very difficult to simultaneously punish a pupil, not hurt her feelings but make her conduct change, and continue to effectively teach a class.

We do not impugn the motives of those who advocate such popular positions. However, we believe this advice is misleading and can be destructive. It generates unrealistic responsibilities for teachers and underrates the resilience of most young people. Such problematic advice is an instance of a widespread error in the educational literature. Practices that may be appropriate for younger pupils are given broadcast endorsement, without the recognition that different techniques may be needed with upper-level high school pupils or students with consistent records of misbehavior.

Natural versus Constructed Consequences

Many educators stress the concept of natural consequences as the essence of punishment. This implies that natural effects are better than artificial, deliberate, or even hostile punishments. Of course, some natural consequences very properly have punitive effects: if we put graffiti on the wall, we have to wash it off. But the natural consequences of much wrongdoing are obscure, ambiguous, often highly disruptive, and sometimes even reinforce offending behavior. For instance, if bullies beat up small children, they may find such hurting conduct enjoyable. If children swear, others may swear back at them, and a general melee arises. Children who stay away from school may be victimized by child abuse. Drug users in the short run may feel exuberant. And, in the adult world, many drug lords attain economic success. As a practical matter, educators cannot always rely on natural consequences to correct misconduct.

Teachers often must invent, construct, and enforce effective artificial consequences through analysis and reflection.

First, let us list consequences we have seen that we consider ineffectual:

1. Sending pupils alone into the hall, where they hang around and bother everybody.
2. Giving pupils tasks, as punishment, without following up on them.
3. Mailing notices of pupil misconduct home to parents, when pupils intercept the mail before their parents get home.
4. Generalized shouting at unruly individual pupils or groups.
5. Sending pupils to a detention room where they engage in chitchat, read comic books, or catch up on homework.
6. Sending pupils to the principal's office, where they act as messengers (a welcome novelty) or are entertained by the passing scene or by the secretary.
7. Sending notes or letters or calling parents of unruly pupils, when it is evident they either "support" their children or cannot exercise effective authority.
8. Scheduling after- (or before-) school detentions at the student's convenience.
9. Sending pupils to deans of discipline or guidance counselors who lack the power to punish or dislike the idea of punishing students for misbehavior.
10. Simply rebuking or suspending pupils who commit criminal acts around the school (e.g., use drugs, bring in weapons), instead of reporting such crimes to the police.
11. Suspending pupils from school if they will not be monitored by the family during suspension, but will instead enjoy themselves out on the streets.

On the other hand, some effective punishments or consequences to misbehavior are:

1. Subjecting pupils to before- or after-school detention within 24 hours of their violation (or, as one school found, Saturday detentions for more serious offenses, since they interrupted student's Saturday games and jobs).
2. Providing an in-school suspension in a designated room, supervised by a stern monitor, with chitchat prohibited and students assigned to do their missed class work.
3. Depriving pupils of their regular daily recess time.
4. Promptly phoning parents, even at work, the moment certain violations occur; or, at least, collecting from the pupil a signed receipt that her parents have read the punishment notice.

5. Granting teachers the power to immediately issue detentions to wrongdoing pupils, without penalties being subject to temporizing review (though such authority should be subject to long-term review).

6. Sharply and suddenly (and sometimes publicly) criticizing individual pupils for particular immediate acts of misconduct, such as treating another student harshly.

7. Having erring pupils write notes to their parents explaining their misconduct, and having them promptly return the notes, signed by their parents.

8. Sending unruly pupils from the class to another class for a short period (e.g., 30 minutes) under prearrangement with a cooperating teacher. The receiving class is usually three or four grades separated from the sending one.

9. Automatically calling the police whenever any student conduct violates the criminal law.

10. Having punished pupils do school clean-up at times that are inconvenient for them (e.g., Saturday morning) under serious supervision.

11. With uncooperative parents, insisting they come to school and meet with concerned faculty and their child. At the meeting, strongly and directly describe their child's conduct. The aim is to involve them in the discipline of their child.

12. When a student continually interferes with the work of the class, using shame. For example, having the child stand at the back of the class face to the wall for a period of time, or requesting that she stand and immediately make a public apology to the class.

13. In certain cases with older children, judiciously applying moderate corporal punishment, when authorized by local laws and school policy.

14. Having specified high school pupils (who are essentially on probation) carry cards, which are annotated by each of their separate teachers throughout the day regarding their promptness and conduct. At the end of each day, designated adult monitors examine the cards.

15. Suspending and ultimately expelling pupils when other measures have not proved effective. It is important to remind parents that (under most state laws) they are legally responsible for supervising their child while she is out of school. An attendance officer may even drop by to monitor this important responsibility.

It is easy to tell if a particular consequence works. Just ask pupils who have been subjected to it, "Would you like to experience that again"?

Classroom Punishment

We have already addressed the role of punishment as a matter of school policy, much of which reaches into the life of the classroom. The existence of clear schoolwide rules will surely spill over into a particular classroom. However, beyond such general policies, issues will arise regarding the punishments individual teachers apply in their particular class. Each classroom is a small community with its own work demands and dynamics.

Teachers, then, must each have an array of punishments appropriate to their classrooms. The punishments should range from mild public or private rebukes for poor work or uncivil behavior, to the authority to recommend (with a high probability of the recommendation being accepted) that the principal temporarily separate the child from the classroom or school. In situations where students do not clearly understand what the punishment will be, the teacher should transmit, orally and in writing, potential punishments to all students at the beginning of the school year. And the penalties should be explicitly linked to the infractions. Most of all, though, everybody in the classroom should understand the rules as part of the teacher's attempt to establish and maintain a place that is friendly, productive, and happy.

Of course, rules alone will not ensure a disciplined, civil, and productive class. Power is a basic fact of human life, and some people have more of it than others. And power has a moral use and misuse. Much of this power is legitimate, such as the power a parent has over a child. Some of it, such as the power of a bully on the playground, is illegitimate. The classroom is a prime setting for learning about power. Teachers have it and legitimately need it. The issue, though, is how they use it. The great potential for misuse of power does not mean that it should be extinguished or surrendered to students. It means, however, that power should be exercised with fairness. This may be the most important message a teacher can give to a child. To achieve fairness, punishment should

+ be applied with consistency and, where there are variations in application, those variations should be based on plausible principles, e.g., a dean of discipline might excuse certain misbehavior by a pupil who had just heard of the death of a parent.
+ in the case of serious punishment (e.g., expulsion), have some system of review or appeal.
+ be the outcome of violating clear or implicit prohibitions.

Rules Under Pressure

Throughout this book, we have stressed that, at this moment in our history, too many public schools are overly permissive. They fail to instill in our young the self-discipline needed for citizenship and full adult development. We believe strict schools (certainly by today's standards) are happy schools and, more important, schools that serve children and society well. We must add, though, that discipline must be the servant of the total educative mission of the school. Often the terrain here becomes tricky and messy.

Each fall the news seems to report a story of a town up in arms over a severe punishment meted out by a football coach. There are variations on this apparently annual story, but there is a basic theme. The school has a written and well-publicized rule against drinking, and this rule is explicitly part of the athlete's code of conduct. Then, key players are discovered drinking to celebrate a victory. The boys are often the ones who have worked hard for years to get where they are. But the coach kicks them off the team and the school board backs him up. Several of the boys claim they had only a single beer. The players and their parents are brokenhearted. The student body and the town cannot understand how the punishment could befall not only the boys, but also the whole school.

Such occasions are painful and difficult for all involved, but it is at times like these that life's most important messages are learned: *Our actions have consequences. Rules have meaning. Not everything can be explained away, or eventually worked out, or made whole again.*

But there are other cases, less publicized. A senior with a spotty academic record in a private school turns in his senior thesis, a requirement for all students in the college track. The school rules prohibit cheating, but do not clearly define all possible offenses. The school also has a strong prohibition against directly lying to a teacher. This misconduct is punishable by expulsion. The student's teacher, correcting his paper, is at first pleased and then suspicious. She confronts the student and accuses him of cheating, or, more specifically, plagiarism.

The boy angrily denies the charge. But the teacher goes on to identify whole paragraphs lifted from various sources. Since the student has committed two offenses punishable by expulsion—lying and plagiarism—he is expelled.

But on final analysis, we should recognize that (a) the student apparently had never received a clear understanding of the relationship of plagiarism to cheating—the rule was ambiguous; and (b) the student's untruthful denial to the teacher was partly due to his misunderstanding of the real nature of his offense.

Fairness and mercy require educators to carefully examine both the principles underlying their discipline codes and their everyday application.

Collective Punishment

We will now consider the question of individual versus collective punishment. Should a whole class or other group ever be kept after school, deprived of recess, and so on for certain group misbehaviors? Such tactics are sometimes warranted, as when the teacher has made it clear that the group as a whole is liable to be held responsible. Here the aim is to stimulate the good students to apply vigorous pressure on the wrongdoers. If punishment occurs, the wrongdoers are punished because of their direct misconduct, and the good students are punished for failing to suppress vigorously their erring peers. But to satisfy the important criterion of fairness, the good students must have a realistic chance of suppressing the behavior. If there are 20 wrongdoers and 2 good students, the good pupils can't do much suppressing.

Group responsibility is a facet of the concept of group achievement, either in prosocial conduct or academics. We have already emphasized that groups of students can win praise or other benefits for achievements. It is equally appropriate to hold groups liable for collective misconduct. Of course, each member of an erring group may not commit the same "amount" of wrong as each other member. But each group member who receives praise probably did not do the same amount of "good" as every other member. Moderate inequalities in rewards and punishments are inevitable in group life.

Enforcement

Assume prohibitions and consequences have been established and published. They must also be enforced by the adults in the school. All adults would like to work in a school with good discipline. But it is not true that all adults, administrators or teachers, are equally willing to enforce discipline. After all, enforcing discipline is hard work. However, without across-the-board enforcement, pupils will violate rules, testing if they are in the presence of a teacher who is an enforcer. Furthermore, pupils will feel emboldened to resist enforcers, to argue with them and criticize them. The pupils will correctly contend that the enforcers are inconsistent with the policies of other teachers. Nonenforcers complicate the work of enforcers, while enjoying the full benefits of the enforcers' responsible conduct.

Principals should emphasize to faculty that the school code, which they have all helped to develop, *must* be routinely enforced by *all* staff. This responsibility is part of everyone's job description. In addition, maintaining a disciplined, civil, and productive educational environment should be a major concern of the school's teachers association. Nothing contributes more to teacher burnout than spending great amounts of energy dealing with poorly behaved students who continually "push the envelope" of permissible behavior or go past those limits. Building-level professional association activities should spend much time on forming a staff consensus on discipline enforcement.

Some Principles for Teachers on Administering Punishment

Punishment can be strong stuff. It makes a deep impression on students. It can arouse long-lasting emotions of anger and resentment. We offer the following principles regarding punishment by individual teachers:

1   The reasons for the punishment should always be clear to the student.
2. A specific punishment should always be administered in a moral framework understood by the student. "I am keeping you after school because you repeatedly bothered your seatmate today, even after I warned you. That kind of behavior shows little respect for others or for what we are trying to accomplish in this classroom."

3. Never punish (apart from giving a low grade) a student for inept performance. Poor academic performance alone is no reason for retribution. However, failure to try is another matter. "You did not do your homework" *can* be a cause for punishment.

4. Focus on the behavior of the student, not on the student's person ("I had you stand in the hall because you were wandering around the room again, bothering other students. I know you can do better than this." Or "You are being denied recess, not because you failed the test, but because you didn't do the homework that might have enabled you to pass the test.").

5. Sometimes engage the student in the punishment process. Give them practice at judging their own mistakes ("What do you think is a good punishment for being late four days this week?).

6. Don't use positive things as punishment. For instance, don't punish a student by having him write a story or read a book. Don't give them what is usually volunteer work or community service as punishment.

7. In all significant cases, quickly involve parents in the adjudication and punishment process. Except in trivial cases, ensure that parents are informed of the violations involved and the consequences generated. Have parents sign to ensure that they have received notes, or phone them at home or work. In some cases, the parents' punishment of a child will be more effective than any the teacher can generate. In other instances, parental permissiveness is part of the cause of the problem, and the teacher may not receive proper support. But even with permissive parents, persistent contacts can often prod them to change their current ineffective policies. All of this takes teacher engagement, tact, and courage.

8. Have several intermediate steps between the relative mild punishments of the classroom and the severe penalty of suspension from school. Some teachers use time out for misbehaving students, where the student is sent to another part of the classroom and separated temporarily from the class activity. Many schools have designed in-school suspension, where students are sent to special no-idling, work-oriented rooms. If offending students do not respond to these intermediate punishments, separation from school is called for. This should be a last resort, but a real resort.

PRACTICES AND POLICIES

1. Can you identify an example of an actual classroom or schoolwide rule you knew of as either a teacher or student that was poorly conceived or drafted? What was it, and what were the effects of its inefficiency?

2. Can you identify a similar instance of a poorly conceived punishment? What was it, and what were the effects of its inefficiency?

3. Provide examples of effective rules or punishments. Why were they effective?

4. Do you know or recall a teacher whom you believe was a poor disciplinarian? What instances of ineptitude come to mind?

5. Describe a teacher whom you believe was a good disciplinarian.

6. Please identify and describe a real discipline problem, existing in either the present or past, in a school or classroom, that you are familiar with. What change or new rule or system of punishment would be useful to correct the situation? Draft an appropriate rule or punishment policy to correct the situation.

7. Find an actual set of published school rules and punishment policies. Critique them in the light of this chapter.

CHAPTER 5

The Moral Nature of the Classroom

In modern times there are opposing views about the practice of education. There is not general agreement about what the young should learn either in relation to virtue or in relation to the best in life: nor is it clear whether their education ought to be directed more towards the intellect than towards the character of the soul. The problem has been complicated by what we see happening before our eyes, and it is not certain whether training should be directed at things useful in life, or at those conducive to virtue, or at nonessentials. All these answers have been given. And there is no agreement as to what, in fact, does tend toward virtue. Men do not all prize most highly the same virtue, so naturally they differ also about the proper training for it.

—Aristotle, 4th century B.C.

Only a handful of educational theorists think that children are naturally good and if the adult world would get out of their way, that they would ripen into fully realized people. But one wonders if the advocates of "natural goodness" theories have ever raised children of their own. For instance, Rousseau placed all of his children in an orphanage. Children do not automatically grow up to be good.

Children are born helpless, and need help from the adults around them well into their teens and beyond. Besides learning how to acquire the basics of food and shelter, and how to stay out of the teeth of furry beasts and avoid large, speeding machines, children need to learn how to live in society. They must learn how things are done in their tribe; how people work together and settle disputes; how to contribute to the survival of the community; and how to balance what they need and want with the needs and wants of the people around them.

The primary teacher of this knowledge is the family. Parents, brothers and sisters, uncles and aunts, and grandparents, all work together to "civilize" the child, to make him able to exist among people with some degree of comfort and harmony. It is a long, time- and energy-consuming task (more so with some children than others), but it is among the most important functions of the family. However, at this moment in our history, the American family is not a very strong teaching entity. One sociologist, Amitai Etzioni, presented his view.

> [Many] of our youngsters grow up in families that are not viable from an education viewpoint. Frequent divorces, a bewildering rotation of boyfriends and parents who come home from work exhausted both physically and mentally, have left many homes with tremendous parenting deficits. Instead of providing a stable home environment and the kind of close, loving supervision good character formation requires, many child care facilities, grannies, and baby sitters simply ensure that children stay out of harm's way.[1]

This condition has had a number of effects. For one thing, the school, a relatively recent social invention, has been pressed into greater service to make up for the lacks and gaps in many families. Since a child cannot get along without the rules of social life and an internalized sense of what is right and wrong, the school is an obvious choice to provide them.

Schools must continue to play their traditional role as a strong secondary source of moral education and character formation. Further, the individual classroom is the inner arena of this learning. Children spend the great bulk of their school days there. Children do not come to school as morally blank slates or without interest and experience in the issues of right and wrong, of good and bad. They bubble over with moral views and concerns. Describing the conversations of children, Robert Fullinwider has written:

> They complain about parents or teachers; they make fun of the weird looking kid
> down the block; they tell tales about people in the neighborhood, spread rumors
> about their teachers, divulge secrets they had sworn never to reveal, and speculate
> about the dark sides of their friends. They confide in one another, sharing their
> fears, hopes, disappointments, and grudges. They make plans for getting even with
> their enemies and imagine the most fiendish ways they could revenge themselves on
> the teachers they hate. They rate and they rank; who's the prettiest, who's the best;
> who's a jerk and who's a snob; who's a good guy and who's a reliable friend; who's
> nice and who's not.[2]

These are some of the moral concerns and ideas children bring with them into their classrooms. These imported perspectives are further agitated by the cauldron of moral matter that lies bubbling below the surface of the typical classroom. The cauldron is seething with issues about the rightness and wrongness of things. The individual child, be he second-grader or high school senior, is up to his neck in moral tensions, issues, and ideas.

"Should I do my best on this assignment or dash it off so I can have some free time?"

"I can't do this work. Should I cheat?"

"I can't stand that girl. Why do I have to sit next to her?"

"If I just keep quiet, watch the teacher, stay out of trouble, I can float right through this course."

"Why should I help him with his homework? If I help him, he could end up getting a better grade than me."

The moral is woven into the very fabric of classroom life.

There is an old saying that claims, "If scientists were fish, the last thing they would discover is water." The same is true for many educators. The environment of the classroom is so morally rich and dense that teachers often do not see it. Like fish and water, we have become habituated to it. We stop seeing how certain children pointedly ignore or even intimidate others. We let troublesome or lazy students, whom we believe can do much better work, simply slide by doing the minimum. We use our own power as teachers in an arbitrary manner. We carefully teach works, such as *Julius Caesar*, emphasizing historical background, language, characterization, and structure, but fail to ask the students critical questions such as, "Was Brutus right to join in the assassination of Caesar?", "Is killing ever the right thing to do?", and "When is it right to turn against legitimate authority?" We go to great trouble developing a final test on arithmetic, but through laxity let some children cheat. For these teachers, habituated by the everyday quality of school, the bedrock moral mission of education goes unacknowledged and unaddressed. As Aristotle's quote at the beginning of the chapter discloses, confusion and uncertainty about the goals of education are not novel. Still, despite such uncertainty, there is a basic reality: the classroom is a moral environment. Ignoring this dimension of classroom life does not make the issue disappear.

This chapter will concentrate on the moral life of the classroom and the classroom teacher. The next two chapters will examine the moral dimensions of the teacher's role and the classroom's curriculum. Our discussion in all three chapters will deal with issues relevant to both elementary and secondary teachers, although some matters will inevitably be more important to one group than the other. Sometimes the distinctions between the two groups will be due to developmental contrasts among different pupil age groups, e.g., the differing capabilities of children and adolescents. And sometimes the distinctions will be due to different forms of school processes, particularly the differences generated by the contrasts between self-contained classrooms and those with departmentalized instruction.

The issues we will look at specially in this chapter are two abstractions, two elements of classroom life that fundamentally affect the moral quality and impact of classroom learnings: the ethos of the classroom and the attitudes of students.

ETHOS

Ethos refers to the shared attitudes, beliefs, and values of a community. Ethos means, too, the spirit of a group or community of people. While not directly observable, the ethos of a classroom or a school can be a formidable force in shaping the minds and hearts of students.

Theodore Sizer's *Horace's Compromise* describes the ethos of an all-too-typical high school classroom, in which the ethos was one of divided expectations.[3] Horace, the middle-age teacher, has struck an unstated but clearly understood bargain with those students who, for a variety of reasons, have little interest in doing the work of the classroom. Horace will work hard to teach those who choose to learn and let the others slip by with passing grades if they do not hassle him, if they do not bother the serious students and his efforts to teach them. Everyone passes, but only some learn.

In another recent book, Tracy Kidder's *Among School Children*, we see another ethos.[4] This book is an account of one year in the life of a classroom, the fifth grade of a school serving the poor in a small western Massachusetts city. The teacher, Chris Zajac, is a fiercely dedicated woman who is in many ways the opposite of Horace. She is all over her classroom, challenging, probing, and encouraging her students. Each of her students is more than known by her; each seems to become a project for her. She will not ease up, even on the weakest, most distracted, and most unconcerned students. Even in the poorest and most hostile students, she will not let the light go out.

From her opening speech to her class to the hugs on the last day of the school year, Chris Zajac was working on the ethos of her class, an environment of attitudes and expectations, rules and procedures, ideas and sentiments. At first her students just passively observe her or seem unaffected. But gradually she and the ethos she has created begin to affect them. It does not affect all of them right away or to the same degree. But Chris Zajac generates a set of expectations, a serious work outlook, and a transforming spirit that reaches and changes her students.

The ethos Chris creates in her classroom, while clearly having academic outcomes, is a moral ethos. She demands respect of her students, respect for her, for one another, and for themselves. She expects them to keep promises, to do their work, and to do it well. If they break their promises, there are consequences (e.g., no recess, staying after, calls to parents). The same is true of incivility and other breaches of good discipline. She expects them to act with respect towards other students. She rewards her students' academic successes and improved behavior. She wins battles and loses them. There are good days and bad weeks. At the end of her year with them, her 180 days of hectoring, praising, confronting, surprising, and challenging them, many of her students are strikingly changed. Some are not. There were no dramatic turning points, no critical incidents where the scales fell from her students' eyes. The demands and expectations she has imposed have been accepted and taken to heart.

Chris Zajacs, however, are rare. The majority of teachers do not share her sense of empowerment. They do not believe they have the authority to be so large in their students' lives. In fairness, Chris taught in an elementary school and monitored 27 or 28 pupils throughout a whole day. On the other hand, Sizer's Horace, in a departmentalized high school, was responsible for handling perhaps 100 to 150 pupils per day. His pupils were also older, and, presumably, less impressionable, than Chris's. We cannot make simple comparisons between the two situations. Still, a significant study of one high school math teacher, Jaime Escalante, by Jay Matthews demonstrates that many high school teachers are often prone to underestimate the educational possibilities around them.[5] Escalante was also the central figure in the biographical film, *Stand And Deliver*. Matthews shows how Escalante's intense caring and his demand for high performance from students paid off in their achievements and renewed self-confidence.

Some teachers in departmentalized schools use another tactic to gratify their aspirations for more morally founded student/adult contacts; they advise clubs or other student activities, or coach teams. These organizations share many of the characteristics of the self-contained classroom. Many of the suggestions we offer that seem to be more aimed at elementary school teachers can easily be adapted to junior high and high school clubs, teams, and similar activities.

Educational sociologist Gerald Grant has written penetratingly about the transformation of the American teacher in *The World We Created at Hamilton High.*[6] Grant's research shows how from 1953 to 1985 a high school was changed. More to the point, he shows how the experience of being in high school was different from one five-year period to the next. What Grant has captured in his study is the modification of some American schools. At the beginning of the period involved, many high schools were relatively intimate institutions, infused with local values, positive and negative, functional and dysfunctional. Gradually, they became increasingly bureaucratized and centralized institutions. Most recently, they have been infused with national, even global, values that too frequently reflect the will of highly vocal special-interest groups.

Grant points out in particular how the existential experience of being a teacher, especially in a high school, was fundamentally different at various times during the period he studied. Many teachers and administrators have changed from believing they were special people, enriching, civilizing, humanizing, and continuing the work of parents and the community, to professionals fulfilling certain prescribed tasks in a contractual exchange of services. Teaching once seemed an honored profession, motivated by interest in helping others; now it is a career that treats term papers, tests, and students as a modern equivalent of piecework. In this transformation from teacher to educational technician, the teacher's moral role has been obscured.

This new legalistic and bureaucratic ethos has altered the relationship between student and teacher in a basic way. The change has engendered an emphasis on established procedures, grievance systems, student rights, and contractual obligations. One example is the labor/management tone among teachers, administrators, and school boards, which has been a by-product of the rise of activist teachers' associations and unions. Another is the prevalence of rights-oriented student handbooks (discussed in Chapter 4) that erode the authority of the teacher and encourage an adversarial relationship. Often, these teacher contracts and student handbooks are silent on the responsibilities of people—children *and* adults—and members of a community, a shared space of common purpose. They say little about the members' moral responsibilities to the community of which they are all part. All too often, since little is asked in terms of a moral obligation, little is given.

Revitalizing or re-creating the moral ethos of classrooms is what is needed. All teachers must be infused with the sense of moral authority possessed by Chris Zajac and Jaime Escalante. We need to reinvigorate teachers with the idealism and compassion that led so many to originally enter the profession, but that has been gradually eroded over the years. This is the task of teacher education, of the school board, of parents, of the administrators, and of senior teachers. Recognizing and acting on one's moral authority is also the responsibility of each individual teacher.

Of course, many teachers now possess moral authority. However, many others have grown up within our contemporary contractual-legalistic ethos. Such teachers often lack understanding about their moral authority and ethical responsibilities. They do not appreciate that they are selected representatives of the community and share with parents the responsibility for the proper formation of their students' habits and moral values. While this larger sense of their role is missing, it is not far from the surface. Indeed, it is built into the very nature of being an effective teacher. The teacher's sense of moral authority and role of creator of a moral ethos in the classroom are inherent in the job. They come with the territory.

Towards Creating a Moral Ethos in the Classroom

Much of this book is about establishing a stronger, more wholesome ethos, one that contrasts with the loose, low standards and self-oriented tone currently permeating many of our classrooms. Making allowances for the developmental level of their students and their specific school situation, we suggest that classroom teachers (or in high schools, the sponsors of pupils' clubs and teams) should

1. continually remind all pupils, parents, and colleagues, through mottos, memos, meetings, posters, or whatever, that education is fundamentally a moral enterprise and encourage that attitude to penetrate all aspects of classroom and personal life.

2. encourage each student to develop or adopt his own motto and strive to live up to it. For example, "Don't wait to be a great adult. Be a great student . . . today!"

3. from the first classes early in the year establish a spirit of high standards and serious purpose. "You are going to accomplish great things this year. We are going to make this class something truly special!"

4. design your classroom environment to reflect the high purpose and moral goals of the class. Put up pictures and other reminders of those goals and ideals.

5. give individual students and the class clear academic and moral goals to be achieved. Regularly keep them aware of their progress towards those goals. Publicly and privately, celebrate their achievements and identify instances when there is a failure to make sufficient progress or fulfill commitments.

6. help the class earn a sense of specialness. Find something that they can take pride in and that makes them stand out from the crowd. Help them to see themselves as a family, as a tight community. For instance, have the class take on an out-of-school project, such as regular assistance to an

elderly couple who need help with getting groceries, house chores, raking leaves, and simple repairs. Or have them plant trees to help the environment, volunteer to clean up part of the school grounds, or hold a car wash for a charity.

7. develop a sense of connectedness among the individual students. Make them feel special ties to their classmates, ties gained through coming to the aid of one another and through working together on shared goals in both academics and sports.

8. have pictures of outstanding people on the walls of the classroom and read to students about their achievements, so these portraits teach more fully.

The ethos of a classroom directs much of this action. It is an intangible spirit that tells students what is important and what is not. Ethos is driven by certain ideas, and these ideas structure how teachers and students behave. Two concepts, one rather new and the other quite old, illustrate ethos-in-action.

Self-Esteem—a Dead End?

Not too long ago our schools reflected the widespread cultural and religious belief that self-love was a perversion and humility was a prized virtue. The social critic Allan Bloom, commenting on a man who had recently been released from prison, where, through psychotherapy, he had "found his identify and learned to like himself," says, "a generation earlier he would have found God and learned to despise himself."[7] Our schools are permeated with a term which is only a slight variation of self-love: self-esteem.

Too many educators treat the pursuit of pupil self-esteem as an unquestionable desideratum. Its current legitimacy is partly due to the efforts of the American psychologist Abraham Maslow. For many decades of this century, Maslow labored to convince social scientists and educators of the importance of gaining self-esteem.[8] He has surely succeeded beyond his wildest dreams with educators.

Rita Kramer described interviews she conducted at 20 schools of education around the country.[9] She found that the cultivation of pupils' self-esteem was the dominant educational theory she encountered. Whether Maslow's ideas and the adoption of self-esteem as a goal have actually helped children acquire a healthy attitude toward themselves is, however, the issue.

Some psychologists have argued that young people who think little of themselves and do not see themselves advancing in life are also students who have not done well in school and are not currently performing well. That is, low self-esteem relates, in some way, to poor performance. These authorities urged all of us, young and old alike, to learn to like ourselves more and, "to be our own best friend." Educational psychologists have made the building of self-concept and self-esteem an essential pillar of teacher education. For instance, William W. Purkey, author of *Inviting School Success*, urges teachers to encourage students to experience feelings of positive self-worth through learning the teaching skills of *invitational learning*.[10] Purkey defines an invitation as "a summary description of messages—verbal and nonverbal, formal and informal—continuously transmitted to students with the intention of informing them that they are responsible, able, and valuable." Purkey's writings and those of other psychologists such as Arthur Combs (the teacher as facilitator), Carl Rogers (learner-centered teaching), and Thomas Gordon (Teacher Effectiveness Training) echo the ideas of Maslow: real learning cannot take place if a student has a poor self-concept.

Ironically, this appealing theory lacks serious research support. For instance, in January 1990 a mathematics test was administered by Educational Testing Services to a sample of fifth-graders from six countries, including the United States. The Americans' test scores were lowest of the six countries. The Koreans were first. The test also asked pupils to say whether they felt they would be "good at mathematics in high school." Of the Americans, 68% said "Yes," while only 26% of the high-scoring Koreans gave that reply.[11]

Another international study compared parents' opinions with their children's academic performance.[12] Of American mothers, 91% thought their children's schools were doing an "excellent," or "good" job educating their children. In other words, they felt their children were doing a fine job of learning. This was more than double the percent of satisfied Chinese (42%) and Japanese (39%) mothers. The average measured academic performance of the Chinese and Japanese children greatly exceeded that of the Americans. Another research report, developed for the California State Commission on Self-Esteem, surely a body sympathetic to the "cause", concluded that no notable proven connection has been found between self-esteem (however defined) and other desirable goals, such as improved academic learning.[13] Finally, a narrative written by a friend of both Maslow and Rogers discloses that, later in life, both became very disillusioned with their earlier pronouncements and the popularized by-products. The "founders" felt that their premises had been unduly optimistic, and typically applied in exaggerated fashions.[14]

Despite such impressive data, many teachers have increasingly seen the raising of students' self-esteem as a primary responsibility. It also is evident that many parents have been infected with this perspective—witness the simplistic optimism many American parents have about their children's mediocre academic performance. Undoubtedly, many children are plagued by self-doubt and a poor opinion of themselves. The reasons for this condition are multiple. Poor performance has many causes, few of which yield to simplistic solutions. Nevertheless, many in the self-esteem movement tell us the answer to this problem is to attack head-on to try to give self-esteem to students. Such an attack usually involves removing all elements of school and classroom life (such as tests, grades, and demanding assignments) that are in some way related to poor self-esteem. Unfortunately, by removing these elements, we also remove the tools that provide students with both realistic feedback about their efficacy and the knowledge necessary to improve their performance.

We must recognize that all wholesome human life is ultimately social. Social life inevitably subjects us to certain stress; we have aspirations, disappointments, and rebuffs. The sociologist Robert Everhart and his colleagues studied several schools that gave priority to directly enhancing pupil self-esteem; pupils were given a broad choice among school activities, so they could avoid disappointment and low self-esteem. The levels of academic learning in the schools were quite low. However, the pupils found their undemanding schools relatively satisfying, good places to spend time. Ultimately, the researchers were critical of the schools' efficacy:

> [the schools] gave minimum consideration to the social context in which individuals live—the competing beliefs, actions and ideologies individuals must confront. This created various degrees of doubt and insecurity among the graduating students. . . . Without some complementary belief about social cohesion and the place of the individual in society, a focus on individual attributes is necessarily incomplete.[15]

In effect, Everhart and his colleagues found the schools fostered a corrosive form of pupil narcissism—surely a fragile basis for self-esteem.

The self-esteem movement puts a false and infectious pressure on teachers. They are more and more expected to keep students feeling good about themselves. In other eras, teachers were expected to provide pupils with an environment and an educational opportunity to grow and achieve. As a result of that growth and achievement, pupils will be entitled to earn self-esteem.

Diligence—The Alternative to Self-Esteem

The idea of requiring diligence from pupils puts the teeth of many on edge. It has an old-fashioned ring about it. It conjures up visions of small boys clutching quill pens, huddled over large desks assiduously copying in their notebooks. On the other hand, it is both a much more worthy and achievable educational goal than self-esteem. If one were to summarize in one word the reasons for the phenomenal academic performance of so many Asian-American students, diligence is that word.

Creating a classroom where diligence is taught and prized means teaching students how to accomplish challenging tasks. It means instructing them how to marshall and focus their attention and energies to accomplish goals. It means setting a great variety of tasks for students in which they can practice perseverance, even when they desire to be doing more immediately satisfying activities. It means, in essence, acquiring the habits traditionally associated with achievement in all fields, whether in school, family life, the arts, sports, business, or the professions. For instance, imagine a student who is careless and casual about his academic assignments, but willing to spend hours honing a basketball jump shot. That student needs to appreciate how diligence can pay off in nonathletic spheres of his life. This may be the most important thing his teacher can give him at this moment in his life.

Many reasons exist why students should learn the habit or the virtue of diligence at their school tasks. For one thing, learning how to attack an assignment and see it through makes homework, recitations, and tests less stressful and much more rewarding activities. And when students leave school, diligence will lead to certain benefits. Finally, acquiring the virtue of diligence is the royal road to developing true self-esteem.

The mistake of the self-esteem movement is putting the cart before the horse. In a paradoxical way, self-esteem does not yield to direct assaults. True self-worth and self-esteem is a by-product; it comes to the student as the secret benefit of whatever goal he has worked to achieve. In life, true self-esteem is never given. It is earned.

Self-esteem and feeling good about oneself ordinarily follow from the effort and the achievements, large and small, that result from that effort. The knowledge that we have worked hard and accomplished a task brings with it as a by-product a sense of personal satisfaction. People who habitually accomplish the tasks life presents them with gain a sense of personal effectiveness or worth. Those who regularly fail, or worse, make the meagerest of efforts, receive instead important, life-correcting messages from their environment, corrective messages such as the old naval adage, "Shape up or ship out." Our lack of personal satisfaction and self-esteem is, often as not, nature's way of trying to get us back on course. Therefore, teachers can aid students to get back on course by giving them advice, offering corrective feedback, restructuring assignments, and helping them acquire the habit of diligence.

Attitudes About Education

Fundamental to being a good and effective student is an attitude, a way of envisioning what one is doing and why one is doing it. In recent decades, attitudes about popular education have changed markedly. Historically, extended schooling—more than three or four years—was something only the relatively wealthy, the sons (almost exclusively) of royalty and of the rich, could afford. As societies gained more security and prosperity, they, in turn, invested more of that wealth in the education and development of their young.

In the 19th and 20th centuries, the concept of universal education seized the public imagination. This occurred particularly in countries moving toward more democratic forms of government. And among these same countries, one after another began making the spread of schooling a national priority. While there was much social altruism in this expansion of education, there was also a good deal of enlightened self-interest on the part of various nations. In a democracy, a literate and skilled populace made self-government more efficacious. Over the decades, then, policy-makers have become more insistent that children be sent from their homes to the local school earlier in their lives and kept there for longer periods. The starting age of schooling has become earlier and earlier, with some advocating that all children be in some form of schooling by their third birthday. Similarly, leaving school has been extended during recent decades from age 10 to 12 to 16 and now some communities require children to stay in school until their 19th birthday (or high school graduation). The school day and year also get longer, taking up more of the waking hours of children. Today, some laypersons and educators are calling for a year-round school calendar. This insistence on students spending more time in school may, at first, have had a salutary effect on the gross national product, in that there has been an increase in the job skills of those leaving our school systems. However, there may have been greater costs, such as the corrosive effect on the classroom as a place of learning.

Consider the attitude of a 19th-century 10-year-old, who is able to leave the arduous and boring tasks of the family farm and go to a warm schoolroom with other children his age and hear about a larger world over the horizon. That child's attitude is sharply different than that of modern 10-year-olds.

Perhaps the point can be made by analogy. A generation ago, if parents sent a child to his room, it was a form of punishment, especially if they added, "And don't you dare turn on the radio!" Today, those same parents would have to add, "And don't you dare turn on the television set, or the VCR, or your CD player. And you can't use your Walkman or your other tape player. And that means no Nintendo! None of those little hand-held games either. And you can't take the cordless phone into your room. And you can't eat or drink anything from your small refrigerator. No sunbathing, either, and stay out of the Jacuzzi. The only thing you are allowed to turn on is your electric typewriter. And if you use your computer, you have to use it for schoolwork and not those video games! And, yes, you can read. What do you mean, 'You don't have a book?'"

Exaggerated? Yes, but accurate for many and partially true for most students. Being sent to one's room today is a release from close supervision.

By analogy, then, going to school for many modern children means leaving their comfortable home with food and drink at the touch, with electronic media to feed them information and entertainment, and where they have few, if any, chores to perform. And what do they go to when they enter school?

True, our student finds the stimulation of friends. However, the environment, again relative to home or the street, makes real demands on him. Students are expected to stay in a particular classroom, if not a particular desk. They are required to follow rules about when and how and to whom they speak. They are expected to cooperate with the teacher, listen carefully, and do the tasks the teacher assigns (teachers who are a good deal less entertaining than the adults who host their television programs). In addition, they are expected to be courteous to fellow students and, in particular, towards the teacher. They are supposed to do this for seven hours a day for half the days of their young lives. Compared with home, school no longer seems the great escape that it appeared to be to our 19th-century child. As a result, the attitudes of students have tended to shift: school, once a rich opportunity for stimulation, has become more of an institution that interrupts their pleasure and places demands and constraints on them.

The most frequent criticism of schools by students (and one that continually saps the energies and creative juices of teachers) is the whine, "This is boring." And, objectively, the pupils may be right. Compared to the cornucopia of diversions and delights the consumer society has laid out before the young, life in school *is* boring. Marshall McLuhan, the media guru of the 1960s, commenting on the information-saturated environment, quipped that the child interrupted his education when he came to school. And this was well before the explosion of the youth-oriented media market. Certainly, the modern child interrupts his entertainment when he goes to school.

From this pattern, another change in attitude has come. School is no longer "something for which I have a sense of responsibility." The prevailing attitude is now "If you are going to force school on me, I must have my rights!" Regrettably, this attitude is often echoed by the child's parents—and by some educators.

Trying to change such a resentful "show-me" attitude to one in which education is seen as something one must live up to is no easy task. However, such changes are crucial for the educative process to take root. It is decisive, too, for the child's development as a mature adult. But attitudes are rarely changed only by verbal assaults such as, "Education is a privilege. You ought to be thankful you are in school!" The teacher needs stronger and more multifarious medicine than this.

In the same way that different medicines work with different patients, so, too, with teachers and students. Some students respond to gentle prodding, some to positive attention in the form of pep talks, and some to punishment. Changing pupil attitudes is usually much more difficult than changing behavior. Indeed, since an attitude is an internal state of mind, it is technically invisible. What teachers actually observe are student behaviors, which reflect such mindsets. We essentially change bad attitudes by changing the behaviors through which they are typically revealed. In fact, the most efficient way to change attitudes is to change behavior. The attitudes will catch up.

We suggest that teachers

1. teach students about attitudes and how they affect behavior and how they can be changed and modified.

2. make it clear to students that student attitudes count. Tell them that while a teacher cannot literally see an uncooperative or negative attitude, he can see antipathetic behavior—words, tone of voice, gestures, postures, modes of dress—and that behavior will not be tolerated.

3. recognize and reward individual and group behaviors that reflect positive attitudes. Give verbal support and group rewards, such as a popcorn party, for the display of appropriate behaviors, when the class shows excellent conduct, or when attendance is perfect.

4. directly help individual students or groups to deal with behaviors that reflect self-destructive attitudes, such as self-pity or anger.

5. display the behavior consistent with a constructive, cooperative attitude.

6. practice empathy. Teach students to understand and interpret the conduct and attitudes of others and to appreciate others' hardships and disadvantages. Use literature and the pupils' own experiences to deepen this compassion.

There is an ancient wisecrack about the college sophomore who is overcome by the great insight into the reality that everything in the universe is connected to everything else. While this is an obvious observation, it is one we teachers forget all too frequently. The *whole* child comes to school in the morning, not a set of separated domains: intellectual, moral, and physical. The student is not a cognitive entity at one moment, the next a moral being, and later on a physical one. As a young third-grader, or adolescent eleventh-grader, leaves his school locker at the beginning of the school day and enters the classroom, he enters as a totality, with a certain amount of knowledge and much to learn. He has certain physical characteristics and a physical potential to fulfill. And he is a moral entity, with things to learn and needs to fulfill. His day and the day of every pupil is taken up with these aspects of his life.

The great bulk of what is written about schools and teaching has to do with the intellectual domain. Next is the physical domain. This aspect of our human nature is formally addressed in schools through the physical education curriculum, through which the school addresses the requirements students have to grow well and develop soundly. Furthermore, concern for the child's physical nature permeates the school. Temperatures are set and maintained for the students' comfort. The lighting is arranged so they see well and their eyes are preserved. Desks are designed with their physical characteristics in mind, and are actually adjusted as they grow. Schools have fire and tornado drills. The need to attend to the students' physical safety and well-being has caused many schools to disallow smoking anywhere in the building, including the teachers' lounge. Unfortunately, in recent years, we have been less conscious of and less direct in dealing with the ethical nature of children and their need for moral safety. The teacher's conception of his own work is critical here. All of us must reemphasize the essentially moral nature of the classroom.

PRACTICES AND POLICIES

1. Informally discuss the topic of moral authority, perhaps using the examples of Zajac and Escalante with several colleagues or teachers in training. To what extent do the teachers they have known possess this moral authority?

2. Part of the chapter discusses student diligence. To what degree do you think you emphasize effective work/study habits in your students? What habits do you emphasize when you teach your students how to work or study? Do you publicly praise students and the class when they have been diligent in completing a task?

3. With several teachers in the same grade level, department, or physical area of the school, compile a list of feasible projects for your students that would contribute to their sense of specialness.

4. Encourage faculty members to share ideas with their colleagues on improving the moral ethos in the classroom and school. On the bulletin board in the faculty room, post teachers' suggestions for improving the ethos in school. Then, implement the ones that are feasible, giving credit to the teachers who suggest the ideas. During faculty meetings, allow five minutes or more for a teacher to present a proposal for improving school ethos or to share what worked for him in the classroom.

CHAPTER 6

Teachers as Moral Educators

Example is the school of mankind, and they will learn at no other.

—Edmund Burke

The great English parliamentarian and philosopher Edmund Burke often wrote of the importance of moral models for the young. He also anticipated many of the findings of contemporary psychologists and researchers, particularly learning theorists like Albert Bandura[1] and Robert Biehler.[2] Much of what we learn is by imitation or modeling. And the younger we are, the stronger the impact of models on our personalities.

Children have one primary aim, one that operates consciously and unconsciously. That aim is to be an adult, to grow up. This is their project, their work in life. The adults that are near and dear to them are the ones they will emulate. If these adults are respectful and caring, they will try to be respectful and caring. If the adults are self-serving and lazy, they will be self-serving and lazy. This principle explains why an overwhelming number of states require evidence of "good character" by individuals applying for teaching licenses.

THE MORAL TEACHER

Teachers have always been expected to be good examples to the young. However, special circumstances of modern life make this aspect of the teacher's work crucial. The circumstances are clearly indicated by the comments of the sociologist James S. Coleman on changes in the American family.[3] He observed that two generations ago the father left the home to work, and that one generation ago, the mother, too, left. His point is that, until well into the 20th century, the majority of parents worked in the sight of their children.

The farmer or small shopkeeper worked, ate, and lived in the midst of his children. The mother was also there, performing farm chores, housework, and food preparation. But that changed with our modern economy, where the father works at a factory or goes to the office. The same trend was followed by mothers. In 1970, 33% of women with school age children worked outside the home full- or part-time. In 1980, the percentage went up to 51% and in 1990 to 67%. By 1995, according to estimates, women will make up 50% of the American work force, and by the year 2000, 80% of American women with children will be working outside the home.[4]

With children rarely contributing to family income, and parents working outside the home, and busy and tired when they are home, parent-child contacts are different than in earlier periods. Related to this is the fact that parents do not have as much to teach their children as in the past. The skills of previous generations (e.g., how to care for animals, sew a dress, keep a fire going through the night) have little meaning to children who will compete for

113

a livelihood in a high-tech culture. Further, most children live in small nuclear families with few siblings, and these small families are increasingly mobile. Children grow up cut off from relatives: grandparents, uncles, aunts, and cousins who, because of blood ties, are concerned about the development of their family members. All of this increases teachers' prominence in the lives of our young.

As the impact of families has receded substantially in the lives of the young, the presence of teachers has grown larger. For some students, their teachers are a major source of stability in their lives. As mentioned in the previous chapter, our children are starting school earlier, spending more time in classrooms, and leaving schooling later in their teens. Young Americans are in the presence of teachers for more time than ever before.

Apart from the simple matter of presence, there are many other reasons why teachers have a powerful impact as models. The teacher is the students' designated leader. This heightens her potential for moral impact, either positive or negative. A teacher immediately controls the lives of children. She gives out rewards and punishments. She assigns tasks in school and tasks to be performed at home. She grades both the students' tangible work and their effort. She decides who goes to recess and who goes to the next grade. She has power over the lives of children. Besides focusing the attention of students on the teacher in a very direct way, this power has another effect. Students examine it as an entity in itself. Few parents or teachers have failed to hear emotional complaints and sometimes tearful sobs about real or imagined teacher misbehavior:

"She's unfair!"
"She gave a surprise test that really counts!"
"He is always playing favorites."
And on and on.

All of us are called to escape from what the late novelist Walker Percy calls the "Great Suck of Self," to learn to be generous, engaged citizens. Educators, though, have a special responsibility to display such maturity: their unique relationship to children. They must be moral models. However, being told, "You are to be a moral model, a moral exemplar" is for most of us unsettling. For some, the idea is paralyzing. For others, it conjures up a vision of some sort of sainthood, secular or religious. They fear this vision must commit them to a role of complete concern for others and total self-denial. Still others worry about being instant fountains of ethical wisdom, a sort of moral Delphic oracle. Such a vision may be behind the unease and suspicion that many teachers feel about this topic. In reality, however, the matter is much simpler, more fundamental, and much closer to the ground.

Characteristics of the Moral Teacher

The teacher needs to be, first of all, someone who is clearly concerned with the good of others, particularly, her students. This does not necessarily mean she must be sweet and obliging to students. Some excellent teachers are hard-driving taskmasters. They come to class every day "loaded for bear" and expect students to come the same way. These teachers may never gush about how much they love their students. However, the students recognize that love. If not immediately, they know it when they have had some distance on the experience.

Secondly, teachers need to show their morality by their actions, particularly the small actions, such as

- presenting well-planned, enthusiastically taught classes.
- getting homework and test papers corrected and back to students promptly.
- not gossiping about students or fellow teachers.
- carrying out small acts of consideration for others such as, cleaning the board for the next teacher coming into the room or taking the wad of used chewing gum out of the water fountain.
- planning a surprise birthday party for a fellow teacher, or the principal, or the secretary.
- going the extra mile for the student who is lost or struggling.

Teachers, like everyone else, are called to humility. Still, it is important that their students sometimes recognize these gestures and civic actions. It is good that they know their teacher volunteers at a homeless shelter or is a fundraiser for her church.

Being a moral model is not waiting for the Great Dilemma to come along. ("Should I go out on strike or not?" or "Should I threaten to resign my position because the superintendent is letting go an outstanding teacher?") The Grand Gesture has its place. Indeed, many of our greatest teachers have taught us by their ultimate sacrifices (Socrates taking the hemlock; Christ accepting the cross.) However, the good example we are speaking of here is much more a matter of the everyday. It is giving one's diligent attention to teaching and to the small demands of our professional life by those around us—students, other teachers, administrators, parents, and staff.

The Morality of Craft

In the novel *The Way of All Flesh*, Samuel Butler wrote, "Every man's work, whether it be literature or music or pictures or architecture or anything else, is always a portrait of himself." The primary moral responsibility of any worker is to strive to be good at her craft—in effect, to be diligent about her principal life responsibility. The surgeon is bound morally to be as proficient at her craft as possible. The shoemaker's moral duty is to repair shoes as well as she can. The autoworker is ethically bound to make the very best car of which she is capable. And, too, the student is morally bound to live up to the demands of parents, community, and school. This principle is particularly binding on teachers. Their work is integral to the growth of children and the progress of society. First and foremost, then, teachers must do their work well. In a later chapter, we will discuss the expectations administrators, typically principals, should have for teachers. But the following points are expectations teachers should have for themselves. There is obviously some overlap between these two perspectives. But truly dedicated teachers should often engage themselves beyond the expectations of their supervisors.

Working Hard. The moral educator works the job. She knows that she teaches students diligence by example. She always comes into class prepared, her materials are the best she can find, and her classes represent the best possible mix of mind and imagination. She gives students demanding assignments that stretch them and get them more involved in the subject. She has thought about where her students are, where they ought to be going, and what they need to get them there. As much as possible, she tries to be conscious of the individual needs, potentials, and learning styles of her students. There is little wasted time in this task-oriented classroom. Students feel her concern that they grow and excel. They recognize she has high standards and they believe that they can, and will, acquire these high standards, too. They feel her insistent but concerned pressure to do their best. And she never works harder than when she senses a student slipping away from her, a student who is drifting or who has began to define herself as a non-student.

Skilled artisan teachers are highly involved in, and identified with, their work. How well they teach and how they are developing as teachers is never far from their minds.

The Continuous Learner. Skilled artisan teachers demonstrate their devotion to their craft through their commitment to improvement. They continuously strive to improve, to learn new competencies and to gain greater understanding of what they teach. They talk about the craft of teaching with other teachers, read professional journals, and seize on opportunities to advance their own professional training. They regularly take refresher courses. They try to stimulate professional development courses and workshops for themselves and fellow teachers. When training is unavailable, they form study groups with other educators. They see themselves on a journey to be as good as they can become, knowing all the time that they can only approach mastery of the craft. Their drive for mastery is motivated by many sources, but one of them is their sense of responsibility to try to excel. They live out the slogan of the teacher as continuous learner.

Concern for Product. Like a fine artisan, the moral teacher is attentive to the final product: the learning of the student. It is critical that the student show significant change in the right direction. She recognizes that learning is often difficult, and that it takes great effort for some students, effort they often are reluctant to give. She is not distracted by the need to win popularity or to have all the children feeling good all the time. She will risk their short-term opinion of her, and even their displeasure. She has in her mind larger stakes with longer time lines. She is attentive to the emotional climate in the classroom, but is not a captive of it. She makes her class into a community, not primarily a pleasant social community, a place for passing time, but a community of learners, a community with a purpose. Her students feel special because of what they have accomplished. They are proud to be one of her "products."

Talking about the morality of craft runs counter to the spirit of the Age of Feel-Good psychology and the relaxed attitudes too evident in many parts of the American workplace. But this fierce sense of craft is exactly what is demanded of the teacher. Think back about Chris Zajac, the teacher in Tracey Kidder's *Among School Children*, or about Jay Matthews' portrayal of Jaime Escalante.

All teachers need to be good at their craft in order to fulfill the social requirements of the work and to realize themselves as fully developed adults. However, there is an even more important reason for stressing excellence: the impact of their example to their students.

Member of a Guild. The artisan teacher is not a solitary worker, plying the trade in isolation from others. She is connected to others, not only to her students. She maintains a special connection with the teachers in the immediate group—the teachers in the building, particularly those at the same grade level or department. They share responsibility to structure the curriculum and its implementation so it is of high calibre. The teacher is a member of a school faculty and takes seriously the responsibilities of a faculty member. The teacher works under the supervision of administrators and imbues those relationships with high ethical standards (rather than an antagonistic labor/management spirit). For instance, the teacher does not think of her allotment of sick days as rest days "owed" to her.

Further, the teacher as artisan sees herself as a part of a professional group, whether or not she is a member of a teachers association or union. If she is a member of such a group, she actively works to help the group reach its highest goals. She feels obligated to improve and enhance the quality of the profession. She is interested in teacher education, taking on student teachers and others learning how to teach. She participates in the activities of her professional group, taking her turn representing fellow teachers in professional endeavors. In all these guild-like activities, though, she is inspired by professional ideals rather than by the narrow, self-serving issues of the moment. She believes, and acts on the belief, that the best interests of the teaching profession are those that advance the quality of education for children.

Some may be troubled with the concept of teacher as craftsperson. Like a craft, teaching involves doing: taking responsibility and control for a process and fashioning something that was not there before. Teaching is a craft because it entails skills, knowledge, and an understanding of the materials being fashioned—the students. But with this sense of craft must come a special conscientiousness. The philosopher, Thomas Green, describes this commitment:

> To possess a conscience of craft is to have cultivated the capacity for self-congratulation or deep satisfaction at something well done, shame at slovenly work, and even embarrassment at carelessness. . . . It is what impels us to lay aside slovenly and sloppy work simply because of what it is—slovenly and sloppy.[5]

THE TEACHER AS DIRECT SOURCE OF MORAL COMMUNICATION

Children and young adults often lose their moral way. They steal someone's property, cheat on a test, or spread a lie about another student. On such occasions, they need direct guidance about what to do. By direct guidance, we simply mean some authoritative person should remind them what is right, and, in a firm but kindly manner, tell them to go and do it. Much of our important moral learning does and should proceed at this simple level. One need not apply psychotherapy. Ideally, the young will get quick and sound direction from their parents, their primary moral educators. But for a variety of reasons, this is not always possible. They need help right away and their parents are not available, or the facts of the incident are unknown to their parents. Being available for this kind of help has traditionally been part of the teacher's work.

When he was in high school, one of the authors got in trouble at home. He found himself in an ugly quarrel with his older sister. He lost his temper (because, he recalls, he was losing the argument), and struck her. Having broken two important family rules, he knew he was in trouble. He fled the house and, after stewing for an hour or so, sought help from a teacher. It was a teacher he did not even like very much, but a teacher who was available at the moment of need. And he received very calming and sane advice ("You already know you made a big mistake. Go home, say you are sorry and face the music.").

The reason for telling this story is because of its ordinariness just a few decades ago. The teacher was not surprised when he was asked for counsel. No one thought it was unusual. Whether we knew Latin or not, we all knew about *in loco parentis*. We knew that in a special way, we "belonged to" our teachers and, equally important, they "belonged to" us. We expected them to be concerned about our behavior in and out of school. We expected them to be attentive to the deficiencies of our character, angry at lapses in honesty, and nagging about our laziness. We knew that this was part of their work. And, whenever we thought about it seriously, we were glad they cared.

There are still many teachers who communicate this attitude of "you belong to me and I to you." One of us recently heard a teacher say to her class about a forthcoming assembly, "I don't care if the rest of the school raises the roof. You will sit there quietly!" And they did.

Unfortunately, such "you belong to me" teachers do not seem to be as common as they used to be. Many teachers simply do not feel they have the support from administrators and parents to feel secure in being a moral educator, particularly in such a direct way. Some teachers feel rebuffed and rebuked and cannot rise to this responsibility. A few believe there is no value consensus or even any basic virtues, so they avoid direct moral education.

Some other teachers say this direct response to requests for moral advice is the job of guidance counselors. However, many counselors would confess they have no special training for this work. Furthermore, in the current intellectual climate, they do not want to be involved in students' moral problems. Helping them adjust (whatever this means) minus morality: yes; scheduling courses of study, or selecting work or college goals: yes; responding to a student's requests for help with a moral problem, such as helping untangle a family feud, or involvement with alcohol, drugs, or promiscuous sexuality: no. For many educators, the role of moral counselor has simply slipped off the screen.

In 1990, Harvard psychologist Robert Coles released an extensive study of the moral character of children.[6] His research team interviewed students in grades 4 through 12 across the United States. They posed more than 90 serious questions (e.g., *Do you believe in God? How do you decide what is right and what is wrong?*) to over 5000 young people. The report revealed many things, among them that different children think about issues of right and wrong in very different ways. Coles' team identified five basic orientations. To an important degree, such differences in valuing were related to the different ages of the respondents. However, there are some notable differences across children in the same age group. Also, children from economically poor families reported greater pressure to engage in immoral behavior (e.g., taking drugs, disobeying authority, joining a gang) than other children. Coles characterized the typical American student as lacking a moral compass, a clear and firm way to deal with moral issues.

One of the most troubling aspects of the study dealt with to whom students went when they had to get advice on a moral problem. Of the high school students in the study 58% reported that when confronted with a personal moral problem they would be most likely to seek advice from another teenager. This is additional evidence for what sociologists have been describing for years: the growing influence of the peer group in the lives of teenagers and the corresponding decline in the influence of traditional forces, such as parents, community leaders, and others.

Students were asked if they would consult a teacher for moral advice. Only 7% said they would, compared with the 58% who would seek out another teenager. The researchers refer to this as the "Wallpaper Factor." The term suggests that teachers and clergy (who only 3% of the students would seek advice from) play a peripheral role in teenagers' moral lives. This fact is especially disturbing since teenagers must cope with the moral problems connected to their new independence. Such independence is an important part of their progress towards maturity. But they should not make decisions about issues such as drinking, drugs, sexuality, and life goals without adult counsel. We are not suggesting that teachers become the primary moral counselors of the young. We simply propose that teachers should be more ready and able to respond to students' calls for help. Administrators and parents should encourage and support this involvement, and teachers should solicit their advice in complex situations.

Ineffectual Instructors

There are innumerable reasons why so many teachers are so unimportant as sources of moral guidance to many teenagers. One simple reason is that many teachers are ill-prepared to provide pupils with moral instruction. This deficiency, in turn, has a number of causes. Let us consider some of these.

In recent decades, the teacher's role has been defined as essentially a technical activity. This emphasis has led to the erosion of the teacher's moral authority. And educators must take substantial responsibility for this development. It is often stressed in the literature that the "effective teacher" uses "wait time" and brings about high rates of student "time on task."[7] The teacher should be largely concerned with conveying information and skills. The dominant professional literature of the 1970s and 1980s dealt with "effective schools" and "effective teachers."[8] In this influential corpus of research and writing, "effectiveness" seems unrelated to fostering moral and character education. Teachers regularly report going through years of teacher education and in-service education and never being told, first, that they have moral responsibilities, and, second, how to fulfill them. A recent study by Alice Lanckton of 30 middle school and junior high teachers did not identify a single teacher who recalled being told about teachers' role or responsibility as a moral educator or developer of good character.[9]

This lack of support has been aggravated by the typical portraits of teachers on television. The medium relentlessly presents teachers in an unsympathetic light: weak, disorganized individuals putting on false fronts for students. Such inept people can barely handle the problems of life themselves, let alone give ethical guidance to others. On the other hand, such distorted stereotypes are similar to the picture of all adults communicated to the young through the popular media.

On some occasions, authorities have licensed teachers to conduct moral education. But the how-to advice teachers receive undercuts their efficacy because it is ambivalent.

For instance, there are the advocates of values clarification, one seriously flawed approach to moral education. These advocates, particularly Sidney Simon, see the teacher's efforts to inculcate ethical principles and habits as wrongheaded *and* failing. In their place, he maintains, teachers should use morally neutral methods. Children should discover moral truths through natural interactions with other children. Whether the advocates realize it or not, this approach separates students from the collective human wisdom about the moral realm. Among other losses, students would lose the moral and ethical principles necessary to maintain a democratic state. The approach compels students to ethically swim for themselves before coming to know the Great Tradition.

Another source of ambivalence is the proponents of the dilemmas approach to moral education.[11] These theorists urge subjecting pupils to a heavy diet of moral dilemmas so they can rise to what they call "higher levels of moral reasoning." In their view, moral education is mainly to teach students how to deal with "hard" and improbable cases (e.g., *If your wife is dying, is it right to steal drugs to help save her?* or *"If you are on an overloaded lifeboat, who should be first forced to leave?"*) The dilemma proponents recommend confronting pupils with hypothetical issues that would have troubled Socrates or the Supreme Court. The proponents almost seem affected with a form of hubris. They believe they can teach pupils to solve problems that perplexed the wise authorities of earlier societies. But the same proponents call it "indoctrination" to stress everyday concerns such as civility, duty, and other basic virtues.

Proponents of the dilemmas approach also undermine the Great Tradition by their hostility to the concept of direct moral education. The proponents believe teachers should be moral bystanders. They object to the idea of a teacher vigorously promoting honesty and demanding it from her students, or directly teaching the necessity of tolerance for minority views or that each of us has a duty to the state. Such positions are labeled "miseducative." They are derisively dismissed as the "bag-of-virtues approach." The formal research relating to such specious contentions has been considered in earlier chapters. But the logic of the contentions still invites direct confrontation at this point. Opponents of direct moral education or indoctrination do accept the view that teachers can be authorities in certain areas of knowledge. For instance, teachers can make definitive statements about poetry, the composition of matter, irregular French verbs, and algebraic factoring. However, the critics balk at giving teachers authority regarding basic moral and ethical matters. The teacher and the schools must shed their authority and pretend that people have acquired no moral knowledge. Supposedly, the institutions of our society have no moral wisdom or moral truth to pass on to the young. Further, the critics do not distinguish between being an authority and behaving in an authoritarian manner.

Preaching Is Often Important and Acceptable

The topic of direct moral instruction by teachers naturally leads to the question of preaching. For many readers, the word *preaching* has strong negative connotations. It transmits images of persons in authority repetitiously and unimaginatively badgering subordinates with arbitrary opinions. Such tactics are usually self-defeating. However, it is important to recognize that the word *preaching* has far broader significance. As we will see, there is both good and bad preaching, and we should carefully examine the distinction. Without such an examination, we will be unable to engage in good preaching. A constraint against good preaching will seriously disarm our arsenal for moral instruction.

It is true that adolescents sometimes talk derisively about preaching: "Don't preach to me." Adults, however, should display more sophistication. They should realize that adolescent remarks sometimes amount to just that: casual, uninformed remarks by young people who have a lot to learn. Adults themselves should be held to more rigorous intellectual standards. Preaching is one form of oratory, a mode of communication. There is a long tradition of complex and profound preaching, and it has always been, and always will be, one of several important ways of communicating moral ideas. The Gettysburg Address was a form of preaching. So were the Declaration of Independence, the preamble to the United States Constitution, and Martin Luther King, Jr.'s "I Have a Dream" speech. The list includes innumerable other statements of principle and aspiration of power and nobility. Of course, as in all fields of communication, there is adept and inept preaching, just like clever and sterile jokes, or good and poor Socratic dialogues. Ironically, persons who deliver blanket condemnations of preaching often are inspired by what they hear in church or at political rallies. However, current educational orthodoxy, perhaps influenced by TV evangelists, has given preaching extremely negative connotations of fanaticism. Granted, preaching should be done sparingly. But this is not the same thing as banning strong, sincere statements of opinion, or well-presented arguments.

One of the authors conducted a simple survey with important implications for the issue of preaching morality. A sample of pupils from several different high schools were asked which type of faculty member they would consult if they had a serious personal problem. Both boys and girls overwhelmingly preferred a gym teacher or athletic coach. Because gym teachers usually also serve as coaches, we assume that the students were expressing support for a "coachlike" style of interaction. Of course, some pupils will prefer different advisors than coaches. Still, the patterns of preference are striking, especially when coaches are sometimes portrayed as insensitive and crude.

Some ideas of what it means to be "coachlike" are indicated in the following remarks—or "preachings"—by Bobby Knight, about college basketball players and drug use. Knight is basketball coach at Indiana University, and has one of the most successful records in America. His team members also have notably high rates of college graduation. He made the remarks to a group of college basketball players at a training camp. (For background, readers should know that Lenny Bias was a college basketball star who, on the edge of a brilliant pro career, died from an overdose of cocaine. Michael Jordan is considered the best basketball player in the world.)

> I don't feel sorry for Lenny Bias, not in the slightest. He had his own mind and his own body to take care of and just wasn't smart enough to do it. Those of you who have been popping pills and smoking dope are doing the same thing Lenny Bias did. Those are serious shots you are taking, boys, serious poor judgments that you're

using with your body and your mind. Lenny Bias was better than anyone here . . . The only college player I've seen in the past few years as good as Bias was Michael Jordan, and I'm not sure if he was as good as Bias was in college, and Bias is dead.

He's dead because he just wasn't strong enough to take care of himself. Somewhere along the way, he wanted to be one of the boys. He wanted to be cool. Well, he was so cool that he's cold right now . . . That's how cool he was.

You boys will be in all types of situations where there are temptations and all kinds of opportunities to do something detrimental to yourself, and when it comes right down to it, there's only one person who can take care of you, and that's you. Your buddy doesn't really give a damn about you, particularly if he's popping pills or smoking dope.

You know what he wants? He wants you right down where he is because he can't handle the fact that you're tougher than he is. [At this point, Knight suggests a profane street phrase to tell the dealer to beat it.]

Take care of yourselves, boys.[12]

Knight is an extremely able preacher. Good coaches have to know how to emotionally reach and motivate players, to stimulate them to go the last mile, and beyond. That is no small talent. And pupils who prefer receiving moral advice from such persons are showing their appreciation of skillful preaching. We do not contend that all—or most—teachers can approach Bobby Knight's level of delivery. Furthermore, Knight's talent as a motivator is due to many factors beyond his considerable skills at oratory. Still, most teachers can improve their current preaching. But they must feel licensed to do so. And they must practice.

Conducting Moral Education

Obviously, we are critical of nondirectional moral education, such as values clarification. Children should not be invited to reinvent the moral world and will surely fail if they try to. This misguided fear, stimulated by values clarification and the relaxed ethical standards of our time, of imposing the wisdom of our culture on students is often held by teachers who have themselves been taught this wisdom. Many teachers have taken courses such as Western Civilization and are themselves culturally literate. Even so, these teachers are often still reluctant to provide their students with this same cultural knowledge and wisdom. The ascendancy of relativism has deprived them of the security necessary to assert and defend their own heritage.

During the last 25 years teachers have heard the message of these fashionable approaches. They tried to become—or were coerced into being—nonauthorities in the moral realm. Furthermore, in both values clarification and the cognitive developmental moral education of Lawrence Kohlberg's, mentioned earlier, the formerly dominant approaches to moral education (i.e., most frequently cited by educational experts and textbook writers), the task of the teacher is to implement a *process*. That process is supposed to have morally therapeutic benefits down the road. Too often, the popular literature has neglected to report that (a) both these approaches have been shown to be ineffective; and (b) many of the advocates of the approaches have abandoned their claims of efficacy, or are currently even recommending more traditional moral education approaches. Nevertheless, these two (obsolete?) approaches have dominated the materials presented to teachers about their responsibilities as moral educators. We have seen few teachers who are actually skilled and active in using these approaches. However, the approaches' message of moral neutrality has been enormously influential in de-legitimizing traditional approaches such as direct moral instruction.

Hard-Case Morality

Parents and educators do have one area of sincere concern about direct moral education. They are afraid that teachers will abuse their responsibilities as direct moral educators. Undoubtedly, there is a potential for misuse. In our culturally and religiously pluralistic nation, there is no strong moral consensus in some communities about certain ethical issues. Some of these issues lacking consensus are abortion, the justification for entering particular wars, the death penalty, and certain issues of sexuality, such as homosexuality. These unresolved areas of ethical life comprise what we call "hard-case morality." It seems that many academics have become fascinated with the intellectual complexities inherent in these topics. They have been excessively engaged with the question, "Can we teach children to solve these complex questions?" In effect, they are urging schools to meet the responsibilities for moral education and character formation by posing hard cases to students. Such concerns reveal a form of arrogance.

Obviously, the unrealistic aspirations of the proponents of moral dilemmas have not threatened the achievements of Socrates. Furthermore, such aspirations have had other deleterious effects. The intellectual focus on hard-case morality has had a paralyzing effect on our schools' efforts to transmit "simpler," traditional morality. The hard-case issues actually involve a narrow band of moral topics. Because we lack consensus on this band, many teachers have been warned off all moral issues. For instance, because there is no local resolution about abortion, teachers have been puzzled about what generally to say to students about sexuality, promiscuity, and, by extension, an entire moral domain. Teachers' uncertainty over the hard cases affects their certainty in teaching about everyday issues, like prohibiting sexually provocative clothes or observing legal prohibitions against drug use. Again, teachers have been unsure of what to do or tell students about classroom cheating, gossiping, vulgar language, and lack of effort. Such withdrawal from everyday morality is not just sloppy thinking; it generates a pernicious spirit, one that undermines the possibility of having a learning classroom and a true school. It not only turns education into a mere exchange of information, (if that!) but even corrodes the concept of teacher.

However, there are still occasional dramatic situations when a student asks a teacher for advice, and the teacher is drawn into hard-case morality. Taking one of the most inflamed issues, consider a high school girl who becomes pregnant. She asks her teacher about having an abortion. In our view, the teacher should urge the student to share the matter with her parents or religious advisor. If the student will not seek help from them, the teacher should suggest the student seek the counsel of some other wise faculty member, school counselor, or social worker. (The teacher should also solicit the counsel of a colleague, ideally the principal, or a school counselor.) Such referrals may not be the most satisfying or most dramatic thing for the teacher to do. Still, they are the correct thing. While the student may prefer not to talk to such persons, that preference may be unwise. One reason people ask other's advice is to possibly be told the course they are following is unsound.

In hard cases, as in other parts of our lives, there is no substitute for good judgment. And a hard case, by definition, is one where we doubt our own judgment. Therefore, we should advise students, when they are unsure what to do, to solicit counsel from wise people around them. When it comes to this narrow band of controversial issues, then, we are urging two principles: first, that students seek advice form their primary moral educators (parents and religious leaders) and, failing that, they seek out truly wise people for advice; second, that they think. Children need to develop their own powers of reasoned thought. The sophistication and level of that thought varies, of course, as children grow up. However, we must prepare them for independent moral thought. These two principles, seeking wise advice and thinking independently, are not in opposition. In thinking through a hard case and coming to their own conclusions, we should urge students to gather as much information and wisdom as they can.

There are, then, limits on the role of teachers as direct moral educators. However, we believe that for the overwhelming majority of teachers, reflection and good judgment are adequate guides. On the other hand, for teachers to withdraw from their responsibilities to be moral leaders of children and become moral eunuchs is a perversion of their calling.

THE MORAL EDUCATION OF THE TEACHER

One perennial question in education is the definition of a good teacher. The most recent form of that question, as we indicated earlier, is, "What is an effective teacher?" Our view is that there are probably a small percentage of natural teachers, people who come to teaching already possessing the social and organizational skills needed to be a success. However, most aspiring and beginning teachers have a good deal to learn about being a teacher.

Trying to identify the candidates with typical needs, and organizing an instructional program to meet them, has been the pervading quandary of teacher education. In recent years there has been great ferment in this field. Numerous alternative approaches to teacher education have been promoted and tried. Most of these new approaches have been based on the idea of the teacher as a transmitter of information and skills. They have focused on equipping teachers with the technical know-how to promote certain intellectual and, to a lesser extent, psychomotor changes in students. This search for the ingredients of an effective teacher has been a vexing challenge. While there have been some improvements, there have also been some big losses.

One of the major losses in teacher education in recent decades is in the moral domain. Teachers in the past learned Socrates' views of the teacher's work: the role of education is to make people both smart and good. Now teacher education focuses overwhelmingly on the first: what the teacher can do to make students smart. Ironically, teachers reduce their chances of making the student smart when they neglect teaching students how to become good. The undisciplined student and the undisciplined classroom are resistant to acquiring knowledge and intellectual skills.

Regarding pupil discipline, one of the authors attended a meeting of practicing educators. At the meeting, various proposals to improve pupil character were being considered. One of the educators remarked, "All of this is to the good, but I hope we are not simply striving to create docile pupils." There were nods of assent among the group members. Later, the author looked up the precise meaning of *docile*. It means capable of being taught, as compared to a wild animal, which lacks docility. Admittedly, we do not know what meaning the speaker and his associates attributed to the word *docility*. But the fact is that, apart from *docility*, it is hard to identify another word in the educational lexicon that means "capable of being taught."

From our innumerable contacts with educators, we feel the speaker's misunderstanding is symptomatic of a widespread problem. The concept of "capable of being taught" can no longer be expressed. If an important concept is indescribable in everyday terms, it has effectively expired: no word is readily available to convey the concept that discipline is a preliminary to instruction. The death of a concept may be one source of many of the deficiencies affecting academic instruction.

One must inevitably reflect on why teacher education turned away from the moral domain and the teacher's role in character formation. The answer to the question is wrapped up with much of the intellectual and cultural history of the United States in the last three decades. During this era, the nation's public morality was questioned on all sides. Our racial policies were revealed to be deeply unjust. Our involvement in the Vietnam War generated, for many Americans, an ethical quagmire. Illegal recreational drugs became widely available and quite acceptable in certain circles.

The moral consensus around our traditional values seemed to be crumbling. Because of this erosion of the consensus, words like "traditional values," "character," "the common good," and "moral principles and habits" became unpopular with some of our leaders and opinion formers. Teacher education, in effect, dropped its focus on these words and their underlying concepts. Instead, it focused on other, supposedly more scientific and noncontroversial words such as "behavioral objectives," "advanced organizers," and "interaction analysis." Due to these changes, contemporary teacher education rarely addresses the explicit moral dimension of a teacher's role. But while many teachers define themselves in this teacher-as-technician way, many do not. Large numbers of teachers are called to teaching primarily out of concern that children grow up to be good people of principles and strong moral character. Some teachers conceive of their work in a religious framework (e.g., providing a religious witness and helping children to do good), others in a secular context (e.g., helping to form good citizens), and others as a combination of religious and secular missions. But to the degree that these teachers are effective in responding to the moral dimension of their work, they are self-taught. Teacher education has had little effect on these teachers, since it does not often speak to this domain. In fact, when education courses *do* address moral issues, their effects are often mischievous. They warn prospective teachers that deliberately encouraging traditional morals values can become indoctrination of the innocent. Many professors decry such moral advocacy as "elitist," "ethocentric," and "narrow." On the other hand, one experienced teacher reported that, "My best source of information and insight into teaching, particularly about right and wrong, values and discipline, has been my mother and grandmother. They have that good common sense you need with difficult children."

A Needed Reform

Throughout the 1980s, there has been a drumbeat of concern about the moral health of our young. Parents, and the public in general, have indicated clearly that they want our schools to take a more direct role in children's moral education. While schools in the 1990s are distracted by many other problems, the message, nevertheless, is getting through to administrators and classroom teachers. It is now time for the teacher education community in universities and in school districts to refocus their energies on moral education. They should help teachers gain the confidence, perspective, and skills they need to take back this fundamental aspect of their work. Four areas emerge where teachers would help. These are

+ understanding our moral heritage.
+ knowing the leading theories of ethical development and character formation.
+ acquiring the skills needed to aid children toward moral maturity.
+ placing the moral dimensions of their work in proper perspective.

Each of these four areas is considered here.

Our Moral Heritage. In the mid-1980s, E.D. Hirsch, a professor of English literature, exposed the great deficit of cultural literacy among our students. Too many students lacked a recognition of the basic events and features of Western culture.[13] He defined cultural literacy as a code that enables those who possess it to function and rise in the society and that blocks those who lack it—the culturally illiterate. The same principle holds for the moral domain.

Moral literacy means knowledge of our culture's moral wisdom. It means knowing the enduring habits or traits needed for good character. We learn much of this moral literacy through the curriculum, particularly literature and history. For instance, we learn about courage from the little Dutch boy who put his finger in the dike, from Joan of Arc, from Horatio at the bridge, and from Harriet Tubman on the Underground Railroad to freedom. We learn loyalty to our country from Nathan Hale, and its opposite from Benedict Arnold and, more recently, from John Walker, who sold military secrets to the Soviets. We learn the importance of persistence from the little engine that could, from Booker T. Washington's efforts to learn to read, from Lincoln's struggle to hold the Union together, and from Alexander Solzhenitsyn's endurance in the Soviet gulag.

Teachers must be masters of our moral heritage. It is especially important, then, that they receive a solid liberal arts education. They must not only know this important knowledge, but reflect on its significance. For instance, they should not only know what a democracy is, how it functions, and how it differs from other systems of government, but know especially how and why it is a moral idea. They should have an understanding of the history of Western ethics so that they are well-grounded philosophically. Moral literacy, then, should be a basic expectation of teachers, one gained from their general and liberal arts education, their continuing study of the culture, and their own personal growth.

Teaching Moral Literacy. The difference between knowing and doing is well known to every sports fan or concert-goer. Every veteran teacher knows this distinction, too. Knowing how to read does not mean being able to teach someone else to read. Knowing the theory of supply and demand does not mean knowing how to get it into the heads of two dozen students with different levels of interest, learning styles, and intellectual backgrounds. Teachers, then, must not only be morally literate, but they must also know how to teach this moral legacy to students. Methodology should teach educators

1. how to focus students' attention on the ethical dimension of the story. "When you read this short story tonight, I want you to ask yourself, `What is the moral of this story? What are we to learn about treating strangers from this story?'"
2. how to lead students to thoughtfully consider ethical principles. "Before we study the principle of radioactivity, I want to read you a short account of the lives of two great pioneers of the field, Pierre and Marie Curie. They contributed immensely to our knowledge of paramagnetic substances and radioactivity, but I want you to listen and tell me what was it about how they lived their lives that enabled them to make such contributions?"
3. how to focus students' attention on the moral aspects of an historical event and how to analyze and discuss it. For high school students: "We have been studying how the founding fathers declared independence and built a new nation. I want you to pause here and think about this from the other side.

Many people at the time thought they were doing a morally incorrect thing. What is the argument on the side of these objectors? Write down your thoughts and we'll discuss them in a few minutes."

4. how to engage students in the moral of a story and see how it may apply to their own lives. "I am going to read you a famous story about Daedalus and his son Icarus. As you will see, Icarus makes a terrible mistake. After the story, tell me what that mistake is, but most of all I want you to think of examples of how second-graders, like yourselves, could possibly make mistakes like Icarus made."

5. how to build among students the skills of moral discourse, which is not just casual argumentation but serious thinking about what is correct and about the "oughtness of life." "What is the correct thing to do?" "As most of you know, last night the school board accepted the new dress code proposed by the Parent-Teachers Association and the new rules will go into effect in a month. I know that some of you are upset about this issue and I think we need to take some home-room time to talk about it. But if we are going to talk about it we must have a rational discussion. First of all, we ought to find out actually what the new code says. We ought to find out what were the reasons given for the change in dress codes. Could there be other reasons? Who, if anyone, is hurt by this decision? Are they moral reasons or is this matter just fashion? If we are going to discuss this, our discussion should be driven by the questions What are the facts?, What is the right thing to do?, and Why?"

Part of knowing how to be an adept teacher of moral literacy is developing a reservoir of materials and techniques that are effective with different students. For example, the middle school teacher needs to have learned ways to get 13-year-old boys interested in the life of a young Jewish girl in *The Diary of Anne Frank* and appreciate her courage. The primary teacher creates activities that enable second-graders to see beyond the story about King Midas and his golden touch to its universal truth about the dangers of human greed. It is this type of craft knowledge that separates the culturally literate knower from the culturally literate teacher. It is at this level that much of preservice and in-service education should be concentrating.

Theories of Moral Growth. Our discussion in Chapter 2 covered topics such as faculty psychology, motivations for learning, and the doctrine of learning as fun. That discourse also identified a variety of pertinent authors and works in psychology and sociology. Materials of this sort should be an important part of the curriculum in any institution helping to teach teachers how to conduct moral education.

In addition to such materials, theology and philosophy are two other major disciplines that traditionally have provided much theoretical support for moral education. Both disciplines are preoccupied by the questions of human nature and how it can improve, and both have been closely associated with the purposes of schools. In colonial America, schools were typically begun out of religious motivation. In 17th-century Massachusetts, theology inspired the famous Old Deluder Satan Act. The act directed towns to start schools. The purpose of these schools was hardly to have children learn "salable skills" or to "reach their full human potential." Instead, their pupils were to learn to read the Scriptures, which in turn would lead to their moral development. As we have discussed elsewhere in this book, Americans are a church-going people and theology is for many Americans an important "meaning-maker" for them, particularly in the moral realm. Concepts such as *sin* and *redemption* should be understood, not only for cultural literacy, but to allow a teacher to more fully understand the moral orientations of students and their families.

Philosophy, too, represented for earlier Americans more than an important repository of human wisdom. The methods of philosophy were tools necessary to guide one's life, in particular, ethics, the branch of philosophy that deals with rationally discovering what is the right thing to do. Philosophy, because it deals strictly with reason, is less controversial than theology, which includes sacred and revealed truths. At present, though, these two disciplines are somewhat out of favor in certain universities. Still, they include many of the most important theories of moral development and constitute valuable resources for revitalizing teacher education.

It takes some reflection to see the connection between disciplined knowledge and concrete problems. This is why instruction of teachers in the disciplines must be carefully managed. But such connections *can* be made evident. Different theological views of human nature help us reflect on the premises underlying different policies of prohibition and punishment. Behavioral psychology helps sensitize teachers so they can analyze the implicit rewards and punishment for good and bad character in their classes and schools. Anthropology can help sensitize us to the important role ceremonies and symbols can have in transmitting moral values. In sum, appropriate theories enrich teachers' understanding of the problem and enable them to pursue solutions. The disciplines and their theories become lenses for us to view practical situations. They can open the door for the teacher to construct the solution. And this is precisely why teaching is a profession, rather than a trade. It lacks formulaic answers to be memorized and applied.

MAKING THE MORAL DOMAIN A PRIORITY

Making moral education a priority means a personal decision by individual educators to take this domain of their work more seriously. They must focus more of their time and professional energy on it. This means devoting more time to the issues of moral literacy and how best to teach them to students. While making this domain a higher priority is partly an individual act, educators work within institutions. One part of their professionalism is to take responsibility for the functioning of the whole. Teachers, whether teaching classes or leading extracurricular activities or teams, cannot simply be concerned with the morality of their own units. They need to feel responsibility for the entire school and raise moral questions such as

- ✦ What is my policy about character formation and teaching moral values?
- ✦ What habits am I trying to promote in my students?
- ✦ Is there a relationship between the way I am treating students and they way they treat one another?
- ✦ Does my class celebrate any heroes? Are these heroes people of character?
- ✦ Have I given the same kind of attention to the moral aspects of my curriculum that I do to, say, the language arts curriculum?
- ✦ Am I contributing to the wallpaper effect? When was the last time a student came to me with an ethical problem?
- ✦ Do our children consider my class as a place where they are learning to be good—good students who are learning to be good people and good citizens?
- ✦ What can I do to foster greater staff solidarity on issues of conduct and values between my students' parents and me?
- ✦ What can we do to get the students to take more responsibility for one another?
- ✦ Does my class discipline policy fit with our goals of promoting responsibility, courtesy, and dignity?
- ✦ Do I let parents "cover" or "bail out" children, or do I insist that students live with the consequences of their actions?
- ✦ Do I show I care about all my students, even when they get in trouble? Or do I abandon them at the point where there is police involvement?
- ✦ Am I as a faculty member giving students a consistent set of messages about discipline?
- ✦ Is the entire staff—bus drivers, cafeteria workers, custodians, administrators, and teachers—taking on moral development and character formation as a priority?
- ✦ How can I do a better job of this?

John Adams, our second president, once stated, "A teacher affects eternity." We realize he was partly considering the transmission of intellectual matter, such as mathematical and verbal skills. However, we also know from his many other writings that his primary focus was on the moral mission of the teacher and the impact the teacher has on the character of students. As we have suggested, *character*, and other words such as *virtue* and *diligence* are making a comeback. Americans are recoiling from the more relaxed child-raising and educational ideas of the last few decades.

The word *character* goes to the heart of the teacher's moral responsibilities. The root meaning of *character* is from the Greek "to engrave." A character is a sign or a distinctive mark. Engravers mark their work with character. People with character have worked day after day to shape their own being. As a result, they have a distinctive pattern of behavior or personality, so that we expect them to exhibit moral strength and self-discipline. People of character are "marked" people. Of course, such marks can be either good or bad; there is such a thing as notoriously bad character too. But character usually refers to good character, unless a negative modifier is used. "She is a woman of character" means that life has left certain enduring marks on her so that we can expect a certain pattern of good behavior from her.

Teachers leave their stamp on us. One confronts our carelessness. Another demands self-criticism and attention to details. Another gives us much-needed humility. And yet another inspires in us a passionate concern for justice. Students, whether 3 years old or 19 have a certain wax-like character, and teachers, consciously and unconsciously, leave enduring marks on their students. This is both the grandeur and the terror of teaching. But for good or ill, as Adams said, teachers "affect eternity."

PRACTICES AND POLICIES

1. When teachers are together (in the workroom, faculty lounge, or the lunch room) approximately how much time is spent gossiping about or criticizing in a petty and unconstructive way—students, parents, or administrators? What are some subtle ways a teacher could constructively and tactfully direct the conversation elsewhere?

2. If your school does not have one already, consider starting a "Sunshine Club," or similar organization. Obtain a copy of the by-laws of an existing successful club. A Sunshine Club periodically collects a small donation from faculty, staff, and administrators and uses the money to recognize important events in peoples lives. For example, Sunshine Clubs usually send a card and flowers for the birth of a child, send flowers or memorial donations for the death of a loved one, or organize farewell parties for departing staff members. Your club could also acknowledge birthdays with a card or an announcement over the P.A. Your Sunshine Club could also announce important days in students' lives, if you wish.

3. Do teachers have input in suggesting particular in-service programs or in presenting in-service programs themselves? Perhaps teachers in your school could volunteer to research and suggest particular in-service programs that would benefit teachers in your building. Or, teachers with specific knowledge or talent in an area could present their own in-service to the school faculty.

4. How comfortable do teachers in your school feel being direct moral educators? If they feel comfortable, why do they feel that way? If not, what are their concerns, obstacles, or reservations?

5. Is it accurate to say that your school's community has relatively homogenous moral standards? How well do teachers know the moral standards of the community? Do they feel comfortable with the moral values of the community? Why or why not?

6. How often are teachers in your school confronted with "hard-case" morality, for example, students asking about contraception or abortion. Generally, how do teachers handle these cases? How invested do teachers get in the hard moral cases of the students?

CHAPTER 7

Curriculum as a Moral Educator

As Aristotle taught, people do not naturally or spontaneously grow up to be morally excellent or practically wise. They become so, if at all, only as the result of a lifelong personal and community effort.

—Jon Moline[1]

A school or classroom's curriculum should be the community's reply to the prime educational question, "What is most worth knowing?" Children are born into an endless universe of facts and figures, theories and opinions, current events and classic stories. Given this array, the curriculum plays the essential role of identifying what of this mass of information should be selected and taught to children in school. The curriculum literally aims to bring order out of chaos.

Planning a curriculum requires us to recognize and resolve a variety of questions. What does a child need to live a good life? To be a contributing citizen? To be a productive worker? To be a good spouse and parent? To be a fulfilled human being? Furthermore, we must confront these vexing questions in a period of finite time. Students do not, and should not, stay in school forever, leaving much important learning to nonschool sources, e.g., the family, the media, religious institutions, the personal initiative of the student or ex-student, the job site. But there still is the question of which learnings should be saved until later or left up to other agencies. Finally, there are questions about which knowledge can be understood by pupils of what ages, and in what forms it should be presented to the young. These questions should guide our selection of what we teach students.

TYPES OF CURRICULUM

Curriculum is one of education's biggest, sloppiest, and slipperiest concepts. We are using it here in its broadest sense: curriculum includes all of the events and activities experienced by the students (as students) during their school years. One way to make discussion of curriculum more manageable is to make some distinctions. An obvious distinction is between the formal curriculum and the hidden curriculum.

In contemporary usage, the formal curriculum covers the academic experiences schools deliberately provide for students. These experiences include the knowledge and skills the school or class will teach. Usually, this curriculum is written and available for examination by concerned persons. It is also called the overt curriculum, since it is out in the open for public inspection.

The hidden curriculum is what pupils learn in and around schools in addition to the formal curriculum. It is all the learnings, personal and social, intellectual and physical, that the student gains from being in a particular school and classroom. It is called hidden because it appears to be unseen. However, the hidden curriculum is very real. It can have a major impact on the lives of students. As a result of being in a particular classroom, a student thinks of himself as a winner or a loser, a community member or an alien. He defines himself in a distinctive manner and relates to teachers and fellow students in particular ways.

The hidden curriculum is intertwined with the ethos of the school and classroom. If bullying is the rule on the playground, it is part of the school's hidden curriculum. If civility reigns on the playground, it becomes a major result of schooling. If teachers ridicule students who, as a result, lose confidence in themselves or interest in their academic work, this is an outcome of the hidden curriculum.

We have been unable to fully trace the history of the phrase hidden curriculum. But we believe it became popular during the latter half of the 20th century. Before that time, the hidden curriculum encompassed the school's efforts to raise children up to the community's highest standards. These activities were the main task of formal education. The hidden curriculum was quite conspicuous—and usually still is. In fact, there is nothing especially hidden about it. It is easier to tell whether a school's students are learning obedience or politeness than whether they are learning arithmetic. Levels of politeness and obedience in a school can be simply assessed. Just walk into the pupils' lunchroom, observe the playground, or watch pupils during an all-school assembly. But whether pupils really "learn" arithmetic is a complex question. We may see teaching in progress or examine textbooks. We can say whether arithmetic is being "taught." But learning is more than exposure to teaching. In the end, we can only assess cognitive learning by applying relatively subtle measures.

Much of what is written about the hidden curriculum has a negative tone. Even the word *hidden* suggests attempts to shape children's behavior in illicit ways. But this is a distortion, and also extremely naive. Such misperceptions are an outcome of the antischool writings of the 1960s and 70s (e.g., Kozol, Holt, and Silberman[2]). The hidden curriculum, just like the open curriculum, can contain much that is either good or bad. The hidden curriculum can stress a spirit of intellectual curiosity, or a strong, but unseen, bond of affection between teacher and students. Such qualities cannot be captured in formal curricula, but they can be core learnings of a school.

There is yet another term that aids our understanding of the curriculum: *the null curriculum*. The term refers to all that is left out of a curriculum. Think what a vast concept this is: the hundreds of languages that exist and the literature and tales of each; most of the immense recorded history of humanity; almost all of our numeracy, only a tiny fraction of which is taught in schools; and most of our physical and social sciences. The curriculum of our schools is—and must be, since life is finite and knowledge infinite—a thin layer from the surface of the known.

The concept of null curriculum reveals, though, another important feature: the dynamic quality of our curriculum. What is a part of the curriculum in one era or one community is in the null curriculum in another time or locale. For example, our first public schools were founded three-and-a-half centuries ago. Essentially, they were created to teach religion. Now, that subject is typically part of the null curriculum. On the other hand, in the same era sexuality, as an area of human experience, was left to the family, church, and the course of life to teach. Now sexuality is very much in our formal curriculum. One of the ironies of education in the 1990s is that, in some public schools, a teacher may be required to teach elementary students the proper way to apply a condom using cucumbers, while on the other hand, the same teacher may be reprimanded and possibly lose a lawsuit if he suggests to students that promiscuity might be sinful. In any event, what is in and out of the null curriculum says a great deal about a culture.

Curriculum as a Social Wager

Many animals have some capacities for learning. However, human beings, unlike our relations in the animal kingdom, face a special challenge in organizing learning. Humans must choose from the universe of knowledge that which is most worth knowing. Even for the higher animals, what they need to learn is programmed by nature. However, as the most complex learning species, humans must consciously seek answers to the core question about what should be learned. Otherwise, we face stagnation or decadence.

The ash heap of history is littered with societies that chose incorrect learning priorities and ended up miseducating their young. This may be one way of interpreting the tensions now afflicting the former Soviet Union. There, the current adult generation was educated in a totalitarian society. The curriculum was designed to perpetuate that society. Now, the adult generation is invited to participate in a shift towards more democratic modes of government. It is unlikely, though, that either the open or hidden curricula formerly presented to Soviet pupils prepared them to participate in democratic life. Because of this many observers are pessimistic about the evolution of democracy in the states of the former Soviet Union, despite popular hostility to past governmental norms. It takes more than a simple desire or a governmental decree to create a democratic citizenry.

In sum, the stakes around the issue of what is most worth knowing are quite high. Still, the answer to this simple-sounding question is complicated by the fact that in answering it we must peer into the future and simultaneously draw on what we currently know. We must design education experiences to help our children to live well (i.e., be strong individuals living in a good society). Building such a curriculum is a huge social gamble.

But an even greater risk is *not* to wrestle with the question. We could just go along with our current curriculum. But as theologian Harvey Cox is fond of saying, "Not to decide is to decide." The school community that has not asked the question has still answered the question. The answer is what students are now being taught.

Many of the questions driving the curriculum, such as "How can people live in harmony with one another?" and "What is a good way to spend one's life?" have strong moral components. The answers to these questions quickly move us into the realm of ethics, morals, and character formation. Our curriculum, by its very nature, then, is our answer to some of our most important human questions. This may appear obvious. But there is little evidence that the moral mission of our school's curriculum (with the possible exceptions of our sex- and drug-education curricula) is currently the subject of public discussion or scholarly debate.

Knowing The Good

Moral education and character formation in schools aim to transmit to pupils the community's best values and ethical ideals. An anthropologist might describe this effort as socializing the young into tribal morality. It seems to be an innate reflex for adults to try to instill in their young the moral values and habits they believe children need to sustain themselves (i.e., to "live a good life.") Likewise, the larger community wants to instill in the young the values the members believe will sustain the community. To do less is beyond being foolish. It is irresponsible.

From where should the content of ethical and character education come? Where can we turn for this most critical curricular material? What do we as Americans, part of a relatively new society, possess that nearly all of us share and are ready to have the school pass on to our young? And how can schools serving the racial, ethnic, and religious mix that is America find core materials to fit the needs of children from all these backgrounds? Our answer is multipart.

1. We must treat the forging of such core materials as a high priority, or our future as a nation is at peril. We need to define our standards of moral literacy if we are to stay a coherent nation.

2. Our schools should return to the source of much of our school content: the moral facts of life and the moral ideals derived from our history and our culture.

3. It is possible that some particular communities or political jurisdictions cannot develop consensus around such matters. Then, parents and educators must be prepared to develop freestanding schools, either public or private, appealing to parents who favor certain coherent values.

The Moral Facts of Life

The late C.S. Lewis provides a useful point of focus for any discussion of traditional American ideals. Lewis spent years searching the writings of past civi-

represent what the wisdom of our species tells us we "ought" to do to be
sonance with the realities of life. There are other things humanity has
d that go beyond these facts of life and lead us to excellence. These we
hical ideals.

Ethical Ideals

earlier chapter, we noted that the United States, at present, is over-
ingly composed of persons explicitly committed to Judeo-Christian val-
ven the majority of recent Asian immigrants share such traditional
s along with already established Americans such as German-Americans
rish-Americans. And, African-Americans are an ethnic group deeply
ed in the Christian tradition.

ying on this cohesion, we have selected eight ethical ideals tied to (a)
eritage; and (b) the antecedent Greco-Roman tradition that enriched the
-Christian tradition. The ideals can serve as a basis for analysis of our
l or hidden curriculum. They represent what some of our great thinkers
e are the proper goals of humanity. (We were helped in the formulation
s section by Thomas Mastu.) The first four ideals come from the Greeks.
are called the *cardinal virtues*, because they are like hinges (the Latin
neaning of the word *cardinal*) on which depend our hopes to reach a
r moral state.

Prudence is the habit of acting with discretion and deliberation. It is
human wisdom applied to the practical. George Washington said, "It
would be the point of prudence to defer the forming of one's ultimate
irrevocable decision so long as new data might be offered."

Justice is the quality of being righteous and fair. One who possesses justice is honest, impartial, and even-handed. Jose Garcia Oliver has written,
"Justice is so subtle a thing, to interpret it one has only need of a heart."
While injustice will always be with us, it is important that we thirst for
justice.

Temperance is the state of being self-restrained in conduct, being under
one's own control. It is having in check one's appetites for life's pleasures. Benjamin Franklin wrote, "Temperance puts wood on the fire,
meal in the barrel, flour in the tub, money in the purse, credit in the
country, contentment in the house, clothes on the children, vigor in the
body, intelligence in the brain, and spirit in the whole constitution." It
should be noted that temperance does not necessarily mean abstinence
from alcohol.

Fortitude is the capacity to withstand misfortune with bravery. It is an
ability to endure pain without breaking or to persist patiently in the face
of hardship. Of fortitude, Joseph Addison wrote, "In itself an essential
virtue, it is a guard to every other virtue."

lizations and seeking their core ideas. Gradually, he saw pa
connecting the great civilizations. These ideas or precepts
tions, but they may also act as a common core. Lewis called
Tao. In *The Abolition of Man*, he wrote:

> It is the Nature, it is the Way, the Road. It is the Way in which the
> the Way in which things everlastingly emerge, stilly and tranquill
> time. It is also the Way which everyman should tread in imitation
> supercosmic progression, conforming all activities to that great
> conception in all its forms, Platonic, Aristotelian, Stoic, Christian
> I shall thenceforth refer to for brevity simply as 'the Tao.'[3]

Lewis goes on to explain that the Tao is not something w
as we choose. It is simply there in the nature of reality. At th
Lewis provides readers with several pages of examples of th
which reflect the Tao. He claims the Tao is present in and
Babylonian, ancient Egyptian, old Norse, Greek, Roman,
Indian, Christian, Hebrew, Anglo-Saxon, and American wr
only some of the cultures.

Many different lists of ideas and percepts might guide t
curriculum for the moral domain. Lewis's approach, with its
emphasis, seems particularly appropriate for our schools. I
illustrations of the Tao and other materials, we have ident
list of moral facts of life:

- ✦ Human kindness is essential to a fully functioning soci
- ✦ We owe a special love, loyalty, and support to our pa:
  lies.
- ✦ We have a special responsibility to posterity, especiall
- ✦ Married people have certain demands on each other
  cific rights and responsibilities.
- ✦ Some degree of honesty is needed for a society to fun
- ✦ We are obliged to help the poor, sick, and less fortuna
- ✦ Basic property rights must exist in any organized soci
- ✦ Some things exist that are worse than death, e.g.,
  betrayal, and torturing another person.
- ✦ Our own inevitable death colors how we view life an
  nature of man's posterity, gives the continuum of life

We should add to this list a warning: we cannot assume
be reflexively applied by all the members of any society, e
Still, these moral facts of life appear to be crucial in orde
with ourselves and those around us. But they are not en

The next three moral ideals are the three virtues of faith, hope, and charity, ideals found in many of the world's religions.

+ *Faith* has two meanings. The original is the capacity to put trust and reliance in God and the confidence that comes from that trust. Faith can also mean the trust and confidence we put in another person or institution. The Bible says, "Now faith is the substance of things to be hoped for." (Hebrews 11:1)

+ *Hope* is the habit of desiring the good, but with, at least, a slight expectation of obtaining it, or the belief that it is indeed obtainable. It is confidence in the future. An old Irish proverb goes, "Hope is the physician of each misery." Alexander Pope penned the famous lines, "Hope springs eternal in the human breast; Man ever is, but always to be blest".[2]

+ *Charity* is a habit of the heart, a disposition to think favorably of other people. It is the habit of acting, too, with affection and goodwill toward others. Roger Bacon wrote, "In charity there is not excess."

+ *Duty* is a disposition to be loyal to those, above us and below us, to whom we have an obligation. It involves our sense of responsibility to something outside ourselves. William Corbett stated, "From a very early age, I had imbibed the opinion, that it was everyman's duty to do all that lay in his power to leave his country as good as he had found it." Duty does not mean blind obedience. It means, though, giving what is expected to those who have a just claim on us. It sometimes means helping those in authority, such as government officials, live up to their obligations.

These, then, are a selection of ethical ideals. The moral facts of life, as identified by Lewis, seem to reside in the human condition and are universal. However, ethical ideals exist in a different form. Philosophers would claim that ethical ideals, such as those above, are a part of the very nature of humans. In individual people, these ethical ideals exist in varied form, from shadowy potential to guiding lights for everyday behavior.

Philosophers and others, of course, may express different preferences regarding the moral facts of life and moral ideals. In this connection, readers are reminded of our earlier remarks about enumerations of moral traits. There, we stressed that perfect lists are not essential or realistic goals. In the preceding inventory, certain virtues, such as forbearance and humility, which are considered essential to some, are not included. Others, such as hope, which are not considered fundamental by some individuals, are included. The aim of our selection is to focus on these facts of life and ideals as exemplars of our moral heritage, a heritage our society ignores at great risk.

The "Practical" Roots of Shared Morality

Sociologists, in contrast to many philosophers, usually perceive of ethical ideals as partially culturally determined. This implies that different cultures highlight or value particular ideals, and that some important ideals are not shared by all peoples. Often, a group or tribe would have one set of values applied among tribe members and another set applied to outsiders or persons outcast from the group. Morality, to the extent it signified "good" conduct, was often solely applied to group members.

Some authorities argue that there are important contrasts among cultures in the matter of morals. Despite such contrasts, one principle still prevails. Societies—long persisting groups of people acting for certain common purposes—must be bound by powerful, shared beliefs. Such beliefs should motivate citizens to make great personal sacrifices for the general good. Citizens' goals must extend past the pursuit of simple, immediate self-interest. Not all group-cohesion activities are wholesome. Group cohesion has stimulated the American civil rights movement, the Nazification of Germany, the crusade against child labor, the public tortures of enemies by Aztec Indians, the European witch-burners in the late Middle Ages, and other activities. But any nation that fails to transmit a common morality to its citizens is extremely vulnerable. It can be disrupted or destroyed by the appeals of internal demagogues or external aggression.

We should also recognize that any body of principles or morals that binds a society can never be applied or invented de novo. Proposals to dramatically and deliberately change American values are either cant or demagoguery. True, moderate shifts in such patterns are always possible. However, the idea of a total values revolution is a solecism, unless some cataclysmic disaster overcomes a society (such as the crushing defeats suffered by Japan and Germany in World War II).

It is easy to identify instances of such values persistence in America. Mature readers will recall the dramatic pleas for community, often voiced by people trying to form "communes", articulated in America during the 1960s and 70s. And there were the many attempts to create new institutions. However, almost all of the communes quickly expired. Typically, they foundered on the members' strong commitments to individualism, a vital, traditional American value. The individualism made the communes' members unable or unwilling to make the sacrifices necessary to intimate communal life. To take a more remote instance, during the American Revolution, some patriots saw the war as a prelude towards a worldwide shift towards democracy. However, shortly after our revolution, the French Revolution occurred succeeded by the Reign of Terror and the Napoleonic Empire. During these climactic events, many Americans discovered important contrasts between the essential incrementalism of our revolution and the more Manichean visions inspiring many French revolutionary leaders.

Absent some total and horrible disaster, America's prevailing values must always carry forward important elements of previous patterns. Thus, serious efforts largely to remake a country through inventing fundamentally different values will merely lead to distortion and disorder. For example, many "revolutions" throughout the 20th century have merely established more profound dictatorships than those they succeeded. Consider the revolution in China led by Mao, the revolution in Cuba led by Castro, or the revolution in Russia led by Lenin. All of these allegedly represented dramatic efforts to shift national values towards democracy; the efforts really led to regimes even more repressive than their predecessors. The revolutionaries carried forward many of the errors and few of the virtues of the old regimes. And these revolutionaries coupled their urgency with an arrogant and ruthless faith in their own virtue. The American Revolution occurred in an already relatively open society, and was far more incremental than many other less successful revolutions that succeeded it over the following centuries. In sum, it is foolish for our schools to broadly resist the teaching and promotion of traditional American values. If such resistance should succeed in any notable way, the end effect will be to endanger the Republic.

Finally, in an imperfect world, we believe American mainstream traditions and achievements are valuable per se, a precious resource for all people. But such universal treasures are not properly cherished in the public schools in their homeland. It is true that efforts to identify or evolve common moral principles to guide the curriculum will be stressful and involve a complex pattern of negotiation and compromise. But this process of development has too long been deadlocked by insensitivity and lack of charity. Relatively small, articulate, aggressive minorities—usually secularly oriented and/or stressing highly individualistic values—have exercised too much influence in this elaborate negotiation. Their energies have been mobilized in court cases, particularistic legislation and regulatory rules, and the constraints created by many interest groups.

For instance, a number of intermediate-level Federal court decisions have supported the right of elementary and high school pupils to refuse to participate in the in-class Pledge of Allegiance if they believe the pledge constitutes a significant constraint on their personal beliefs. The students are not obligated to relate their objections to any significant, external patterns of belief, e. g., being members of some established religion. In some classrooms, this principle has led to distressing scenes: the teacher and a few pupils awkwardly participate in the pledge, while perhaps twenty indifferent adolescents sit sullenly at their desks, supposedly expressing their deep personal beliefs. Undoubtedly, the few pupils willing to express their patriotism feel like deviates. The extreme individualism of the non-saluters has often been supported by our national media and certain intellectual and academic groups.

The inhibitions on the articulation of a protradition curriculum should be removed or, at least, moderated. Schools (and their immediate constituencies) should formulate more coherent statements of moral principles and ideals, from which educators can develop morally vital curricula. For Americans about to enter the 21st century, the moral facts of life and ethical ideas we discussed are the framework we recommend for this purpose. Schools should be given freedom to put these principles into effect in their programs and activities. These principles should appear early in stories and games in kindergarten and be developed and elaborated as the child grows. If these are our Tao and our moral ideals, it is imperative that we teach them thoroughly.

One concrete and successful instance of deliberately changing American values may be instructive. It shows us how and why success in such matters is rare.

Over the past 30–40 years, American attitudes about smoking have conspicuously changed, and education has been one notable cause for this shift. The process of change relied on (a) incrementalism and persuasion; (b) enormous persistence by the antismoking camp; (c) powerful, persuasive antismoking evidence that was gradually developed and disseminated; and (d) subjecting the pro and con evidence about smoking to a searching and conspicuous public debate. Only a moderate degree of compulsion was applied (until very late in the game). The collection and analysis of supporting, objectively verified data was a high priority. The overall aim of suppressing smoking was consistent with the American tradition of prohibiting harmful substances, e.g., alcohol.

Ultimately, the actual changes generated by the antismokers were not extraordinary. Only a moderate proportion of persons actually permanently gave up smoking; what was more typical is that succeeding age cohorts grew up more disposed to dislike smoking. We should also recognize that rearing an increasing proportion of nonsmokers does not necessarily amount to some vast change in national values. While this development may prolong typical life spans, it does not signify the spread of a lifestyle dramatically different from that which prevailed in the past.

In sum, the special circumstances surrounding the successful campaign against smoking have ironic significance. The circumstances emphasize the narrow parameters limiting the role of education in dramatically shifting human values. Only in extraordinary occasions can such efforts to foster change generate large-scale success. On other occasions, the results of such efforts may range from simply wasted energy and resources to aggravated disorder. While it can be realistic to have a campaign to encourage schools to reaffirm traditional values that have evolved over hundreds of years, it is probably naive to campaign to establish dramatic new ones.

If a Consensus is Unattainable

For many reasons readers can appreciate, a consensus on principles to guide curriculum development may not be feasible in particular communities, even given notable leadership by local educators. There are also situations where such a consensus may be feasible, but where inadequate leadership has failed to bring this possibility to fruition. In any event, it is important to consider situations where purposeful, good-faith efforts still fail to establish a community consensus on basic education principles. Essentially, three alternative (and possibly overlapping) policies can evolve. One is relatively popular, and quite wrong. The other two are sometimes applied, and make more sense.

The wrong policy is to try to develop a body of curriculum and related educational policies that simultaneously apply a variety of conflicting principles in each affected school. In effect, this results in something for everyone, but no coherent whole.

For example, in the same school or even classroom students may: participate in the Pledge of Allegiance to stress patriotism; be taught a body of history or social studies denigrating many national traditions in order to foster pluralism (e.g., being taught how the framers of the U.S. Constitution were largely motivated by selfish considerations); regularly practice values-clarification exercises to decide how they individually feel about ethical issues; be shielded from serious academic learning demands to moderate their stress; and be told they are uniquely gifted to raise their self-esteem. Other absurd mixes can easily be imagined. Such divergent materials make neither good psychological or pedagogical sense. Many pupils may be able to survive such incoherent fare; however, even at best, these policies waste a considerable body of faculty and pupil time, as energies are dissipated in divergent directions.

Another, and sometimes sound, tactic when consensus is lacking is for the majority to simply compel the minority to follow its dictates. In other words, assume the majority has a clear vision of its values and believes certain issues are properly urgent education priorities. Some of school desegregation court cases are an example. In those situations, the courts—in effect, representing the majority of the country—forced the majorities in certain school districts to carry out nationally determined policies. Those policies usually did not deal with formal school curriculum. Still, the underlying principles are applicable to curriculum issues: in some instances, the state—representing the majority—is justified in suppressing certain local curriculum priorities. Then, the majority may be justified in applying such priorities to a recalcitrant minority. Indeed, compulsion may even be justified if the "minority" is actually the majority in some particular district or other jurisdiction.

Majority compulsion can sometimes be morally justified in curriculum policy. However, it is a desperate alternative. As a practical matter, in most situations parents are and must remain their children's primary educators. This reality is one reason for America's longstanding support for local control of education: it is awkward and impractical to compel all parents in a large heterogeneous society to submit their children to a relatively uniform curriculum. The fact is that there is no historic instance of any culture (except perhaps the ancient Spartans) inventing a large-scale effective substitute for the family as a child rearing agency. Of course, there are cases of schools adopting important policies contrasting with the values of a substantial minority of their pupils' parents. In such instances, it is safe to forecast troubling times ahead for educators as well as pupils.

One instance of such parent/school conflict is the conflict around mandatory desegregation of public schools, particularly those involving compulsory busing. In fact, there is considerable evidence that busing often failed to encourage desegregation. It failed due to white flight—the refusal of white parents to move into, or continue to live in, communities subject to busing. In many cases, it seems these mandatory policies actually inspired greater segregation than existed previously. In a democracy, one can only push large numbers of people so far before other options for such malcontents begin to arise.

A third, and usually optimum policy, can be applied when a community lacks a values consensus. The state can allow families the freedom to choose schools that reflect, within certain parameters, their own values. Such schools of choice can be fostered by diverse means, e.g., vouchers, parents opting to use privately supported schools, or public schools providing families with choices among various genuine alternatives, such as magnet schools. Elsewhere in this text, we have discussed the merits of these approaches in greater detail.

Thinking Through the Moral

We have written much here of adults establishing rules and procedures with the clear expectation that the young will follow these rules. Through such mimicry, students will acquire self-discipline and cultivate virtuous habits. We have stressed the duty of the older generation to indoctrinate the young with what they are convinced are the essential moral realities and ethical truths the young will need to live well. Such measures are important. But they hardly represent all of moral education or character development. With equal vigor and skill, we need to teach the young to think about issues of right and wrong, good and bad. It is essential for the school continually to engage the child in reflection about moral principles.

Teachers should not aim to produce students who are solely rule-followers. Instead, teachers should help students toward moral autonomy appropriate to their age level. By moral autonomy, we are not suggesting the typical 20th-century antihero, a moral Lone Ranger, a solitary person who is either ignorant of our ethical heritage or has rejected it. Rather, we are talking about a student who knows and understands our moral heritage and is capable of applying that tradition to various situations. For instance, we want a student who knows how to respond to the common classroom situation of several students picking on a classmate. Our moral student should have learned certain principles: ganging up on the weak is unfair; we must be tolerant of the new and the different; and that good people protect innocents threatened by others. These principles derive directly from our moral facts of life, which should be firmly set in each student's memory. The student's total experience in school—the rules of the classroom, the events in the lunchroom, stories read for homework—should be his moral curriculum. The student *must* be able to think through these issues.

Philosopher Edwin Delattre, writing in *Education and the Public Trust*, addressed the intellectual role of schools:

> Schools should teach our children the three Rs. We want students to learn to use words and numbers well, to read, write, and translate with understanding, to do

calculations, and to conduct experiments. We want them to learn how the past is related to the present, and to be able to look at a painting or listen to a symphony intelligently. Many of us expect our children to study English, mathematics, languages, science, literature, history, and the fine arts. We want our children to achieve reliable study habits and self-discipline through the curriculum, the classroom, homework, and extracurricular activities. When we successfully teach, learning is no longer drudgery. Education cannot be neutral to the difference between good and bad habits. The work of schoolchildren is to become good learners. Teachers must design their courses and assignments so that good habits of learning and success—even the appearance of success—are not separated. A good learner can learn things on purpose, rather than by accident or luck. Working hard is not enough, because the student must know how to work, what to concentrate on, and which skills to use. Good learning depends on one value above all others: the value of intellectual honesty. Children who never learn this have slim chance of significant benefit from school.[5]

An important part of education, then, is regularly posing to students the question, "What is the right thing to do?" This is a central question in any society, and asking it should begin early and continue through to graduation. When people lose the habit and the capacity to ask the question, in the words of Yeats, "things fall apart." Specifically, then, students need to learn the skills of ethical thinking. Like the scientific method or certain mathematical formulae, these skills can be learned and applied. In particular, students should be skillful with the following:

1. Students must be able to identify behavior that is good and contributes to the general good.
2. Students must be able to identify behavior that is wrong, violates social and moral norms and unjustifiably harms others.
3. Students must know how to think through the question, "What is the right thing to do about this issue going on right now in my class or in this story?"
4. Students must be able to sort out the facts of what is going on and discover who is doing what to whom and why. They must learn what evidence is, and how to get it, and how to apply it.
5. Students must be able to recall similar incidents or principles that apply to the situations in front of them.
6. Students must be able to think through various solutions to the problem or issue in front of them.
7. Students must be able to select the best (most ethical) solution, based on the solutions they came up with.

Learning the good is not enough—we must strive to live it. It is a bedrock responsibility of our schools.

LOVING THE GOOD

Much is known about "knowing the good" and, as we shall see, about "doing the good." However, we seem to know much less about "loving the good." Love is like fire, a consuming energy—dangerous, vital, difficult to contain. But life without love is shrunken and impoverished. Love out of control endangers life. Thus, like fire, love must be harnessed.

Learning to love the right things is the work of a lifetime. As parents we know how important it is for our children to love good people and good ideas. We anguish over their self-indulgent friends or the way they want to spend their free time (i.e., the things they love to do). We worry most about the idealized image of themselves they construct—the self they are trying to become.

The Curriculum and the Hero

The educational response to the perceived values crisis in the 1960s and 1970s was to create and adopt new "values curriculum." These materials typically were permeated with the moral neutrality of two seriously deficient approaches: values clarification and cognitive developmental moral education. The approaches had somewhat different emphases. However, many of the differences required considerable subtlety to identify, and most laypersons, and many practicing teachers, treated the approaches as interchangeable. This considerably enhanced the short-term effects of each approach. It seemed as if all serious concerns about moral education were to be treated with one uniform prescription.

The approaches dramatically contrasted with our schools' traditional moral curriculum. That curriculum aimed to engage the young in the most important ideas and content of our mainstream culture. (Again the question, "What is most worth knowing?") Out of this quest came the content of schooling. Out of it came the mathematical and scientific material students must master. Out of it came the knowledge of their world that future citizens must possess. Out of it, too, came our great narratives, the stories and histories that carry within them the moral facts of life and ideals that the young need to know to order their own lives and participate in civic life.

But our curriculum must also touch the heart. To be morally educated and ethically disposed to life involves more than just our minds. As Warren Nord has recently written, "The relationship between feeling and reason in ethics is complex and controversial, but certainly morality is grounded to some considerable extent in the moral feelings—compassion, guilt, hope, despair, dignity, mercy, and love, for example. When ethics is stripped of its emotional dimension, it becomes artificial, abstract, and lifeless."[6]

Our great narratives and literature fulfill an important need here. Through encounters with these materials, students learn

✦ to have both an intellectual and emotional understanding of the lives of good and evil people and what drove them to do what they did.

+ to acquire an incarnate sense of justice and compassion and of greed and cruelty, learned through the study of the narrative's characters.

+ to be emotionally touched by some lives and repelled by others.

+ to continually be deepening their understanding of and feeling for moral facts of life and ideals by seeing them lived out in the narrative's heroes and villains.

+ to enhance their moral imagination and moral sensibility as they vicariously experience lives of characters.

+ to have greater insight into the lives and stories depicted in literature and history.

+ to have a storehouse of moral models to guide them when they act.

As students encounter the story of civilization in history and literature, they come to know Julius Caesar and Marc Antony, Henry the Eighth and Macbeth, Joan of Arc and Elizabeth Bennett, Adolf Hitler and Willie Stark, Martin Luther King, Jr. and Atticus Finch, Thomas Edison and Huck Finn, Walter Reuther and Hester Prynne. In them, the young see abstractions, such as loyalty, compassion, and betrayal, come alive. For younger pupils, the message will also be transmitted by mythology and stories in readers. From Aesop's "The Hare and the Tortoise," they see the dangers of self-indulgence and the importance of staying the course. Patriotic tales, like Horatio at the Bridge, tell the young that life was not always the way they are experiencing it, and that others before them made great sacrifices so that we can live well. Further, these tales should alert them that they, too, may need to make extraordinary sacrifices for their neighbors, fellow Americans, and others in need. Our pupils live the experiences of real and imaginary people from our past. They measure themselves against their motives and accomplishments, challenge themselves to reach their levels of excellence, and warn themselves against their weaknesses and mistakes. These figures become their models or their caution signs. Or so it ought to be.

Heroes and Villains

The 20th century philosopher Alfred North Whitehead argued strongly for the place of heroes in our education. "A sense of greatness," he wrote, "is the groundwork of morals." To Whitehead, it is impossible to have a moral order apart from "the habitual vision of greatness." Our young, therefore, need to be enveloped by heroic individuals and images.

William Bennett, the former U. S. Secretary of Education, grew up in Brooklyn in the 1940s and 1950s. He has written engagingly about his boyhood heroes. There was Gary Cooper as Marshal Will Kane in *High Noon* and ballplayers Lou Gehrig and Roy Campanella. But there was also Sir Edmund Hillary, Esther, Odysseus, and Abraham Lincoln. These latter heroes were consciously presented to him by parents and teachers. Referring to the heroes of his youth, Bennett writes,

In all of them, it is fair to say that there was a certain nobility, a largeness of soul, a hitching up of one's own purposes beyond the self, to something that demanded endurance or sacrifice or courage or resolution or compassion; it was to nurture something because one had a sense of what deserved to be loved and preserved.[7]

But who are our children's current heroes? Three times during the 1980s, the *World Atlas* conducted a large-scale study of students from eighth to twelfth grade. The question was simple: "Who is your hero?" Among the 30 designated by the respondents, there is no Jefferson, Washington, or Lincoln; no Eleanor Roosevelt, Jane Addams or Mother Teresa; no Edison or Jonas Salk or Madame Curie; no Henry Ford or Lee Iaccoca; no Abigail Adams or Annie Sullivan; no sign of Bush or Dukakis. Instead there was Eddie Murphy, Arnold Schwarzenneger, Prince, Michael Jackson, Burt Reynolds, and a smattering of sports stars. Individual parents were frequently mentioned. But what emerges from these surveys is a picture of children confusing celebrity with the virtue and enduring fame that are the accompaniments of heroism.

During the last four years of the 1980s, one of the authors routinely surveyed his undergraduate and graduate students. All of them were preparing for careers in teaching. They were asked two questions, "Who is your hero?" and "Who (other than Hitler) do you consider evil?" Some students had difficulty identifying a hero. Approximately 15% percent mentioned their parents or grandparents. A smaller percentage (5 or 6%) designated Jesus Christ. Close behind were Martin Luther King, Jr. and Mother Teresa. At that point the list of heroes breaks down and becomes quite particular (e.g.,my fifth grade teacher, Mr. Masty). However, 55 to 60% of these young adults named popular and contemporary personalities, the type of "heroes" who fill the pages of *People* magazine.

These same students had even more trouble with the question about whom they considered evil. Many answered, "No one is evil." The most frequently mentioned evildoers were people in the news when the question was asked. As a result, one class would have 20% identifying Jimmy Swaggart and the year after an equal percentage would have Jim and Tammy Bakker. (And Jimmy Swaggart would go unmentioned, as would the Bakkers the following year.) Saddam Hussein was quite evident in the period of the Gulf War. Khaddafi and the Ayatollah Khomeini had smaller percentages, but they showed up each time the survey was given. Television serials were the source of imaginary evil individuals for some, though the question asked for real ones.

These two separate surveys, one of high school age youth and a private one of future teachers, have relatively consistent themes. They provide serious food for thought. Suffice it to say that our traditional heroes and heroines, our Jeffersons and Jane Addamses, are not large in the minds and hearts of our young or tomorrow's teachers. The findings are more than simply a curious artifact of contemporary life. The inability of our culture to project its best and brightest as models—or its worst and most heinous as villains—should be a source of alarm.

Another pattern of denigrating heroism was discovered in the research of Paul Vitz.[8] He surveyed hundreds of school readers, literature anthologies, and history and social science texts used in American schools during the late 1970s and early '80s. As educators know, such books often contain stories and portraits aimed at identifying role models for pupils. Vitz statistically demonstrated that such materials had high proportions of recent figures, liberal politicians, and important female personalities. There were very few "traditional" leaders, heroes, or persons in business or industry. Again, three-quarters of the array might have been lifted from *People* magazine. These deficiencies provide a partial explanation for the limited and shallow perspectives displayed in the student surveys. The students' curriculum, riddled with transparent and naive ideology, failed to supply most of them with vital, relevant heroes. And so they turned to rock stars and TV personalities.

Some, however, might complain that in a democracy, there is no need for heroes, that such concerns are elitist. The German playwright Bertolt Brecht said, "Unhappy is the land that needs heroes." Another line of reasoning states that heroes feed elitism, and elitism is contrary to the egalitarian spirit of democracy, In fact, nothing could be further from the truth. Democracy requires heroes and heroines. Thomas Jefferson spoke of democracy's need for a natural aristocracy, a class of persons who would lead the nation and inspire others to think about and work for the common good. In particular, society, through the appeal of heroic models, must arouse in the young a vision of the worthy life and a love for the ideals of democracy. The British poet Stephen Spender has written:

> *I think continually of those who were truly great*
> *The names of those who in their lives fought for life,*
> *Who wore at their hearts the fire's centre.*

Sophie Barat, the founder of a religious community of teachers, once said, "Youth is not built for pleasure, but for heroism." But to call out the best in an individual usually takes strong stuff. It involves teachers making powerful demands on themselves, in order to make such demands on others. And even what seem to be our individual best efforts may not be enough for life's challenges. The poet May Sarton has written, "One must think like a hero /in order/ to behave like a merely human being"—another justification for surrounding our students with our best.

Developing the Moral Imagination

The psychologist William Kirk Kilpatrick wrote,

Moral development is not simply a matter of becoming more rational or acquiring decision-making skills. It has to do with vision, the way one looks at life. . . . It follows that one of the central tasks of moral education is to nourish the imagination with rich and powerful images found in stories, myths, poems, biography and drama. If we wish our children to grow up with a deep and adequate vision of life, we must provide a rich fund for them to draw on.[9]

Teachers are responsible for feeding their pupils' moral imagination, for ensuring that our young truly encounter models of human excellence and frailty. Such figures should not simply be the focus of examination questions. Some of the things teachers can do to ensure students come to know these characters are

+ assign students biographies and biographical sketches of great contributors to society.

+ give students individual projects to report on the lives of significant, wholesome members of their family, community, religion or ethnic group.

+ display pictures of heroes (or texts associated with them) on school and classroom walls and bulletin boards and make them part of the curriculum, regularly calling students' attention to them and their contributions.

+ have students role play and dramatize crucial moments in the lives of great people.

+ in social studies and history lessons, linger over the human factors involved: identify the negative and positive results that flow from human desires and actions. Do not leave students with the impression foolish wars or cruel despotisms are simply the product of impersonal forces. This widespread view is another flawed intellectual attitude. Historian Richard Hunt has labeled it our "no-fault theory of history." In contrast, earlier societies preferred to emphasize, perhaps even overemphasize, the role of individual choice. A classic example of such an approach is Plutarch's *Parallel Lives of the Ancient Greeks and Noble Romans*. The book stresses the difference that human wisdom and determination can make in complex situations. Composed in the first century B.C., it is still engaging reading. Its emphasis on personal responsibility provides learners with strong motivation to strive towards self-control. The emphasis contrasts strongly with the personal irresponsibility transmitted by deterministic doctrines such as Marxism.

+ in reading, teachers should stress "the heart of the matter." It is important to read literature for language and plot. However, the motivations and moral struggles of the characters also need to be highlighted and analyzed. Richard the Third's treachery should not be sacrificed in favor of Shakespeare's language. Nor should Huck Finn's ethical anguish over helping the slave Jim escape be lost to a study of Twain's symbolic use of the river or the steamboat's contribution to opening up the West. Teachers should try to bring these heroic and villainous actions into sharp relief for students, asking, "What has Huck done that you admire, that you would want to imitate?"

Everyday Heroes

The effort to surround students with heroes and heroines, and to help them acquire a sense of altruism, should not be confined to history and literature. Science, arts, and music classes should study the lives and contributions of great scientists and artists. The disciplined toil and persistence involved in creativity should be an integral part of the study of these fields.

The formal curriculum is not the only source of ethical models or moral stories. Teachers should not ignore events in the world around them. Each day brings reports of people doing heroic and villainous things: a bystander dives into a frozen river to save drowning passengers after an air disaster; an engineer persists in the face of repeated failure and finally develops an important safety device; a businesswoman gives up a lucrative career to work among the poor (or, conversely, a politician uses his prestige to hide the criminal behavior of a group of bankers; or a researcher distorts her data to justify a desired conclusion). We should always be careful about canonizing the living. Still, we should point out to the young that there are heroic people among us, such as ex-Vietnam P.O.W. James Stockdale and Rosa Parks. And, at a more proximate level, there are individuals in every community who work heroically for the good of others, either in business, service activities, or community affairs. These people and their works are legitimate subjects for examination by our young. As Willaim Damon has suggested in *The Moral Child*, perhaps these virtuous people can be encouraged to visit classrooms or other school activities, telling their stories to pupils and being available for conversation—and, we hope, for emulation.

Alexander Pope said it best: "The proper study of mankind is man." There are heroes and heroines in every community. Imaginative administrators and teachers can find ways to weave these people into students' lives.

DOING THE GOOD

When asked, "How do you make someone virtuous?" Aristotle responded, "A man becomes kind by doing kind acts. He becomes brave by performing brave acts."[10] A curriculum that aims to form the good student must, then, give students occasions for moral action. However, our youth lack opportunities to become moral actors.

In an influential book, *Youth: Transition into Adulthood*, the sociologist James Coleman described how the experience of youth in America has been radically altered.[11] The change was caused by many forces: by shifts in the means of production, the distribution of food and other goods, and the size and structure of the American family. The modern world has fundamentally revised the way we prepare children for adult life. Among the major changes is that youth has little role in the economic survival of the family. The typical child no longer lives on a farm or helps parents with a small business. He has little to contribute. Because of smaller families, there is less opportunity to be responsible for younger siblings. What responsibilities youth has, such as making the bed, doing the dishes, and folding laundry, are not the kinds of tasks that help forge a sense of self-worth and competence. At the same time, today's young people exist in a world that urges them towards a self-focused mentality. They are surrounded by cultural forces vying to capture them as consumers of passive pleasures and luxuries. Many children become captives of such systems, unable to satisfy even the minimal expectations of home and school.

Today's youth is caught up in an world of mediated sounds and pictures. Much of this world plays on their curiosity for the new and different. While they may "know" much more than their predecessors, it is an eccentric knowledge. Coleman describes American youth as "information rich and experience poor." Certainly many young people learn self-discipline through academics and athletic programs, activities that stress the capacity to persist at difficult tasks and other virtues. But many students do not participate in such activities. Their physical and intellectual capabilities do not mesh with these particular endeavors. Because such activities are a source of failure, they avoid them. It is here, though, that educators can provide experiences of fundamental importance to those youth who need to break out of their envelope of self-interest or escapism and develop as mature adults. Educators can give pupils opportunities and training to be moral actors by creating an appropriate mix of prosocial activities in the classroom. As for the use of schoolwide activities to foster such ends, Chapter 3 provides a number of proposals.

Moral Action and the Democratic Schools Movement

There has been a good deal written about moral education being fostered in "democratic" schools and classrooms. John Dewey was an early proponent of such concerns. Certainly our schools should contribute to the maintenance of our democratic government and institutions. As stated earlier, we recognize that democracy, with its respect for individual rights and responsibilities, is a profoundly moral idea. Possibly in recognition of this fact, and of the need for schools to assist in the maintenance of democracy, a number of educators have begun what might be called the Democratic Schools movement. The Harvard psychologist Lawrence Kohlberg was notably associated with this movement.

Kohlberg and his followers did not believe educational democracy was an ideal for pupils to learn now and apply in the future. Instead, they thought it should be fully present in pupils' current lives:

> Schools in which everyone has a *formally equal voice* [our emphasis] to make the rules, and in which the validity of the rules are judged by their fairness to the interests of all involved. If the best learning is learning by doing, then students can best learn justice not only by discussing its claims in the abstract, but also by acting on its claims in the here and now of the school day.[12]

The exact formulation of what a "democratic" school is varies from school to school and place to place. However, the core idea seems to be to give students (usually high school students) a direct experience in democracy. The movement involves students much more directly and provides them with more authority than the typical student council. Students in democratic schools are allocated areas of authority typically reserved to the adults in the schools. (Sometimes, such programs are not whole schools. They really are programs for special groups of pupils in otherwise traditional schools.) For instance, they have a direct participation, sometimes the majority vote, in school policies, such as the rules of discipline and the behavior code. They have control of certain public funds to use as they decide. They receive petitions and requests from administrators, teachers, and other students, and they discharge them.

A *New York Times* article described one democratic public school. In the school, the students voted whether sex and knives should be prohibited at the forthcoming school picnic.[13] Fortunately, the prohibition forces won after lengthy debate. Presumably, if the vote had gone the other way, sex and knives would be licensed. One of the authors was incredulous about the report. As a result, he phoned the school to check the story's accuracy. He was told the story was true, that the incident had occurred under the school's former principal.

Probably very few American public schools have seriously applied these remarkable ideas. But the influence of such ideas extends beyond their precise number. For example, if a school innovation is carefully described in the *New York Times*, it has attained a considerable level of attention. And Professor Kohlberg, the founder of the movement, is one of the world's most frequently cited psychologists in the professional literature. The practices in these schools have established an image of what "education for democracy" means. Few Americans are prepared to be against education for democracy. Thus, we are led to an anomalous impasse: either people are led to tolerate, or sympathize, with what are often dubious practices, or they feel guilty for opposing "democracy."

The principles underlying democratic schools are quite different from the basic governmental modes that have long prevailed in the U.S. We are a *republic*, a society where most government decisions are made by elected representatives of the people, not by direct popular vote. The plebiscite is not a typical form of American political action. (The legendary New England town meetings, where such direct democracy is practiced, have only affected minute numbers of citizens for many decades.) The founders deliberately selected a republican mode of government instead of a direct democracy for innumerable practical and theoretical reasons. Ironically, the educators and intellectuals who founded the movement seem unfamiliar with our 200-year-old political traditions. In reality, the model of the school student council, where certain decisions are made by student representatives, chosen after election campaigns, is more like our republican system of government.

Actually, this prescribed direct experience in democratic self-government rarely even meets the theoretical requirements of a true democracy. Historically, democracy means an assembly of all the interested parties, each with a vote. But when votes are taken in democratic schools, no parents vote, though they clearly have a strong interest in what their children are licensed or required to do. No taxpayers vote, although they usually foot the bill for almost all school activities. Teachers often have a vote in these councils, but they are equal with students on a one-person-one-vote basis. Allegedly, the purpose, again, is to give students real responsibility for moral action—to practice doing the good.

The movement is also seriously flawed because it continuously stresses the theme of student responsibility. But responsibility means accepting the consequences. If we break your window, our responsibility means we should pay for its repair. However, students will rarely have to pay money out of their pockets if something goes wrong due to their decisions. They will not have to pay the costs if someone gets stabbed on a picnic where they have voted to allow knives. That will be left up to taxpayers, the school board, or the injured pupil's family. Students will not be expelled if the policy they vote for proves unsound, although the principal allowing that policy may get fired. And so on. The talk about responsibility appears to be so much cant. It would seem that students in these democratic schools are given authority, while the responsibility remains with others. It is only play acting. It is very unhealthy.

We do not question some of the impulses underlying the Democratic Schools movement: to prepare students for participation in civic life and give education a more hands-on quality. Perhaps such experiments have done some good (e.g., teaching some individual students the skills and habits of public deliberation). However, we are skeptical. Our observations of these experiments in action and conversations with students who have participated in them lead us to conclude that, at best, they waste enormous amounts of valuable student time in labored discussions of the obvious. At worst, they give students a distorted perception of our political process and, even more importantly, what they, as students, should be about.

There is an old truism that we must crawl before we can walk and walk before we can run. And, again, "For everything there is a season and a time to every purpose under heaven." The same is true for learning about democracy, and republican government. Schools are not, should not, and, indeed, cannot be either democracies or republics—just as there cannot be democratic gas stations or democratic hospitals. The very nature of a school requires a hierarchy of knowledge and responsibilities. This hierarchy must be under the control of adults and accountable to representative external agencies that create and finance the school. In the classroom, the teacher must be the authority and have authority over his students. Without this relationship, school quickly turns to chaos. The essential nature of the student is to be a learner, not a policy-maker.

In the 1930s, the prominent academic George Counts issued the challenge "Dare the teachers of America build a new social order?"[14] It seems that, since that time, educators have been confusing education *for democratic living* with education *as democratic living.* Surely, one of the important subject matters of our schools is democratic (or republican) citizenship. However, this is learned in many ways, from the give and take of the playground and the Student Council to the careful study of the *Federalist Papers* and our Constitution. All education should not necessarily be hands on.

Other Moral Action

Moral action is consciously doing the good. While there is heroic moral action, such as giving one's life for another, the occasion for moral action is usually rather ordinary. The schoolwide prosocial service programs we urged in Chapter 3 should have their classroom counterparts. Students should learn that helping other students and teachers is a normal part of classroom life. Fortunately, there exist unending opportunities for students to be of service and to "do" ordinary moral action in classrooms. For example:

+ doing one's assignments as well and carefully as possible
+ befriending a new or lonely student
+ working on a cooperative project with others, sharing what one knows and does not know
+ volunteering to help the teacher or other school staff, particularly when this exposes one to ridicule
+ breaking up a fight or patching up a disagreement among classmates
+ not joining in when the class is taking advantage of a substitute teacher, or opposing such unfair behavior
+ quietly helping another student having difficulty with an assignment
+ participating actively and well in school ceremonial events (e.g., saying the Pledge of Allegiance clearly and respectfully and learning the school song and singing it well)
+ performing simple, everyday acts, such as bending down to pick up the discarded paper in the main hall, and risking being called a "goody-goody" (or worse!)

COOPERATIVE LEARNING: AN UNCERTAIN REMEDY

Cooperative learning is often proposed as a means of teaching pupils both cooperative values and academic skills. It would seem to be an ideal means of fostering good pupil character. Unfortunately, from our considerable experience, we feel the approach is often misapplied, or applied in trivial ways. And so some qualifications must be considered.

One of the authors has surveyed hundreds of graduate and undergraduate students about their personal experiences in cooperative learning. The survey particularly asked the students whether and how they participated in cooperative learning in elementary and high schools. Their replies are similar. Almost all of the students, on some occasions during school, were grouped with other students to work cooperatively on projects. Many of these projects were brief—15 minutes to perhaps a few hours. These activities can be entirely legitimate education exercises. But it would be simplistic to suggest they advance important character development through encouraging prosocial conduct. The brief time periods involved cannot supply the challenges necessary to stimulate profound learning. Such brief cooperative activities—especially as pupils mature and are capable of more elaborate exercises—are not very significant for character formation.

Many students also reported they were occasionally asked to participate in more elaborate cooperative projects with other pupils. The length of such projects ranged from several hours to several weeks. Assignments of this scope do have the potential for encouraging the practice of significant prosocial skills. They *can* assist in the formation of good character. The students were asked how they were graded for their work on such projects. If their work was not done for a grade, and their other academic work was for a grade, it is probable that they dedicated little or no effort to the cooperative project. Logical students would assume that their teacher expected them to concentrate on their traditional academic subjects, where good or bad grades could be earned. In other words, without an allocated grade, a time-consuming cooperative exercise is of no great academic importance.

Still other students reported their teachers gave elaborate group assignments and did grade their projects. In such cases, the teacher often gave the whole project one grade. Then, each of the cooperators received that same grade (to be counted for their report card) for their work. According to the findings from the study, such uniform grading is common among teachers who assign substantial team projects. However, we believe it is an unsound practice. And so did the students who had been subjected to that process. They frequently reported that, during the projects, the dedication or skills of team members was not uniform. Often their groups included one or more freeloaders, pupils who consciously determined not to work very hard and assumed that other responsible pupils would be pressured to do the work, while they would receive a high, unearned grade. Indeed, this expectation of freeloading was so common that the author's pupils regularly looked towards his forthcoming class (which would emphasize long-term group projects) with disfavor. They expected to be again exploited by freeloaders, as had usually occurred in their earlier classes. In other words many pupils' previous experience with significant in-school cooperative learning had been unhappy. It taught them to try to avoid substantial future cooperative work.

Some other pupils reported other grading systems their teachers applied for longer cooperative projects. Without going into cumbersome details, it seems that most of these "solutions" were seriously inadequate. The systems failed in diverse ways:

+ They did not realistically accept the fact that there are, or may be freeloaders, or seriously inept pupils (whom the able students see as an unfair burden).

+ The teachers undertook the task of policing each group to maintain appropriate pressure, an extreme (and unrealistic) practice that actually shields pupils from the great learning experience in serious cooperation—monitoring cooperation in their own group.

+ Students in each group were given two separate grades: one for their individual efforts, and one uniform grade for their team project. The individual-effort grade really reflected the teacher's assessment of that student's particular element of the whole project, e.g., the chapter the student contributed. However, the individual grades were the only ones entered on their report cards. This grading system would provide students will little incentive to engage in serious cooperative efforts. The system simply encouraged students to work hard on their isolated segments of the project, but not to care about the overall task assigned to the whole group.

+ Students were explicitly or implicitly asked to monitor and pressure their own freeloaders. However, they were supplied with no effective tools for generating pressure. They could not physically attack freeloaders. All they could do was practice social withdrawal. And if the freeloader determined to bull through, he could get away with it—surely a disheartening lesson to teach all concerned. In some instances, the freeloaders comprised the majority of a group. Then, they could simply coerce the dedicated minority to do the bulk of the work.

One author has applied a system that seems to meet the foregoing objections to team assignments.[15] The system is a relatively elaborate simulation, a structured process that attempts to replicate in classrooms, the pressures that surround group cooperation in out-of-school life.

We will briefly describe this system. We do not suggest it is the only way of solving the problems outlined, nor can it be mechanically applied to students in lower grades. Still, the system provides an example of how the problem should be attacked if we hope to encourage student cooperation in academic work.

To apply the system, at the beginning of the course the instructor randomly divides students into teams of three to five students. During the course, all teams must complete two assigned writing projects. The projects, both done for grades, comprise the principal academic work for the course. The first project is relatively brief—a practice exercise. The second is quite elaborate: find and describe in some detail a real operating school. Throughout the course, the pupils are given instructions, through lectures, exercises, and readings, on how to conduct their research and write the necessary papers.

The instructor grades each of the two papers in toto. They receive numerical grades, e.g., 3, a B; or 2.4, a high C. Each team determines the grades of its individual members by deciding how to subdivide the overall grade for their project. Thus, a four-member team with a B paper might (a) give each member a B, or (b) subdivide the grades so there were two Bs one C, and one A. Note that in the second case the total grade still averages B. In other words, the instructor is qualified to decide the overall values of the work. The team is qualified to divide that grade among the group members. They know who really did the work. The instructor does not accept any final paper unless a majority of the group's members have signed their assent to a proposed grade division in the paper. That division is expressed as proportions of 100%. When all members simply got the same B, that division would consist of four grades of 25% totalling 100%. Or with the two Bs, and a C and an A, there would be 25%, 25%, 20%, and 30%.

Problems have arisen in the simulation, and its design has been altered in response. Sometimes, the real workers only constitute a minority of the group and may be exploited by freeloaders. Furthermore, most students need advice about how to handle the novel problems in cooperation that arise. And students must be helped to arrange away-from-class meetings of their groups, since there will not be enough time for all meetings during class.

We will consider the simulation's solutions to such problems briefly. Students are given some freedom to switch groups on their own, after a short introductory phase. The instructor provides students with both generalized advice about cooperative work through lectures and arranges a series of instructor/group and one-to-one sessions to provide more focused counsel. Some meetings occur in class time, to permit the instructor to observe and offer advice, while others occur out of the instructor's sight, to give students a chance to operate on their own.

The consequences of the simulation are interesting. Many of the groups produce excellent papers, providing far richer descriptions than any one student could ever do. The instructor finds himself working more like a coach and less like a disengaged lecturer. All of the pupils agree that their interstudent contacts in the class are far more intense than in most other classes. A large majority of the students say that such contacts are far richer and more gratifying. They are more likely to make friends as a result of the course. A few of the students, 5 to 10%, believe their interstudent contacts in the class are much worse than in typical classes. This is quite plausible. When human relationships become more intense, some of them are likely to change for the worse. The instructor is convinced that such dissatisfactions would diminish if the students could take similar courses over several semesters. The students who "erred" would be likely to correct their mistakes. However, it has not been practical to arrange such continuity.

The sum of the matter is that the concept of cooperative learning is fine. However, if we want students to experience more elaborate cooperation, we must analyze the learning systems we design. It is no simple task to create a learning system that consistently operates in a wholesome manner. Many existing cooperative systems are probably teaching questionable skills and attitudes.

In conclusion, there are currently great pressures for the curriculum to include more and more material (e.g., environmental education, studies in pluralism) and more and more goals (e.g., students' self-esteem, media literacy). One of the growing voices is for greater emphasis on moral education and character formation. We believe that, rather than a new voice, this emphasis is a rediscovery of the curriculum's core intention.

Curriculum is the knowledge, skills, and attitudes we transmit and promote in school. The aim of the curriculum is to forge the "good student." Teachers and administrators should not look for special programs or imported panaceas to improve moral instruction. Instead, they can find their most potent instrument in the form and substance of their curriculum. Unfortunately, many educators have lost the habit of using the curriculum for this purpose. Therefore, we must look among ourselves to see how we can use what we have to help form the "good student."

PRACTICES AND POLICIES

1. In general, how aware are the teachers of the school's hidden curriculum? List several ideas that seem to be promoted through the school's hidden curriculum.

2. Analyze your own classroom or have a colleague observe you for one or two periods. Do you discover anything about your own hidden curriculum of which you were not aware? Is the hidden curriculum that is being promoted in your classroom consistent with your explicit curriculum and your perceived roles as a moral educator?

3. Do teachers in your school have a common understanding of the most important goal in the school's formal curriculum? Are there explicit moral/character goals in the formal curriculum? What are they? How could they be improved?

4. Consider the ethical ideals presented in Chapter 7. To what degree do you think these principles are taught directly and indirectly in your school or classroom?

5. List several activities or lessons currently being taught in your school that directly support any one of the ethical principles. With some other teachers, list units or possible lessons in which these ethical principles could be infused.

6. With your students, identify and discuss the characteristics of heroic people. Then, each month, prominently display a picture of a hero or heroine and discuss that person's contribution to humanity. You could, depending on your grade level or discipline, expand the concept of heroes and heroines to become a thematic unit for your class.

7. Are there service activities that you, other teachers, or the school as a whole could sponsor as part of the curriculum? For example, could you and your students, or some club or team you monitor, take responsibility for picking up trash from the playground or "adopting" an elderly couple needing help with household chores? Volunteering at a homeless shelter? Volunteering to clean up a local beach, park, or riverbank? For teachers with older adolescents, perhaps you could become involved in a blood drive. With several other teachers, list such projects in which you and your students could participate.

CHAPTER 8

Fostering Community in Schools and Classrooms

. . .liturgy is not simply a function of religion but an inevitable feature of the life of the city. The Greeks were, I think, the first to define it . . . each citizen was assigned a portion of the material work of the city as his personal responsibility: the repair of so many feet of wall, for example, or the construction of so many yards of drainage facility. The word they used for this was leitourgia. They saw that community of life meant community in things, and that unless the citizens joined in the doing of the things, the city would not thrive. Each was to have his particular liturgy; but it was to be his as a member of the body politic, not on the basis of his private taste. As cities became larger and more complex, of course, it became unwieldy. But it is precisely the absence of visible liturgy that nowadays makes the common life less obvious to common men.

—Robert F. Capon[1]

Earlier, we referred to the Great Tradition, which essentially focused on the moral aims of education. The Great Tradition envisaged children reared in a community, a social environment where relatively supportive, intimate, persisting, and predictable relationships prevailed among the inhabitants. In 1620, the first English settlers in New England arrived in a wilderness. They quickly realized their children were being reared away from the routine supports typical of the English communities they had left. The settlers were appalled at the implications of their wilderness environment for their childrens' values. In 1647, they passed laws providing for systems of public education, "lest by degrees we sink into savagery and barbarism."

The settlers understood that New England lacked the communal structures prevailing in England; it became essential for them to make a deliberate effort to "invent" local communal forms. Without such forms, their children would not grow into vital adulthood.

COMMUNITY AND SCHOOL SPIRIT

Even in our own era, many educators give a high priority to the maintenance of community in and around schools. But they usually describe their efforts with the popular term *school spirit*, rather than the more academic term, *community*. However, the two terms, school spirit and community, have the same operational definitions, and so we will apply them interchangeably. This matter of interchangeability is quite important; there is considerable literature on the development of community. We will tap the knowledge in this literature in our analysis of how to improve school spirit.

Many educators conceive of school spirit as a by-product of successful athletic teams. Team success is often due to factors outside of school influence. A school may be lucky enough to have a good collection of athletes enrolled at

one time, or its attendance area may tap some neighborhood especially interested in encouraging their children into athletics. And some schools, e.g., elementary schools in many situations, for various reasons cannot participate in
competitive athletics.

If athletics is an important component of school spirit, and partly outside of
educators' control, it may seem that school spirit is largely due—for better or
worse—to unmanageable forces or random chance. This is incorrect. Success
in competitive athletics is not irrelevant to school spirit. However, there are
innumerable other factors that also determine the quality of school spirit. The
management of these other factors is largely in the hands of educators. But to
make wise decisions about how to foster school spirit educators need a theory,
a structured body of ideas, about what to do and why.

A DEFINITION

First we have to define what a community is. Then we can identify steps
schools can take to improve their levels of community—to enrich their school
spirit. Elements of a community include:

+ A community is a bounded environment, persisting over time.
+ Its inhabitants share important common goals, articulated by significant
  rites and symbols.
+ The inhabitants cooperate with one another to attain such goals, and
  with certain external institutions.
+ Frequently, such cooperation is managed by some system of benign hierarchy.
+ In vital, large communities, the members simultaneously belong to the
  larger group, and various "subcommunities." These subcommunities
  replicate, on a micro-scale, the essential factors of the supracommunity.

It will be profitable to dissect and analyze the definition. Simultaneously,
the analysis will identify concrete applications of relevant principles in school
settings.

About Boundaries

Boundaries are means of keeping outsiders away from a community. Outsiders
are persons or groups unsympathetic or at best neutral to the community's
values. Boundaries, however defined, are critical to community. Indeed, without boundaries, there is no "commonality." A randomly collected group of people are unlikely to form a community, since they will not have a common point
of view about most complex issues.

Boundaries can exist around a school, or around certain programs, classes,
or other activities in school. Much of the following discussion will focus on

single schools. But readers should recognize its applicability to intraschool situations. Indeed, later in this chapter, such applicability will be explicitly considered.

Some schools are situated in disordered neighborhoods. It is important for such schools to establish boundaries that separate them from external disorder. They must control their doors to ensure that strangers and exploiters cannot easily penetrate into the school environment. If the school's tangible boundaries, its walls and doors, can be easily penetrated, the school's inhabitants will not feel safe. They will, quite understandably, withdraw from people they see in the building to protect themselves from danger.

One of the authors recalls visiting a school where all control of external boundaries had been lost. The administrators could not arrange for all the building's doors to be either closely monitored or securely locked. As a result, each teacher locked the door to her classroom to protect the class from the dangers in the halls. In such a situation, the level of community among classes was nearly nil; they were too afraid to try to contact each other. The first step to fostering school spirit in such a school would be to regain control of the school's external doors to reestablish certain tangible boundaries.

Schools, especially if they are located in disordered neighborhoods, apply a variety of means to maintain tangible boundaries. They ensure that almost all doors are securely locked during the school day. They post guards and monitors where the active entrances can be observed. They require visitors to first go to the office and/or secure passes. They have bells visitors must ring to be admitted. They maintain closed campuses to restrict pupil involvement with the neighborhood during the school day and cut down traffic into the school.

Another school-bounding device is of a semi-symbolic nature: plastic I. D. cards containing a photo. Cards are typically provided for both faculty and students. The cards implicitly recognize that in larger schools, it is impossible for everyone to recognize everyone else. There must be some simple, immediate means of identification to separate community members from intruders. Hence, the cards, a form of boundary. Only community members have cards. In some schools, faculty and students are required to wear their cards at some visible place on their clothing. Then, persons walking by can determine identity through observation, rather than requiring monitors to ask for identification from each person.

It is obvious that I.D. cards work better if everyone wears them publicly. But in many schools the administrative and disciplinary problems involved in enforcing such a "wear a card" rule are too vexsome. Then the cards lose some of their efficiency. People are less safe, and the level of community is lower, partly because community members will not cooperate with a simple rule made in the interest of all.

Another symbolic boundary is sometimes applied, usually in private schools. Students wear uniforms. This practice has a variety of effects, but one is to cause strangers in the school to be conspicuous. They are not dressed like other students in the school; they "violate" that boundary.

At this time, there is increased interest in encouraging or compelling pupils to wear uniforms in some public schools. This development is simply an example of the revival of traditional values.

Conceptual Boundaries

Schools or school programs can be surrounded by conceptual boundaries as well as physical ones. Such conceptual boundaries are extremely important. Essentially, they determine who is eligible to enroll in the school. They can be community-building devices. The boundaries may foster a sense of commonality among school members—or may encompass an extraordinarily disparate collection of pupils. A variety of concepts are applied, in both public and private schools, to define boundaries. Schools, either by deliberation or coincidence may restrict enrollment to

+ children of families living in the immediate area of the school, which is the practice in public neighborhood schools. Pupils share many common away-from-school experiences due to living in proximity.

+ children from a common ethnic group, who share similar concerns and by coincidence or policy are served by a single neighborhood public school.

+ children from the community (or one-school district) served by the school (common in some suburban or rural areas).

+ children who have unique talents or interests, which a particular public school is specially designed to serve.

+ children whose families enroll them in independent schools, where enrollees may be of a particular religion, pay a significant tuition, or display other common unique commitments.

These patterns of school-boundary definition are not free from criticism. For instance, at one time race was another criteria for school-boundary formation. We all know the injustices and controversies resulting from that practice.

Many forms of conceptual boundaries for schools have been under intellectual attack due to their elitist implications. Despite such attacks, there is also a widespread tendency among members of all racial and intellectual groups to favor certain forms of boundaries. The boundaries enable group members to relax among their own kind. In schools, they play a role akin to that served by walls and doors in a family home. It has been cynically remarked that many opponents of school boundaries have ensured that their children are educated in schools "protected" by various boundaries. Even when such schools are racially integrated, measures are often taken to ensure that such integration does not generate a broadcast socioeconomic integration.

The conflict between open and closed boundaries will be perpetual. It involves certain emotional truisms. On one hand, we need to mix with variegated groups, to engage in certain forms of complex learnings and exchanges. On the other, such mixing is inevitably attended with various tensions since, by definition, these groups possess only diffuse common values. We push for diversity, to include the excluded. Sometimes, the intended results are achieved. Sometimes, as the excluded are included, they form support groups of their own and, after a certain point, even the supporters of diversity become uncomfortable. Then different forms of community dissolution reoccur.

Boundaries also persist because many institutions cannot operate unless certain levels of commonality prevail among members. If many adolescents in some neighborhood really do not like studying for school, it is hard for a school grounded on voluntary student cooperation to be academically effective. One of the authors was told by an experienced principal that the most difficult ethnic conflicts in schools arise in urban high schools where two or more large student ethnic groups are of nearly equal size. Each group may try to control the environment (and the other group). An enormous amount of adult energy is invested in moderating intergroup conflict in such schools. Conversely, when one group is clearly dominant, smaller groups can honorably accept a subordinate role. Then, everyone is more relaxed. Academic learning proceeds more smoothly.

Boundaries may even take on a special importance when they concern children. Children are usually more emotionally vulnerable than adults and have less ability to withdraw from distressing situations. Therefore, one might conclude that children are more in need of coherent communities—strongly bounded environments—than typical adults. Ironically, just because children are relatively powerless, adults may use their power to apply policies to put children in noncommunal environments most adults would reject. Sometimes, such noncommunal placements occur because the adults believe heterogeneity is in the interest of some larger cause.

Intellectual confusion sometimes arises when public nonneighborhood schools say they are open to all, but really apply implicit entrance criteria. These schools are offered as examples of open environments but this assertion is inaccurate. Almost all open-enrollment public schools necessarily "discriminate." They favor families with the energy and initiative to carry out certain bureaucratic steps (collect information, file accurately completed forms by a certain time, arrange interviews). Some of the families applying to such schools may be rich, and others poor. But, regardless of such differences, all applying families are different from families without the initiative. Thus, any public school with an application process, in contrast to the typical practice of drafting students, is defined by an important conceptual boundary. Furthermore, once a school has an application process with any form of screening, it is extremely difficult to stop the school from "creaming": choosing the most academically able students. As one principal of such a school frankly told us; "I do my best to select the most promising students from among the applicants. Wouldn't you do the same thing?"

The basic issue is highly paradoxical. The absence of choice among schools and communities discriminates against families with the energy and judgment to make wise choices. They are often forced to send their children to schools they believe are unsatisfactory. Conversely, the existence of choice discriminates against families without the competence to make wise decisions or to make any decisions at all. We do not aim to propose some ultimate answer as to how inclusive or exclusive boundaries should be. We simply want readers to (a) recognize the tensions generated by urgent approaches from either perspective; (b) become more informed about how to handle particular personal or group conflicts; and (c) increase consciousness of the hypocrisy sometimes prevailing around this issue, when policy-makers assign children to noncommunal environments they would not accept for themselves or their own children or grandchildren.

Magnet Schools and Community

There is also the matter of special-purpose (public) schools, with diverse, selective entrance criteria. These are sometimes called magnet schools. We have no doubt that such schools, with their particular boundaries, will persist. It is impossible to teach some subjects unless students have met certain rigorous academic criteria or demonstrated significant commitment. We already have considered some of these themes elsewhere.

If a school is a school of choice, educators should use its boundaries to intensify its level of community. First, the school must identify what particular values it stands for, e.g., making pupils diligent, having all members of the school display respect for one another. Families and prospective students should then be told, in writing, and in clear, warm, attractive terms, what the school stands for. Families should be informed they are expected to help their child meet the school's goals, e.g., promptly respond to school requests for conferences, monitor their child's homework. Parents should be warned that their child's continuance in school, in some sense, may depend on their willingness to display such engagement. We even know of a public high school where an able staff member is assigned as part-time recruiter, equipped with an audiovisual display, literature, and other resources. The recruiter's program is available to pupils and families in the seventh grade in elementary feeder schools.

The processes of screening should solicit commitment to the school's aims and discourage unsympathetic enrollees and their families. Similar systems can be applied to recruit students into special (i.e., bounded) programs in schools.

School Philosophies

Whether schools are magnet or not, educators can take many steps to enhance the vitality of their conceptual boundaries. Obviously, such steps can also have some bearing on their curriculum policies. Educators can identify and articulate principles that regularly remind school "inhabitants"—teachers, students, and families—what their community stands for. This uniqueness and clarity can be fostered by drafting and publicizing a strong, coherent statement of school philosophy. Even if students and their families have been drafted into the school, such clarity can persuade them to choose to accept the school's artfully stated principles. Of course, many school statements of philosophy are a medley of conflicting principles, pervaded with empty rhetoric. But our experience and research have shown us other situations where public schools have adopted statements of philosophy or principles that are significant and distinctive.

As another identifying device, community members can be encouraged to recite pledges articulating the school's basic values. Such pledges can be recited along with the students' daily Pledge of Allegiance. Some idea of the power of such patterns can be seen in the Oath of the Ephebi, a pledge administered in about the second century B.C. to all male Athenian youths on their entry into adulthood:

> I will not disgrace the sacred weapons [I have just received], nor will I abandon the man next to me, no matter who he may be. I will bring aid to the ritual of the state and to the holy duties, both alone, and in company with many. Moreover my native commonwealth I will not transmit lessened, but larger and better than I have received it. I will obey those who are judging; and the established statues I will obey, and whatever regulations the people shall enact unanimously. If anyone will attempt to destroy the statutes, I will not permit it, but repel such person. . . .[2]

The sum of the matter is that the forms of boundaries established for a school have much to do with its potential levels of community.

In some situations, school administrators do not have much control over the conceptual boundaries that define their student body. But even so, boundary definitions apply to other educational entities beyond whole schools. Recall that our definition of community said that schools can and should have microcommunities, in classrooms, clubs, etc. In our later discussion of microcommunities, we will see how such entities are critically affected by issues of boundary definition.

Persisting Over Time

Ideally, people should remain community members for a notable period of time. Then, they have the time to learn and apply common values. Furthermore, community members should see that the community existed before their enlistment and will continue after their exit. Conversely, if people are only together for brief periods of time or perceive their central values were invented yesterday, their mutual coherence is diminished. After all, values invented yesterday may well be abandoned tomorrow.

By definition, it is harder to generate community feelings in schools with high levels of staff or student turnover. It is also harder in schools where pupils' length of enrollment is short, e.g., two-year junior high schools, rather than K-8 schools or four-year high schools. Length of enrollment can also be an issue where one school actually encompasses two or more campuses. Sometimes this is done with a freshman/sophomore campus in one building and a junior/senior campus in another. Then, in the eyes of many students, they spend two years in one school and two more in a different one—not much time to lay down roots there.

Persistence also means the prevailing common values existed *before* the entry of the current students—and will continue *after* them. The fact that we still honor the past gives a certain power to prevailing contemporary values. Persistence can also encourage current community members to more deliberately consider the values they create or revise. Persistence invites the question, "What do we want to transmit to the future?" The question can generate wholesome introspection.

There are different ways administrators can foster persistence through longer enrollment. Higher level administrators and school boards can favor policies encouraging longer enrollment in particular schools, with K-8 preferred to K-5 and 6-8. Various incentives can be developed to lessen student, family, and faculty turnover. For example, one medium-sized district we know has a policy of favoring staff promotions from within the district. The policy encourages able staff members to remain employed in the district; if they stay put, they have a reasonable chance of being promoted.

Listening to the Past; Speaking to the Future

Members of communities both listen to the past and speak to the future, and the effects are closely intermingled. They engage in these patterns because communities exist in time, with a past and a future. The community members' knowledge of these two time dimensions structure their current life patterns. Because community members know of their past, they (a) know of the successes and failures of the past; (b) have some gratitude for the benefits they are receiving due to sacrifices in the past; (c) have their present conduct shaped by such knowledge; (d) assume that their current lives in the community will form the past for some future community members; and (e) conduct themselves in the present with the expectation of such future surveillance and assessment.

Students listen to the past when

+ their school is filled with memorabilia from past classes, such as photos, trophies, and gifts from graduating classes.
+ there are important, still observed, school traditions inherited from the past.
+ the school's namesake—if one did exist—is conspicuously honored and his or her feats described in the school (e.g., on the wall or by a bust outside the building).
+ the school's graduates frequently return to the school to receive attention

and to offer gifts to their school, and deceased graduates are honored. (One school sold to pupils a calendar of activities. For each month, a photo of a graduate was included with a description of his life. The ages of the graduates described ranged from 21 to 57.)

We recall a public high school where a graduate was posthumously awarded the Congressional Medal of Honor. A plaque was mounted on the wall of the school, reciting the commendation describing his heroism and including his picture in uniform. It seems likely that many American high schools have graduates who were publicly recognized for acts of heroism. Why is this "concealed" from pupils?

Students speak to future classes when they

+ carefully maintain, or constructively reshape, previous traditions. (In one southern school, black pupils complained about a statue recognizing a white Confederate war hero. A school committee arranged for the erection of a second statue honoring a prominent local black leader.)

+ provide the school with significant, designated gifts, trophies, and decorations.

Sharing Common Goals

Community members must share common goals. To paraphrase the famous statement of the Pilgrim leader John Winthrop, they "must rejoice in each other's success, and mourn for each other's disappointments."

It is critical to realize that common goals are different from similar goals. Two boxers have similar goals: knocking out the other. But if one wins, the other loses. They would only have a common goal if they fought together to overcome a mutual opponent. Then if one won, the other would win too.

Sociologist James S. Coleman emphasized that, in many schools, students have *similar* goals, but not *common* goals. Most students are not better off because another student did well on an exam. The exam is akin to a prize fight, where winning fighters transform other fighters into losers. To elevate school or class spirit, administrators and faculty must identify and design more constructive activities that increase the number and intensity of common goals among school inhabitants. Then community members will care more about each other.

Interscholastic athletic competition is one classic means of achieving this result. The team represents the whole school; the whole school feels better if it wins and is distressed when it loses. Even the team members share similar feelings towards each other. Even second- and third-stringers gain some prestige if the team wins. But athletics is more than a means of stimulating school spirit. It can also serve as a metaphor for many nonathletic activities that can attain effects just as beneficial. The trick is to transform individual (i.e., selfish) activities into collective activities representative of the whole school. Then everyone gets some benefit from any individual success. Furthermore, most people experience a special thrill when they achieve something that is of immediate benefit to others. It is one thing to do well on a math exam and excel your previous performance. It is another, and possibly more significant, to do well in some activity when others desperately depend on your success.

There are many ways to achieve this effect. Find nonathletic forms of inter-scholastic competition where school representatives can compete: band contests, debates, choral contests, spelling bees, dramatic contests, academic contests, and so on. Where such activities do not exist, work with other educators in your school or area to create them. Publicize the efforts of the different representatives from your school or class. Emphasize the tie between their success and the school's prestige. Send them off with cheering. Welcome them home with celebration. (One poor urban junior high school won national attention for having a championship chess team. Pep rallies cheered them off to their contests. Outside the school was a large sign that read "Home of the Bad Bishops.") The more such activities, the better. Then there are more things for everyone to applaud, and there are more pupils lauded by their peers.

These patterns have important implications for the treatment of a school's academic successes. Of necessity, such successes will always have important individual elements. Still, there are ways to increase the collective benefits of individual academic success. Educators can emphasize that individual scholarships and other academic honors bring prestige to the whole school. Furthermore, contests can be devised where schoolwide academic attainments, e.g., the school with the best average on the such-and-such exam, are also valued. Then everyone looks better if the average goes up, and everybody's efforts can help raise the score.

Something also should be said about the matter of publicity. Large, well-budgeted schools often have a staff member responsible for getting the school favorably mentioned in the community media. But even without such resources, a school can have an active publicity committee or some engaged faculty member who finds such work gratifying. It is an important means of building school spirit.

Significant Symbols and Rites

If we want pupils and faculty to learn to see the school as a community, we must sensitively apply profound forms of instruction. Ceremonies, symbols, and rites are among the most important kinds of instruction for this purpose. Such activities and forms of art can be frequently repeated and conspicuously displayed, have significant aesthetic content, and often involve body management.

Schools use a variety of symbolic forms to emphasize the nature of the school as a community. They use assemblies ritually to communicate vital messages to students in which students entertain each other, commemorate important occasions in school life, and relate to the external society. At graduations, the graduates and remaining pupils say farewell to each other (this requires graduation to be managed so graduates "perform" in some way before the remaining students). Each day, students and their teachers may stand together and salute the flag.

Class gifts to the school, symbols of generosity and affection, may be clearly designated and scattered throughout the school. Students may know and frequently sing the school song. There may be a school flag. Some public schools have school pledges that are often collectively recited. Banners commemorating school achievements may be created and hung in the building. One school participated in contests where banners were not provided to winners. The school found some money and paid to have banners made and hung to memorialize the occasions.

Such patterns of symbolism and memorialization require adult ingenuity and application. One high school principal wanted his school to have a school song, an alma mater. He kept asking the music department to do the job, but nothing happened. Finally, he found someone in the community, paid him $100 from his own pocket, and got the job done. Another principal had her school develop a faculty social committee. The committee made sure that all important public emotional events, happy and sad, in the lives of the faculty were properly demarcated.

Art can play an important part in community-building activities. Notable works of past or contemporary art can enrich the community: student actors can perform Shakespeare for the school; a choir can sing choral works; or the halls can be decorated with reproductions of important art works. In other cases, locally produced art, often designed and created by students, can serve the same purpose, e.g., decorating floats for homecoming or designing costumes for a masquerade. All great and enduring institutions have recognized the importance of mobilizing the enormous powers of art to enhance their vitality. A study of life in 19th-century English boarding schools quoted a visitor's remarks on pupils' singing at Harrow during mealtime: "When you hear the great volume of fresh voices leap up as larks from the ground, and swell and rise, till the rafters seem to crack and shiver, then you seem to have discovered all the sources of emotion."[3]

We want to say something about the role of pupil discipline in such matters. Many spirit-building activities require the faculty to bring together a large number of pupils and have them display decorum. Some schools cannot maintain discipline on such occasions. As a result, the gatherings do not occur, and the sense of community declines further. It is important for schools to work at maintaining discipline on public occasions. The problem is not pupil disorder, but lack of adult skill and organization. Careful faculty planning for gatherings and, where necessary, practice drills for students, are undoubtedly the keys.

Cooperating With and Serving One Another

We have already emphasized many ways members of the school community should help and serve one another, through prosocial activities and cooperative learning projects. The community also includes faculty members. But there are still some unique considerations to be identified.

Cooperation includes having fun together. Together may mean both adults and pupils being appropriately silly: a student/faculty volleyball game played before the whole school, a dress-silly day for everyone, a day for students to take turns being teachers and vice versa. Such occasions remind all community members of their common humanity and, incidentally, provide a significant test of school discipline. Indeed, they even provide students with a reason to maintain discipline: unless there is good discipline, the school cannot plan lively activities where there is a risk of serious disorder. (One principal, before lively assemblies, announces to students, "If you do not believe you can control yourself during this assembly, you are free—without criticism—to leave now and go to study hall. But if you choose to stay and then cannot show control, the consequences will be serious." The assemblies are interesting and well planned, and no one leaves.)

Helping and serving (in essence "caring for") imply that community members are sensitive to one another's sorrows and joys. We have already mentioned the important role of a faculty social committee. But in an organization as complex as a school, other concerns must also be kept in mind. For example, there should be ways of identifying, reorganizing, or supporting students who are experiencing joy or distress in their family lives, e.g., a sibling born, a death or divorce, a fire at home. Teachers should show appropriate engagement and, in some cases, encourage students to respond, write cards, throw a party, or send a delegation to the funeral. Students can also be encouraged to display solicitude to teachers; one school held Teacher Appreciation Week and the Student Council carried out "Thank you" activities.

Some observers bemoan the inarticulateness of many American adolescents. This phenomenon is due to an adult defect. We do not offer adolescents useful instruction and practice responding to complex social situations. Adolescents used to attend dancing classes, where they learned both dancing and proper social conduct. The aim was to transmit conventions that simplified public socialization in a complex situation, i.e, an adolescent's first dance. A school with a high level of community invents and transmits conventions that help students learn to display solicitude, partially remedying this deficiency.

THE NEED FOR HIERARCHY

Communities do things: the members cooperate in various ways. To get things done, community members consult and plan together. However there must be some effective system of decision making and administration under the direction of one identified person. Otherwise, members will engage in a frustrating and tedious pursuit of consensus, and nothing important will be settled. It is very rare for a community to be born or persist under such circumstances. In the end, someone must have authority—a leader, a boss, a manager, or even a "coordinator," as long as the reality belies that ambiguous title. The person in authority must also be accountable. But that is different from subjecting each decision to endless discussion, or making the leader powerless to direct subordinates.

These obvious and commonsensical principles are opposed by the advocates of the egalitarian tendencies that afflict education in our era. We have already discussed the deficiencies of these tendencies. We will simply note one irony: many Americans decry the decline of community, while simultaneously resisting the exercise of legitimate authority, on which community must finally be grounded.

Microcommunities

Healthy human beings are embedded in concentric circles of communities: their nuclear family, their extended family, their neighborhood, their city, their state and nation, and so on. Each successive circle serves a different function: it is larger and helps members relate in more complex and abstract ways. And each smaller circle satisfies more profound and intimate needs. A typical school is too large a circle to meet all the emotional needs of the students who inhabit it for long periods of time. There must be smaller circles within the school. These circles should replicate many of the generic characteristics of the school community: have boundaries, persist in time, have common goals, display symbols and practice rites, and so on.

Many of these patterns are found in the traditional self-contained classrooms in many elementary schools. In some classrooms, there are further subcommunities, e.g., blocks of pupils grouped as a row, or seated with their desks together into a table. All of this is just what we are prescribing when we talk of microcommunities.

The problem arises when pupils advance to "departmentalized" situations, where they pass through several different classes during the school day. In some schools, departmentalization begins in the fourth grade or earlier. Furthermore, in passing, pupils may be grouped and regrouped, to bring the appropriate mix of capabilities together before the right teacher. This means that pupils in some junior high and high schools may share their classrooms with 200 different pupils and 6 teachers in one day. In four years this may total perhaps 500 different pupils and 30 different teachers, leaving little chance to develop microcommunities.

In typical junior highs and middle schools, less interaction is the norm. Still, American schools, in general, are too prone to shift students and teachers around to serve academic instructional goals, to the detriment of sound moral and emotional development. Many other commentators, including Theodore Sizer, have voiced the same criticisms.[4] Furthermore, even in foreign countries with greater academic press, there is less pupil shifting. In Japanese high schools, subject teachers are assigned to freshmen classes and stay with them for four years, as they progress through the school, to foster a sense of community. To the Japanese, it is more important the math teacher know the pupils and vice versa than for the pupils to be taught by four different teachers, each skilled in one area of math. The Japanese seem to be doing fine teaching math. In German schools, a different, but relevant, adaptation occurs. German students stay enrolled in the same "class" throughout high school. If a student flunks one subject, he does not stay with the class and simply drop down for the failed subject. Instead, he is dropped down to the next-lower class. All students in any year group take all of their classes together. As students move through school, they come to know well the others in their year group.

Different formal and informal adaptations occur in American departmentalized schools to moderate the problems we have identified. Some pupils find vital microcommunities in sports, clubs, and other extracurricular activities. Some students take a focused academic program that develops a cohesive group of students, under the direction of a limited number of faculty members. Other students make a less satisfactory adaptation. They become part of a group or gang without constructive adult monitoring. They may drift to, or beyond, the edge of trouble.

In many departmentalized schools, too many students are left without vital, constructive microcommunities. Options such as extracurricular activities are available. Most adults do not believe academic learning should be left to chance. Likewise, we do not believe communal life in school should be left to chance. Educators should establish systems that engage all students in significant microcommunities under adult monitoring. There are a variety of ways to achieve this goal, e.g., each student must participate in at least one extracurricular activity. Here are two proposals, possibly complementary.

The House System. The house system is one way of organizing social settings in schools. Houses, discrete, limited groups of students (50,100,250) are assigned to a specific area (with a boundary) in the school. They regularly attend classes, eat, and study in this area. They take their classes from a small (5 or 10) group of teachers. Each house has a distinct identity in the school. Students may wear symbols identifying their particular houses. The teachers for each house work together as a team. Depending on the school's policies, houses can engage in other community-building practices.

Homerooms. Instead of houses, homerooms (or "divisions") may serve similar purposes. Many departmentalized schools already have such units, where teachers make announcements to students, take attendance, and handle other school business. But, too often, homerooms are not organized to serve microcommunity functions. For instance, students in a homeroom may not stay with each over their total school enrollment, or the homeroom teacher may change each year. Sometimes very little time is allocated to homeroom, so that little interaction can occur. Educators sometimes deprecate the idea of vitalizing homerooms since, they say, many homeroom teachers do not know what to do with their charges. The confusion is understandable; planning and leadership are needed to resolve this problem. Here are a few suggestions.

- ✦ Homeroom teachers, ideally, should teach their whole continuing class one academic subject each year.

✦ Homerooms should be assigned service responsibilities on behalf of the school, with the homeroom teacher overseeing the group—schoolwide contests might be held to identify the most helpful homerooms.

✦ Homeroom teachers should be expected to counsel their students and help correct their academic deficiencies (this might involve asking students in the homeroom to tutor each other).

✦ Homerooms should engage in intramural athletic or academic competitions.

✦ Homerooms might be composed of a mixed age group of pupils; the older pupils, under the monitor's supervision, might counsel and tutor the younger ones. (One school we have seen using this system has had excellent results.)

The point is there's plenty to do in homerooms, if we choose to reorganize the way things are done. It is also true that, with the forms of organization that now often prevail, homeroom time is not well spent.

PRACTICES AND POLICIES

1. Some public schools, or programs in particular schools, have elements of discretion in whom they enroll or recruit to enroll. If your school is in this situation, consider, in consultation with others, including active parents, whether steps should be taken to improve the clarity of the recruitment and enrollment process. As one educator in such a situation told us, "We enroll families, not students." But family enrollment cannot occur unless each family has a clear understanding of the significant policies and values of the school.

2. Does your school hold frequent, well-organized, enjoyable assemblies, often involving presentations by student groups? What steps, if any, should be taken to improve the school's assembly policies?

3. Should the school have a beautification committee? Its charge would be to devise and carry out activities to improve the appearance of the school's grounds, halls, library, floors, assembly hall, and public wall space.

4. What is the quality of the school's programs in music and art? Is student participation enthusiastic and widespread? Are the students' creations used to enliven the school's halls, ceremonial life, and other appropriate occasions?

5. Does the school have notable decorations or other memorabilia that provide students with reminders about the past life and traditions of the school?

6. If all or part of the school is departmentalized, to what extent does that program prevent each student from developing a powerful, adult-moni-

tored base group in the school? What revisions, if any, are appropriate for the program?

7. Do or can the pupils and faculty of the school sing together? Develop a list of ten good songs that all students and faculty should learn (as part of music class?) and sing together.

CHAPTER 9

Leadership in Moral Schools

The intention to be effective in teaching, not to be incompetent, is more than simplya professional expectation implied by an employment contract; it is a positive, internalized psychological force pressing teachers. Teachers say they enter the profession because they want to have a positive influence on the lives of youth.

—Daniel C. Lortie[1]

If we assume a school is to transmit moral values to its pupils, then the school must conduct itself in a moral fashion. The concept of the morality of the school, rather than the morality of the teacher, is relatively novel. Most traditional authorities focus on the individual teacher as the moral transmitter. But, as we have indicated, the development of institutional schools has thrust new responsibilities on educators. We need to propose new concepts to meet this challenge. Many of the themes expressed so far in this book relate to the moral management of the school; they describe schoolwide policies necessary to generate moral learning. We have also identified other schoolwide policies that frustrate this learning. Still, apart from policies directly impacting pupils, many other school policies also affect pupils' moral learning in vital, but indirect, ways. Most of these policies involve the principal's management of staff relations: how faculty are hired and supervised, and expected to work together. The principal usually implements such personnel practices.

This chapter will focus on the principal's role as a school leader. The concepts we will describe are not entirely original. We have derived them largely from the practices of able educators managing morally oriented public schools. But the practices have rarely been explicitly examined in terms of their moral efficacy.

At this time, considerable research is focused on the idea of "effective schools." "Effective schools" generate higher levels of measured academic learning than other, similarly situated schools. Higher achievements are typically measured by better pupil scores on objective tests. From our study of the literature, it seems that such schools are, in many ways, like the moral schools we are proposing here. It may seem that we derive some of our recommendations from the effective schools literature. We are not concerned with establishing first rights on such insights. However, the fact is that the effective schools research and our moral school concerns have been moving along somewhat parallel lines. But the effective schools research has not yet extended to carefully describing the moral environments of the schools it has studied. Perhaps further research will show the soundness of our tentative contention about the two areas of study being somewhat similar.

What does the concept of the moral school mean? It means that public schools are agents of society. They are established and organized according to public statutes and are supported by payments from taxpayers, some of whom are parents, others not. The ultimate morality for a school is for it to conduct itself according to the wishes of its "owners." Essentially, this means it should strive to be an efficient and diligent organization, teaching its pupils about character, academics, and discipline. It should be accountable within the organizational hierarchy established for it by society. It can transmit vital morality to pupils only if it meets this standard. Assume some educators strongly object to important priorities established by "society", i.e., the voters and taxpayers who create and support the school. If these educators refuse to obey such injunctions and can see no way of developing a livable compromise, then it is best for them to leave the school.

Discussion often centers more on school accountability to parents than on the school's organizational structure. But accountability to parents is often mere rhetoric. For instance, one high school teacher, in one day, may teach children from 100 different families in four separate classes. And each family may relate to two to four different teachers. It is impossible that the diverse educational procedures that all of such families desire, or that the different teachers apply, can satisfy everyone. There must be a process for shaping such complex patterns into a coherent whole. This requires compromise, deliberation, planning, delegation, and obedience. Thus, in practice, public schools are usually accountable to representative institutions designated to speak on behalf of individual families, taxpayers, and voters.

There are efforts underway to shift the focus of school control. Voucher plans imply that some schools should have greater accountability to parents, who may shop among different schools with different values or academic emphases. This shift may provide some educators with greater freedom to design, or pursue employment in, schools with values or academic emphases congenial to certain families. Such potential changes have many attractive characteristics. Despite increased diversity, we assume that taxpayer-supported schools (voucher schools will receive taxpayer support, merely via different mechanisms) will be subject to many external controls. These controls, for better or worse, will inhibit principals' freedom of choice and surround schools with many demands beyond satisfying parents.

Discussions of school efficacy often center on the role of the principal. We share much of this concern. If one person in a school must be identified as critical to school efficacy, that person is the principal. However, the principal should not be seen as isolated from the sum total of school activities. In most activities, the principal acts through agents, such as teachers and other staff members. A key responsibility of principals is to ensure the school is staffed with highly competent and active staff members. Unless such broad-scale efficacy is achieved, any principal's assumed competency will go for naught. Furthermore, if the principal is to foster morality, he must have a broad-gauged vision of the school's overall role. This book has described the elements of such a vision. This chapter focuses on the supervisory aspects of the principal's work.

BEING NIMMUKWALLAH

In the early 19th century, the Duke of Wellington, a prominent English states-man and military leader, expressed his concerns about personal responsibility with some poetic words. A friend asked him why he persisted in accepting political responsibilities, though he had long ago earned honorable retirement. In his youth he had served in India. Relying on such experience, he replied,

> In India, the native troops said it was "becoming nimmukwallah." The term means, "I have eaten the King's salt." The eating of the King's salt was a ritual which signified the formal enrollment of recruits. By voluntarily taking the "gift" of the valuable salt, the recruit signified his willingness to repay the gift with loyal service. And I, too, am nimmukwallah.[2]

By "voluntarily" taking and keeping a job as an educator—accepting the King's salt—school employees become *nimmukwallah.* They obligate them-selves to try to carry out the wishes of their employers. Of course, their wishes are often ambiguous and contradictory, and there are inevitable issues of inter-pretation and extrapolation. Employees are licensed by circumstances to adapt and invent. But, in acting on obscure directions, responsible educators are best advised to apply Wellington's dictum: to follow the difficult path of duty and hardihood, rather than to opt for cynicism or petulant resistance. Or, if their conflicts with the status quo are deep and important, such educators should exercise one of the precious freedoms available in a democratic soci-ety. They should seek employment elsewhere. Every day, we see many gradu-ate students who have wisely chosen to exercise this right to learn new skills to pursue different work. Many other educators work at lower pay levels than are typical in public schools in order to teach in private schools they find con-genial.

What policies should administrators follow to gratify the best aspirations of their employers?

The first step is to recognize that the issue of maintaining a moral environ-ment in schools, public or private, extends below the top. It also encompasses the relationships among school faculty and between faculty and pupils. Such relationships are critical to pupils' learning character, academics, and disci-pline. Thus, we must say something about how moral relationships among adults in schools can be formed and monitored. The clearest foundation for such relationships is to simply recognize that school faculty are employees. By virtue of receiving a paycheck, they must be held accountable for establishing a moral environment. They, too, are nimmukwallah.

Next, administrators must carry out a system of supervision in the school. The system should ensure the school is meeting its responsibilities and that the employees are correctly doing their work.

For example, the work of faculty members necessarily involves many mat-ters of judgment; as a result, there must be a process of coordination so that a vital exchange of ideas and new information occurs among faculty. In addition, children are uniquely vulnerable, and teachers have considerable authority over the lives of other peoples' children. Obviously, such power may be abused. A review system is necessary to prevent serious mistakes. Finally, adults need encouragement and praise from other adults as they carry out their employment; teachers need some structure to provide them with this support. All of these themes intimately relate to the quality of the moral life of the school. The themes are encompassed under the concept of the moral school.

The matter of morality also touches on hierarchy. The acceptance of hierarchy has been an important theme pervading traditional values. Indeed, without appropriate hierarchy among the adults in a school, how can pupils learn to observe discipline? But vital hierarchy should not be equated with authoritarianism. In a moral environment, even people with authority should be subject to many constraints. In schools there should be some framework for the exercise of temperate, legitimate authority over adults. Finally, persons with authority must participate in polite but searching exchanges with their subordinates, or team members. Without such discussions, superiors cannot obtain essential feedback. Without it they will inevitably commit serious errors. In sum, a school should have a well-conceived system of administration that will provide for the accountability of its leaders and faculty. The task of developing such a system is not insurmountable, but it involves a number of difficulties.

The topic of school-based management has received considerable professional attention. As with many other reforms, the term is vague and has different meanings to different persons. For example, the term is sometimes construed to mean that the majority of issues concerned with managing a school should be settled on the job site, not determined by remote authorities. However, even if many decisions are to be settled on the job site, the question arises of which person in the school should have the final say. Some authorities imply that school-site decisions should be made through a highly consultative, semidemocratic process, with a great stress on consensus. The dictionary definition of consensus stresses attaining a high level of agreement, ranging from 75 to 95%. We believe such a stress on consensus is unwholesome and unrealistic. Too much time will be spent in consultation and, since a consensus often will not be attained, many necessary decisions will not be made. Such management policies will not provide the clarity and energy necessary to school efficacy or moral vigor.

Furthermore, when authority is too decentralized, it is difficult to enforce accountability. No one can really be held responsible for serious errors. A story collected by one of the authors illustrates this point:

The high school was in a disorderly neighborhood. Drug dealers infested the streets near the school. The students mixed among them when they went out for lunch recess or on breaks between classes. Some school staff members wanted to declare the school a closed campus; students would have to stay in school throughout the whole school day. The declaration would affect the work day of the teachers; they would give up their lunch period and be able to go home earlier. Under the union contract, a majority vote of the teachers, by a secret ballot, was necessary for the administration to make the change. The principal made such a proposal, and a vote was held. The closed campus proposal was defeated 40 votes to 60. One teacher said she believed the proposal lost "because many of the newer, younger teachers believed the proposal deprived students of important personal rights."

Assume some citizen believes the school should have such a closed campus policy. Or suppose some parent, whose child was hooked on drugs obtained during recess or injured in a drug-related fight while out on break, sued the school for not having a closed campus. What school employees can be punished or criticized if the open-campus policy is held fundamentally unsound? The 60% of the teachers who voted against it?

If an unwise policy is adopted by a consensual or voting process, exactly who is responsible? In important institutions, there must be clear points of accountability, not merely an amorphous group of faculty members. Without *focused* responsibility, the clarity of decision making will be greatly impaired. We are not suggesting that principals, as individual human beings, are necessarily wiser or more moral than particular teachers. Nor, in most circumstances, are we opposed to strong faculty input into decision making. Our argument is that in education, the stakes are high. The pupils' immediate health and safety can even be involved. There must be one person clearly in charge. There must be a clear system of accountability. Where such accountability is not practiced, the solution is not to further diffuse responsibility, but to clarify who's in charge. In many site-based management proposals, this clarity is lacking.

Identifying Good Teaching

A school must establish criteria to define what kinds of faculty conduct are desired. After such criteria are established, employees will have clearer ideas of what is expected of them. Furthermore, the principal and other administrators can collect information to see whether employees are working the ways they are supposed to. Employees who consistently violate the criteria can be compelled to leave. However, the matter of criteria is quite complex, especially when we recognize that the criteria should be partly related to moral concerns.

The first criterion for evaluating teachers is their ability to cause pupils to learn appropriate academic and character-related subject matter. This is the prime moral obligation of educators. It is so important that the ability to cause desirable learning in pupils may override almost any other teacher deficiencies. However, if adequate learning is not occurring, we must be able to provide teachers with constructive criticism. Thus, beyond examining learning, we must identify particular traits and behaviors that are also relevant to teacher competency. The traits will enable us to offer advice to unsuccessful teachers.

In addition, teachers' specific traits are important because most learning effects on pupils are due to a myriad of influences. The influences often include the efforts of several teachers. Assume we can recognize that desirable pupil learning has occurred. Even so, we often do not know which teachers are responsible for the success or failure. Furthermore, even if one teacher was clearly responsible, teachers have other important duties, e.g., cooperating with peers and administrators, that go beyond their immediate classes. Finally, when teachers are being hired, we often cannot obtain precise evidence of their previous formal teaching success; and some new teachers may never have taught before.

In sum, the assessment of teachers must often be based on criteria separated from actual teaching outcomes. To apply such criteria, we will propose certain basic traits of good teachers. These traits relate to the general educational goals we have already articulated.

Desirable Traits

We start by identifying desirable traits in somewhat general language and will expand our definition later. The traits are listed in order of priority. Such a classification contains artificial elements; it is often difficult to display one trait without displaying others. Still, the list provides a considered hierarchy. Furthermore, the list has been subjected to extensive empirical analysis. Trained graduate students have conducted hundreds of interviews with practicing principals, asking them to identify desirable teacher traits and priorities among such traits. The priorities in the list are congruent with those indicated by the more experienced and thoughtful interviewees. Readers, whether they have supervisory experience or not, are free to justify their own alternatives. Some of these alternatives appear in the following list.

1. The trait indicated by terms such as *commitment,* or *dedication.* A willingness to work hard, cheerfully to accept extra responsibilities, and to try to do the job better. To walk the extra mile. It has some of the overtones of *nimmukwallah.*

2. An adequate *knowledge of the subject matter.* But, as many principals emphasized, new or different subject matter can usually be learned, if commitment is there.

3. A *liking for children* and/or adolescents.

4. A *sense of humor;* one that is not employed at the expense of others, particularly students.

5. *Being a good role model*—routinely displaying conduct we hope pupils will want to emulate and avoiding bad conduct.

6. *Having a set of principles* of teaching and classroom management that fit together logically.

7. *Being committed to the philosophic goals of the particular school,* if such goals have been identified, e.g., if the school is sympathetic to tradition, the teacher should believe in the importance of character, academics, and discipline.

8. *An ability to work cooperatively* with other adults—peers, school administration, and parents—and accept significant supervision.

9. *Good communication skills*—able to make oneself clearly understood and to understand others.

10. Finally, *intelligence and imagination*. These are good things, but perhaps rate below the preceding virtues. Clearly, a certain level of intelligence is required. But, after all, if a teacher was not committed to doing his job well, how valuable would his intelligence be to his pupils?

Causing Pupil Learning

Once basic traits have been identified, we must translate them into observable conduct. Then, teachers can know how they should act, and supervisors can know what behaviors to look for. But first we must apply the key measure. *Are pupils learning?* To see, we have to search for signs of pupil learning, in character, academics, and discipline.

How do we know that pupils are learning good character? We can see if they regularly display courtesy, good humor, and helpfulness. Are they frequently engaged in class and schoolwide activities where they display such conduct?

As for academics, do the students' different academic work products—oral recitations, projects, exercises, written exams, essays, writing activities, art—show significant application and learning of the subject matter? Are pupils learning at an appropriate pace? Is a relatively rigorous but fair grading system maintained? What are the pupils' grades on exams and report cards and scores on relevant standardized tests? Is there any way of comparing such outcomes with those attained by similar pupils in other classes or in previous years?

Regarding discipline, do students promptly and pleasantly obey their teacher? Is good order generally maintained in class and while the class is moving throughout the school? Are school and classroom rules obeyed? Does the class have many discipline incidents? Is student attendance good, and are tardies low?

But teachers' supervisors can rarely afford to focus solely on direct measures of learning. Many proxy measures, largely related to the previously listed traits, also must be considered. We next identify specific teacher behaviors that should be associated with the desirable learning outcomes.

Translating Traits Into Observable Conduct

Observing human conduct is a subtle process that cannot be governed by formalisms. In other words, principals who are skilled observers must pay attention to indicators that have little or no legal weight: the tone of someone's voice, his pattern of dress, and small factors in his demeanor. Such information will rarely, in itself, justify supervisory intervention. But it can provide clues about when and where further attention is appropriate. After all, principals are expected to be sensitive to matters such as child abuse by teachers, inadequate preparation for lessons, or alcohol or drug abuse. Such deficiencies are often deliberately concealed from other adults. They become apparent in very subtle ways. Without a system of identifying clues, a principal cannot sort the vast number of incidents that occur in a school.

Teacher diligence and commitment are disclosed by regular and prompt attendance at work; coming to class well prepared; beginning instruction promptly and moving it along at a vigorous pace; a willingness to accept extra assignments; being freely available to students, peers, and parents; and staying informed about professional developments in the school in particular and teaching in general.

Knowledge of subject matter is shown by previous formal training; displaying knowledge of the pertinent information and skills; and being an active member of an appropriate professional group.

Liking children and adolescents is shown by the teacher's previous commitment to working with children (e.g., camp counseling, Sunday-school teaching, being a scout leader); the teacher's good relationships with pupils around the school; and a willingness to sponsor student activities.

Good humor extends far beyond being able to tell a joke. It is being able to be silly when appropriate, or to turn ambiguous situations into tension-relieving funny occasions.

Having a good philosophy of teaching means the different plans and policies of the teacher—grading criteria, lesson plans, system of examination, amounts and forms of homework, policies of in-class discipline, and modes of instruction—are integrated in some consistent fashion. Students, supervisors, and parents are not constantly surprised by the unpredictable (and "unfair") policies the teacher applies.

Being dedicated to the school's philosophy means being knowledgeable about that philosophy; being able to identify its operational implications for teaching; and applying those implications in work.

Being able to work cooperatively with other adults requires tact; courtesy; knowledge of group processes; insight; determination; communication skills; and the abilities to handle confrontation and accept appropriate hierarchy.

Having good communication skills means being able to communicate to, and receive communication from, groups and individuals, by speaking and listening (face-to-face or over the phone) or by writing and reading.

Imagination is disclosed in education by a teacher's using a variety of effective teaching modes; and displaying ingenuity in devising incentives to encourage learning, as well as punishments to discourage misconduct.

Intelligence is disclosed in the teacher's ability to quickly master new teaching material; plan novel instructional arrangements; and work with other teachers in devising original policies and procedures.

Role Modeling

It is complex for a teacher to be a good role model. First, it involves being a diligent teacher, showing pupils that work should be taken seriously. Secondly, it means not being publicly connected with questionable conduct. Obviously, different people and different communities will have different opinions about what is questionable. But being a role model implies that teachers have a larger obligation than simply observing the criminal law. Even if a teacher is not breaking the law, he may still be a poor role model. If such *public* conduct persists after due warning, or the first offense is flagrant, he should not be kept as a teacher.

In a moment, we will list a variety of sensitive role-model issues. It is important for readers to recognize the parameters of questionable conduct: public drunkenness; extramarital affairs (with another teacher?); teaching while conspicuously pregnant with an out-of-wedlock child; a public avowal or advocacy of homosexuality; aggressively boasting about sexual conquests; being a centerfold nude model; disorderly dress; conspicuously antipatriotic (even though legal) acts, e.g., publicly burning an American flag; smoking cigarettes on the school campus if such behavior is banned; or being a member of a racist organization.

Note that most of these acts are legal. We still believe that public school teachers might be removed from their jobs for such conduct, just as General Motors employees can be fired for going around advertising they believe Chevrolets are lousy cars—even though such opinions are legal. We do not propose to weigh the liability of teachers if any of these acts is committed. Where *we personally* would draw the line is not critical. Still, most readers will agree that some forms of legal acts should subject teachers to serious criticism and perhaps discharge. Furthermore, we have urged that teaching extends far beyond academic instruction. If that principle is accepted, than pupils' learnings about morals, character, and discipline can be undermined by public breaches of morality by teachers they respect. Being a good citizen means more than merely obeying the law.

However, the line of discharge will be different in different communities, and among pupils of different ages. And different supervisors will draw the line at different points. Ultimately, in making such decisions, we believe the values of pupils' parents should receive very great weight.

Educators sometimes answer hypothetical questions about role model issues with the qualification, "This conduct is OK, if it does not affect his teaching." Unfortunately, such an answer is excessively qualified. How can one finally know when someone's teaching has been "affected"? That is a matter of definition. Consider this scenario:

Mr. X, a teacher who is known publicly to be involved in an extramarital affair with Mrs. Y., another teacher, still comes to work and applies himself to teaching. His pupils may work quietly at their seats. But isn't it realistic to assume many of his 12-year-old students' minds are focusing on the ramifications of the episode, rather than on their work? Will Mrs. Y again spend the night at Mr.X's apartment? Query: have such episodes "affected" Mr. X's teaching?

Publishing Criteria and Behaviors

Assume criteria and behaviors have been identified. Then they must be clearly disseminated to current and prospective faculty members. In many schools, this is done through a variety of informal means. But it is better practice, especially in larger schools, and/or ones with high staff mobility, to formally communicate such standards. The process must rely on documents (e.g., job applications and evaluation forms, faculty handbooks, bulletins to staff) and oral communications in group gatherings and one-to-one meetings.

The aim is to (a) inform faculty and prospective employees what is expected; (b) explain why certain expectations are established; (c) translate the criteria and behaviors into specific examples and requirements, applicable to immediate situations; and (d) invite faculty to apply their experience and perspectives to refining the monitoring process.

A large part of the work of a principal or other supervisor must be dedicated to such dissemination. There is always some employee turnover, and most new employees need "education." Even with experienced employees, people sometimes slip back into bad habits. Furthermore, new situations requiring reinterpretation of existing criteria are always arising.

Applying Criteria to Job Applicants

A key way principals ensure morally cohesive and efficient schools is to hire only competent job applicants, sympathetic to the schools' goals.

The applicant selection process is especially important in education. As is well known, it is extremely difficult to terminate incompetent tenured teachers. And, even if teachers are terminated, they are almost always kept until the end of the year, leaving time to cause a lot of trouble. Furthermore, for reasons to be considered later, teachers have peculiarly large areas of independence compared to many other types of employees. A poor teacher has more freedom to cause harm than employees in many other jobs. The multi-step criteria outlined should be used to assess job applicants and potential teacher transferees.

There are variations among schools and school districts as to the control individual principals have over their school's hiring or transfer-in process. Despite such variations, in many different districts strong and effective principals acquire more control over staff intake than less vigorous leaders. Regardless of a district's formal procedures, there is usually some room for principals—by hook or crook—to assert influence. Better principals find ways.

Of course, most principals, on being assigned to a school, usually inherit a staff. It is rare for a principal to hire or choose, all at once, a number of new teachers or transferees. But many schools have active staff turnover, and will gradually need new blood. Furthermore, if a principal has a strong vision of where he wants his school to go, he will gradually encourage unsympathetic teachers to seek transfers or just leave. Over a few years, vigorous principals can create the opportunity to choose most of their staffs. But these principals need to know the characteristics a good staff should have. Otherwise, they will squander a precious opportunity.

Teacher applicants (or potential transferees) must be told (orally and in writing) what will be expected if they become employees and invited to ask questions about the information. Of course, some job applicants are hungry for employment and may disguise their real feelings. But other applicants, with different motivations, will be more straightforward. Indeed, one of the challenges for interviewers is to identify an applicant's basic values. Inevitably, some applicants will try to disguise their feelings—and take a job with reservations. But even these persons will be more likely to apply correct principles in their later work, if they have been told, at application, what will be expected.

In many situations, it is appropriate for two or more staff members to participate in the screening. This is especially true in departmentalized schools, where teachers are more strongly subject-focused, and department chairs are expected to have special knowledge of such competencies. Furthermore, using more than one interviewer allows multiple perspectives on particular candidates. Multiple interviews also help candidates get a fuller picture of the spirit of the school, permitting them to make more informed decisions about where they want to work. In other words, the aim of screening is to avoid hiring unsuitable candidates. Certain candidates should be kept out by the process, and other candidates should be allowed to decide on their own that the school is not for them.

Applicants' past experience can be examined, through searching questions and careful listening, to see if they have previously satisfied some or all of the school's criteria. Helpful information can be gleaned from the application form (some districts even require applicants to submit brief essays or other expository documents). References should be carefully scanned and evaluated, often using phone calls as backup. If the applicant has significant prior teaching experience, skillful questioning and checking should eventually produce a portrait of previous performance. We even know of principals who, when choosing teachers to be transferred in from other schools in their district, observe classes taught by the applicants in their old schools.

The point of entry is also important because it begins the socialization of new teachers into the school. The information in the interview should prepare new teachers to work more effectively in the school.

Challenges Surrounding Information Collection

Assume criteria for teacher performance have been established and translated into behavioral terms. Furthermore, suppose teachers all have been clearly informed what is expected, and why. Next, principals and other in-school supervisors must collect information to see whether teacher conduct meets the criteria. Otherwise, they can allocate neither praise nor blame nor can they identify better practices and share them with others. At best, the school will stagnate; at worst, undesirable and even destructive practices may persist and spread.

The matter of collecting information about teachers is complex. Teachers usually work in individual classrooms, isolated from other adults. This isolation makes it difficult for principals to observe teacher behavior, compared to supervisors at other work sites. The isolation also socializes teachers to working without regular observation. Research has demonstrated that such socialization makes many teachers uncomfortable with the forms of monitoring and observation typical in most adult work sites. For instance, many experienced teachers routinely see their supervisors in a highly critical light. Conversely, most noneducation employees usually see supervisors in a more supportive perspective. Some teachers say this shows principals are unusually insensitive supervisors; other persons might conclude that teachers are especially defensive employees. The matter of supervisors' insensitivity to teachers' concerns is especially ironic. Due to state laws, probably more than 98% of all principals are former teachers. This makes school principals perhaps the most inbred supervisors in America.

None of this discussion about teacher defensiveness is to belittle the general virtue of many teachers. However, as Willard Waller first dramatically demonstrated, the isolating effect of the self-contained classroom makes teachers especially prone to fear intrusion. One of the authors recalls interviewing an experienced teacher, who reported that no supervisor had visited her classroom during her 14 years of teaching. (The 14 years is the longest period of nonvisitation to ever come to the author's attention.) The author remarked that, under such circumstances, the teacher would be fearful if a threat of such a visit ever arose. But the teacher replied, "I would welcome such a visit."

The author responded, "I believe in the sincerity of your remarks. However, the psychological probability is that, after 14 years of seclusion, the real prospect of a visit would trigger understandable fear and tension. Such fear and tension would complicate the task of the 'intruding' supervisor."

Waller saw the process of teacher supervision as bordering on tragedy. He felt that teachers often fear the people who (usually with good intentions) want to help them. The helpers, who began their efforts with goodwill, often became angry and frustrated because of such (unjustified?) teacher resentment and fear. Then, because of such anger, the teachers' fears seemed partly justified. And so on. A number of thoughtful books and articles have touched on such themes, talking about "loneliness in school."

Supervision of teachers is also complicated by the matter of span of control. This term refers to the optimum number of subordinates a supervisor can monitor. Typical desired ratios run between 1:7 to 1:15. In other words, assume a supervisor has to oversee 20 employees. It is unlikely that he can give 20 people adequate supervision, e.g., identify their mistakes, provide them with deserved praise, encourage communication among coworkers. The supervisor will be spread too thinly.

The optimum range for span of control is affected by many factors: the amount of discretion allocated among employees; the depth of their work experience; the levels of their prior training; the selectivity of the hiring process. The more routinized the work, the greater any supervisor's span of control.

Most supervisory structures in education drastically violate the principles of span of control. For instance, it is not uncommon to have a principal for 25— and even more—subordinates. This means that, compared to most work environments, especially considering the sensitive nature of their work, teachers are grossly undersupervised. Their levels of intercommuncation are poor, their on-the-job training skimpy, and their advice and support inadequate. None of these contentions are inconsistent with the prevailing research on teachers and teaching. Such factors generally handicap the evolution of collegial supervisor/teacher relationships, regardless of the good intentions of the persons involved.

In the short run, employees supervised by an overextended supervisor may be relieved. They are shielded from observation and possible criticism. In the long run, such employees may feel ignored, unsupported, and surrounded with disengaged colleagues—at the same time they are fearful of serious supervision. Everyone knows feelings of isolation, frustration, and anxiety are common among teachers.

Collecting Information

The basic principles about supervisors collecting information in education are simple: it is a top priority matter for administration; it must be pursued energetically and ingeniously; a great diversity of techniques must be applied; and it will frequently meet with resistance. For instance, some teachers will consider their classrooms their personal property and be very defensive about supervisor's visits.

Sometimes, the matter of collecting information is contrasted with the supposed key role of the principal: instructional leadership. The phrase implies a principal directly counseling individual teachers about improving instructional techniques or otherwise directing instruction in a hands-on manner. Research has often deplored the fact that few principals spend much time on such activities. In general, our experience is congruent with these findings, especially in larger schools. However, we also believe that many excellent principals see the concept of instructional leadership in a far broader light. They think that improving instruction, or sustaining good instruction, depends on many factors beyond immediate principal/teacher interaction around instruction. Good instruction also depends on who is hired or not hired, what general instructions faculty are given, how well discipline is monitored, the efficacy of teacher committees, the quality of school spirit, the standards established to identify good and poor teaching, and other factors. The narrow connotations sometimes attached to the phrase *instructional leadership* do not fairly characterize the realities of school administration.

The following recommendations are conditioned on the size of the school involved. Some principals supervise 200 teachers, and some 15. In large schools, tasks nominally assigned to principals are, or should be, delegated to other supervisors. We will regularly use the word *principal*, with the understanding that the actual tasks, in some schools, may properly be assigned to others.

It is important for principals to often see and hear what happens in classrooms. Much of this information-collecting is the by-product of activities, e.g., dropping into a class in session for a quick chat with the teacher, walking down the hall and listening to the chatter in classrooms with their doors open, glancing into classrooms through the windows on their doors, noticing the state of array or disarray in a temporarily vacant classroom. Many effective principals have told us that, on a typical day, they "examine," in the way we have described, 10 to 20 classrooms.

Such examinations have many limitations. But their great strength is frequency. In a medium-sized school, each classroom may be examined in this way 20 to 40 times a year. And we know principals in small schools who visit every classroom at least once every day. Large numbers of observations, even of brief length, of many situations by a trained observer provide a rich base of information. Furthermore, such frequent contacts desensitize pupils to "intrusion" by the principal. Eventually, the visits become routine. Then, pupils, despite the principal's presence, continue their normal behavior.

Quick, drop-in visits should be supplemented by more prolonged, focused visits. The information obtained from drop-ins should be used to schedule more lengthy visits, e.g., to classes with exceptional problems or novel strengths. Some visits should be scheduled with relative deliberation—"This week, I will be visiting classes in grades five and six."—and others should be completely unannounced. Some visits should be entirely at the teacher's request, to observe and comment on some new technique or provide necessary advice.

During visits or drop-ins principals can observe a variety of matters: the state of pupil discipline; the level of pupil engagement; the tempo of instruction; the quality of the teacher's presentation and preparation; the teacher's engagement with pupils; the nature of the materials posted throughout the room; the relationship between the instruction offered and the teacher's lesson plan; the quality of pupil learning disclosed by recitations and other performances; and the teacher's dress and demeanor. Such observations relate to criteria such as commitment, philosophic coherence, knowledge of subject, communication skills, good humor, and being a role model.

Principals can also collect information about staff performance by other means. Diverse methods are often necessary, due to the inherent problems of school supervision (e.g., the attenuated span of control, the comparative seclusion of teachers in classrooms). Information can be obtained through

✦ reading and skimming written reports and other data from and about teachers, e.g., reviewing lesson plans and grade books; pupil report cards; pupils' test scores; samples of pupils' academic work made available to the principal; copies of notes sent to parents by teachers; teachers' (and pupils') attendance and tardiness records; records of pupil discipline incidents.

✦ observing teacher/pupil contacts outside the classroom, e.g., in the halls, assemblies, play areas. Do mutual respect and good discipline prevail?

✦ frequently participating in small and large meetings with teachers, to observe their demeanor and hear and consider their comments and suggestions.

✦ judiciously listening to remarks made by other teachers, pupils, and parents.

✦ examining empty classrooms to observe cleanliness and the state of the bulletin boards.

✦ interviewing individual teachers about their work and plans and asking them to submit periodic written reports and other documents.

Fostering Collegiality Among Teachers

On most work sites, rank-and-file employees have important responsibilities for supervising one another. They help newcomers break in, share ideas about increasing their skills, and make plans to coordinate their efforts. Peer "supervision" is an especially important element of any vital profession; it should be pertinent in teaching, where aspirations for professionalism are frequently voiced.

Ironically, the level of peer supervision is much lower in teaching than in most work, even including production-line work. Peer supervision and support are lower because teachers work in classrooms cut off from one another. Furthermore, because their work schedules also often isolate them, they often lack occasions to cultivate peer engagement. Finally, many teaching responsibilities are assigned to individual teachers, rather than to groups or teams. Thus, unlike many other workers, they do not seem to have to cooperate to attain their goals.

Due to these factors, when teachers are provided time for peer interaction, their discourse often drifts into small talk. It does not focus on analyzing and improving teaching. It seems that, being ignorant of the specifics of one another's work, they are reluctant to talk shop in a focused way. Such discussion may disclose sharp divergences in principles, which could be very upsetting.

Well-managed schools strive to increase true staff collegiality. They often succeed. To attain this end, they may

✦ require teaching staff to participate frequently in small group meetings. Such groups are assigned definite, relevant, work-related responsibilities, are guided by agendas, and generate conclusions and minutes. The groups deal with matters such as curriculum, scheduling, various subject areas, publicity, safety, discipline, counseling, and grade coordination. Principals and other administrators monitor committee activities, and their recommendations and decisions are taken seriously.

✦ structure school activities so teacher social interaction is facilitated: a faculty room with appropriate amenities; a faculty social committee to plan and conduct a variety of engaging activities throughout the year.

Some principals, far from encouraging staff collegiality, see such cooperation as threatening their own status. As a result, they fail to stimulate collegiality or even take active steps to discourage it. But effective principals foster such cooperation and make sure it is directed at wholesome goals.

One commentator on this text asked our suggestions for teachers who work in schools where the principal is an inept or even irresponsible leader. Obviously, there's no simple answer. For instance, many employees believe their particular supervisors are inept or even immoral—and those employees are sometimes objectively wrong. So our first reply is that one employee's opinion—or even the opinions of a number of irresponsible employees—can be in error. Our first counsel is to be patient and solicit the opinion of other wise people.

Next, we would be concerned with the nature of the particular irresponsible acts. There's only so much subordinates can or should be expected to do, unless the conduct involved is directly criminal (e.g., embezzlement). Then it may be a matter of going to the law. Absent such overwhelming evidence, our counsel would turn to practical realities: Can the teacher get a transfer? Does the principal directly intervene in his or her work in significant ways? How strong and helpful is the union likely to be? In other words, as in handling many other life problems, aggrieved teachers may have to optimize the situation, just as many competent principals, discovering themselves supervising inept teachers, have to make their situation as effective and functional as possible.

Providing Teachers With Feedback

Once a principal has collected information, he must feed it back to affected teachers in a useful form. Most often, the feedback will be brief, simple, oral praise. Sometimes praise will be written. Sometimes, the feedback will be a mixture of praise and constructive criticism, either written or oral. Other times, the feedback will be largely critical. When feedback is critical, it should be couched in constructive terms. What changes in behavior are necessary to attain the desired results? When the criticism is about complex matters, the principal should supplement written remarks with formal and informal discussion.

Designing an appropriate mix of praise and criticism for particular teachers can involve delicate questions. What rate of progress should one expect of new employees? When does it become relevant to begin "developing a case"?

There are no firm answers to such questions, but it is our impression that good principals often err on the side of formality. They regularly put things, often including sincere praise, in writing and in personnel files. If there is a fairly routine output of various evaluative documents, written comments become less threatening. And, if it becomes necessary to develop a record, the groundwork has been laid.

One principle is more easily settled. Employees should not be shielded from warnings or criticisms because the supervisor is afraid of a confrontation. Our impression is that the most common moral deficiency among principals is the reluctance to engage in such confrontations. Such reluctance is often portrayed as a form of charity or kindness. And surely criticisms must be carefully considered. But teacher defects can lead to serious deficiencies in pupil learning, either of academics or character. Good principals realize their first obligations are to the pupils under their charge.

Maintaining Rewards and Sanctions to Affect Teacher Performance

Just as in the case of pupil learning, able principals strive to relate teacher performance to systems of rewards and sanctions. One obvious reward is the granting of tenure. Of course, the prevalence of tenure seriously undercuts a principal's power to provide additional sanctions or rewards. Still, it is our impression that too many principals use a teacher's tenure to avoid taking controversial, but feasible, personnel decisions. In other words, many principals use the existence of tenure to excuse their failure to build a case to pressure poor teachers to either improve or be terminated. This is not to say that such cases can always be won. But too many principals fail to fight, even when they might win.

But there are sanctions beyond direct discharge. Skillful managers should be able to devise means of putting marginal employees (even those with tenure) under pressure to either improve or choose other fields of employment. The precise tactics towards such ends vary from case to case. Usually the tactics require courage and ingenuity. But the basic point is simple. A school is neither a site for early retirement while holding full-time employment, nor a base to sustain a second career in real estate or other entrepreneurial field.

Good principals also work to invent various rewards and benefits for their more committed employees. The forms of such benefits differ among schools and districts, but they rarely include direct salary increases. A very common and powerful reward is specific public praise.

For instance, one of the authors has had contact with several teacher-recognition programs, which exist in different forms throughout the U.S. The winning teachers identified by such programs usually come from well-managed schools, undoubtedly, partly because strong, elaborately written recommendations from principals are invaluable in attaining such awards. But some principals do not want to go to that much work, and others lack the skills to produce persuasive recommendations. However, able principals know it is important to recognize dedicated service and put time into helping teachers win deserved awards. Even where efforts fail, the praised teachers appreciate the support.

The Principal as Role Model

Some recognition must be given to the concept of the principal as role model for teachers. If the principal tolerates shoddy performance from teachers, many teachers will act the same way towards students. If the principal strives to avoid difficult discussions with parents and teachers, teachers learn from that. If the principal has a poor attendance record, and otherwise evinces disengagement, such patterns will be mimicked by the staff. If the principal walks away from challenging pupil discipline situations, the staff will apply the lesson being taught.

We are always teaching others by our conduct, especially if we are in positions of authority. The trouble is that, sometimes, we teach the wrong things.

PRACTICES AND POLICIES

1.   Can you identify any schools that are striving to be, or already are, moral schools? What characteristics cause you to reach this opinion? How near are they to attaining such a goal?

2.   Every principal, perhaps with some faculty assistance, must analyze his routines to see how and whether he can increase the frequency of some of the supervisory items on the checklist, e.g., frequency of classroom visits, regularly reviewing lesson plans. Should some of your principal's current responsibilities be delegated elsewhere? Which ones, and to whom? Should some of them be discontinued?

3.   Should the principal seek any additional training or counsel to improve his performance of supervisory activities? Where and how can he obtain such help?

4.   Are teachers now clearly informed of their work responsibilities? If the situation is now ambiguous, how can it be improved?

5.   Does the district provide the principal with adequate discretion and information in hiring and transfer situations? Does the current process ensure that competent, well-informed applicants are chosen? If not, what improvements are needed?

6.   Do faculty members now see most, or all, faculty meetings as productive? Are faculty members actively involved in the planning of most meetings? How can current meeting policies be improved?

CHAPTER 10

Planning Ceremonies for Moral Schools

The historian Polybius (202–125 B.C.) described the Roman ceremony of honoring deceased notable family members. Masks of all such persons were kept in family homes. On important occasions, the masks were worn by citizens who were clothed in the robes of honor awarded to their predecessors. The masked images were carried through Rome on chariots, finally assembled at a prominent place, and seated on ivory thrones. Polybius said, "It is hard to imagine a more inspiring scene for a young man who aspires to win fame or practice virtue."[1]

Educational research has paid little attention to the role of ceremonies in schools. It has not provided educators with information about how to improve in-school ceremonial life. Ceremonies are an important means of emphasizing and transmitting moral values. This does not mean that ceremonies always communicate good moral values. Just like books, ceremonies can communicate desirable or undesirable things. Books and ceremonies are morally neutral. But despite such neutrality, morally focused ceremonies are essential tools for transmitting good conduct and values.

Educators should design and conduct school ceremonies to transmit or teach moral values. Many educators already conduct a variety of in-school ceremonies, such as assemblies, graduations, the Pledge of Allegiance, homecoming week, recognition banquets, and various forms of induction. Such ceremonies can be conducted in either whole schools or individual classrooms.

WHAT ARE CEREMONIES?

Ceremonies are reiterated, collective activities, occurring at determined times and/or locations. They often require participants to wear special garments, articulate and/or listen to certain formal words, assume prescribed postures, and give or receive gifts or tokens. Frequently, they involve honoring important symbols and engaging significant works of art, e.g., music, paintings, or architecture. They are often accompanied by parties or other forms of good-spirited activities.

Ceremonies are important because they teach. They encourage participants to adopt new values or to practice current values with greater rigor. They are often powerful teachers because they are public, collective activities. Public collective activities have teaching power because we are properly impressed with values to which large numbers of persons display dramatic, conspicuous allegiance or respect. Traditional ceremonies are, by definition, ceremonies that have persisted. In part, they possess power because their persistence implies that they have been designed with considerable imagination and insight and that many previous generations have participated in them.

Ceremonies always have certain formal elements. However, they also often include cognitive appeals. The inauguration (a ceremony) of a U.S. President includes an inaugural address. Abraham Lincoln composed the Gettysburg Address for the consecration (another ceremony) of the war cemetery at Gettysburg. Much of the intellectual impact of such addresses is due to the ceremonial elements of the occasions, e.g., the public gathering, the beginning and closing activities, the site of the event. Obviously, many school assemblies can have important ceremonial elements.

Ceremonies are often the subject of controversy—which is, in fact, one sign of their psychological importance. They incite conflict because they express values. But not all persons in a society or other environment automatically share the same values. Some people object to certain ceremonies. Their real objection is not that a particular ceremony is meaningless. Instead, they simply resist acceding to its particular meaning. There is a conflict of values.

An instance of such a ceremonial controversy was a dispute during the 1988 U. S. presidential campaign. The dispute was about the Pledge of Allegiance in schools. One candidate, Governor Michael Dukakis, said that he did not approve of placing public school teachers under pressure to lead their classes in the pledge. Vice-president George Bush, the other candidate, took a contrary position. Governor Dukakis said he loved America, but simply did not believe in forcing teachers to pledge. (He also mentioned he believed Constitutional issues were involved; but it seems evident that he, personally, did not believe in "coerced" salutes.)

The intellectual differences between the two candidates centered around whether public employees, particularly teachers, should be compelled to show loyalty, regardless of their states of mind. One side said yes, and the other no. In other words, the pledge was designed as a ceremony to compel schoolchildren (and perhaps their teachers) to show loyalty through publicly saluting. Governor Dukakis did not believe in compelling professions of public loyalty.

Elements of Ceremonies

Some readers may also be troubled by compulsion. However, school life is filled with compulsion. Students are compelled to come to school, to study, and to learn many things. Unless teachers want to be fired, they are compelled to come in on time, file lesson plans, assign homework, complete periodic reports, and so on. All public (and many private) institutions use compulsion, though it is poor taste to go around rubbing it in. The basic intellectual issue underlying the pledge debate was not whether compulsion, per se, is wrong in education. Instead, the question was, should the compulsion already widely applied in schools be applied to cover the pledge?

Compulsion, often tacit, is associated with many important ceremonies. The compulsion arises because certain people oppose the values underlying particular ceremonies. Some people are uncomfortable accepting the formal obligations of marriage. Anti-Hitler Germans felt uneasy giving the Nazi salute.

Witnesses in court proceedings may resent having to publicly swear or affirm their truthfulness. But many ceremonies deliberately aim to stimulate people to publicly commit themselves to positions where they may have some uncertainty. For example, do I really want to stay married to this person "until death do us part?" Once someone has made a public declaration by participating in a ceremony, that person is less likely to reverse her commitment. Clearly, some compulsory ceremonies are so intrusive that they should be resisted by informed adults and not applied to young persons. But the question remains of how should one decide what ceremonies to resist, especially when the costs of dissent may be quite high. We cannot tell readers which ceremonies they, or other persons, should resist or assent to. The answers lie at the center of each person's moral and emotional being. There is also an enormous body of writings to assist explication. However, settling such ultimate questions is beyond the scope of this book. All we can do is recite a variety of truisms: Many particular ceremonies have their moral pros and cons. Important communities rely on mixes of ceremonial volition and compulsion. All social life rests on a considerable foundation of compromise. Sometimes the costs of particular compromises are so high as to be worth the pain of public dissent. Sometimes heroic dissenters, in the end, only create new and more elaborate systems of compulsion. Both heroes and demagogues have publicly resisted important ceremonies.

Sometimes, ceremonies "work" better if participation is voluntary, such as choosing to take an oath of enrollment in an organization. Many scholars have concluded that, after people take public positions, they are less likely to revoke their commitments. They invest emotionally in acting consistently with their declared positions. Furthermore, compulsion can help ceremonies teach because our own beliefs become strengthened when many others conspicuously share them (even though some of the sharers are really secret objectors).

None of this means that compulsion works perfectly. The matter remains probabilistic; in general, people who take public positions on certain issues by participating in ceremonies are more likely to act on those positions than those who did not participate.

Something also should be said about the connection between ceremonies and religion. Almost all religions give considerable emphasis to ceremonies to communicate and intensify their members' beliefs. America is a relatively religious country, more so than other industrial nations. Thus, it is understandable why many Americans concerned with designing ceremonies interweave religious and secular themes at important occasions. For many participants, such interweaving increases the power of particular ceremonies. The president takes the oath of office swearing on the Bible. The pledge refers to "one nation under God." When public schools celebrate Christmas, it is often difficult to design activities without religious content.

Undoubtedly, our current legal and philosophic environment regarding religion greatly complicates the design of in-school ceremonies. Everyday experience reveals that different public schools and communities draw the line regarding religion at different points. But even where no possible religious entanglement is permitted, reasonably effective in-school secular ceremonies can usually be carried out.

A Multiplicity of Purposes

School ceremonies serve a multiplicity of purposes, and even individual ceremonies typically meet a variety of needs. Let us consider high school graduation as a typical example.

Graduation can obviously have many ceremonial elements. The basic ceremony can be anticipated by various preliminary activities, e.g., the prom. Pupils, and sometimes teachers, wear special garments and caps. The adult audience is usually dressed up. Often, the pupils formally march into the site of the ceremony. Solemn music is played. Unique decorations may be displayed in the assembly place. Special dignitaries are present to heighten the occasion's significance. Each graduate typically has her name announced to the audience, proceeds to the stage, and is presented with a formal document. Graduates receive bouquets of flowers and other tokens from family and friends. Hugs are exchanged, and sometimes tears are shed. A student representative addresses the audience, symbolizing the students' advancement towards maturity. A printed program is distributed, listing the names of the participants and some of the honors awarded. The graduation is often followed by elaborate family parties at the students' homes. The graduation reflects real changes in the status of the students: they no longer attend their high school, and they may totally cease school attendance or go away to college. Many high schools also enrich ceremonies with different local embellishments and traditions.

Graduation is actually a rite of passage, an important traditional form of ceremony common in many cultures. A rite of passage "instructs" both the initiates and their family and community. It teaches the onlookers that the initiates are leaving an old role and going on to a new and more responsible one. The rite is also a reward for the graduates; they enjoy the pleasures of unqualified public praise and sympathetic attention. As a result, it stimulates the remaining students to look forward to, and work towards, the happy day of their own graduation. Indeed, many students are very sensitive to the threat that, if they are irresponsible, they will be excluded from the public graduation.

Other rites of passage common in our society include weddings, induction into various organizations, and rites surrounding birth and death. Obviously, in the case of birth and death rites, the person directly involved, the infant or the deceased, does not learn anything from the rite. But, because of the rite, the audience is "instructed" about how to respond to a critical event—the birth or death of someone important to them.

The Heart of Ceremonies

Important ceremonies symbolize events and values that operate in the world.

They represent real tangible or structural relationships, or changes in such relationships. Where the underlying subject matter—the meat of the occasion—is not really important, the ceremony loses vitality. Conversely, where there is no ceremony (or a poorly organized one) to symbolize an important real event, that event may be misinterpreted. The heart, in effect, is missing.

High school graduation is an example of a ceremony that has been undermined by the diminishing significance of school completion. This is not to say that completion is a meaningless act. But in too many schools, most students know, long in advance of completion, that they will graduate unless they die. There are very few surprises. Furthermore, many other important indices of adulthood—attaining a driver's license, being allowed to vote—do not coincide with graduation. Many graduating students also know that, next fall, they will be sitting at another school desk in college. Due to such patterns, the impact of high school graduation has been undermined. On the other hand, in earlier eras, one might strive to finish high school and still fail, and far fewer graduates went to college. Then, graduation marked a more dramatic passage.

In sum, many contemporary patterns necessarily undermine ceremonial vitality. Still, there are elements of school life that invite greater ceremonial emphasis, including graduation. Our own research shows that schools that emphasize ceremonies transmit vital traditional values and increase the integrity of their programs.

Ceremonies in schools are not costless. They require pupil and faculty time, both for actual participation and often for rehearsal and planning. They use resources to manufacture apparatus and symbols and require talent and imagination, always scarce resources, so activities will be well designed.

Still, most important and effective organizations have routinely used ceremonies to heighten individual and group commitment to important goals. In the case of schools, goals can include academic achievement, maintaining pupil discipline, improving pupil character, strengthening parent/school ties, improving attendance, and increasing school spirit.

CONCRETE EXAMPLES

Let us consider examples of two different public schools we have studied, one secondary, the second elementary, with different forms of rich ceremonial life. There are two principles that apply to both of the schools, despite the differences in the ages of the pupils involved.

1. Each school's ceremonial life emphasizes good pupil discipline. Discipline enables the faculty to bring large groups of pupils together, have the pupils participate in novel and stimulating activities, and expect good pupil conduct. Discipline is the product of determination, foresight, and planning. In the elementary school, it often includes individual teachers conducting rehearsals for their classes about how they will enter and leave the assembly site or proceed to the stage. In the high school, planning often means

developing a seating plan for teachers, so they will be strategically placed throughout the hall. Pupils are also clearly warned about the serious consequences of individual misconduct. In a sense, the ceremonies are a public test of each school's discipline. Furthermore, the humor often generated by the occasions increases pupils' affection for the school.

2. In each school, faculty work hard and enjoy their work, students like being in the school, parents are generally pleased, discipline is excellent, and pupil test scores are good.

The High School

The school had many awards and recognition assemblies. The occasions demonstrated support for pupil achievements in academics, athletics, and school and community service.

All of the athletic teams, and most major clubs, had individual annual recognition banquets. At the banquets, notable achievements were recognized, and all group members received lavish praise before their parents and faculty. Everyone was formally dressed. Jackets, trophies, athletic letters, certificates, written reports of the accomplishments of the team and its members, and symbolic gifts to faculty members were distributed. Appropriate addresses were delivered. The school's booster clubs raised the funds for the banquets. Each athletic team and significant club had its own award banquet, instead of one overall banquet, which considerably personalized each occasion. The school had 30 banquets a year.

The school understood the instructional value of ceremonies. For instance, each year it actually held two successive graduations, with slight formal distinctions. The first graduation, the Senior Award Assembly, was held before the whole student body. The formal graduation was held three days later before parents and family members. The first graduation enabled the school's students to see what opportunities for winning honors lay before them—if they applied themselves. The process recognized that ceremonies are largely designed to affect their audiences.

The school had many other forms of ceremonial activities: an elaborate homecoming week and pep rally, graduation, induction into the Honor Society, farewell occasions for departing faculty members.

A variety of dances and other well-managed fun activities were held in conjunction with many ceremonies.

The advice and help of the Student Council and other student organizations were solicited in planning and carrying out many ceremonies.

The Elementary School

Many ceremonies were conducted in individual classrooms, e.g., the daily Pledge of Allegiance, Christmas or holiday parties for younger grades. But schoolwide expectations were concurrently established when a different member of the Student Council recited the pledge each day over the school public address system. This practice signaled the prompt start of daily instruction. It also encouraged each class to simultaneously recite its own pledge. In addition, many classroom teachers with skills or interest in music taught their pupils to sing patriotic songs along with the pledge.

Ceremonies almost always included fun elements appropriate to the pupils' ages. At Halloween, there was a costume parade through the neighborhood, after a costume contest in the auditorium. The parade also symbolized the opening of the school's attendance contest. In conjunction with ceremonial assemblies, dances for the seventh and eighth grades were held several times a year (towards the end of the school day). Parent help was often enlisted to carry out such activities.

The various ethnic groups in the school were encouraged to perform different entertainments from their traditions as gifts to the whole school, at which students were encouraged to applaud warmly. At the same time, the school placed such activities under an umbrella of quite emphatic American patriotism.

The students, as part of their training in music, learned to perform choral pieces for the enjoyment of the whole school or for classes of the appropriate age.

Since the community had strong religious traditions, the school felt comfortable including expressly religious values in some of its assemblies, e.g., at the Christmas assembly some of the classes sang traditional carols.

The annual graduation included a "practice graduation" before the student body, except the seventh grade, at which the graduates wore attractive street clothes, not their robes; a graduation dance in the gymnasium later that day; the final graduation in robes, witnessed by parents and the seventh grade; an entertainment for the audience presented on both occasions by the graduates; and a reception after the real graduation.

Assemblies were held to distribute awards for a variety of individual and group pupil achievements, and to emphasize the important role the Student Council played in the school.

PRACTICES AND POLICIES

None of the following materials exactly cover how to design a ceremony. But they describe and analyze ceremonies in many different environments and provide readers with concepts and insights to apply to their own situations.

Triumph of the Will.   A powerful and provocative 1934 film of an enormous Nazi party rally in Nuremburg, Germany. Available on commercial videotape. Seeing it gives one a new perspective on the power of ceremonies— for good *or* evil ends.

Deal, Terrence, and Allan Kennedy. *Corporate Cultures.* Reading, MA: Addison-Wesley, 1982. A discussion of anthropological concepts applied to modern businesses.

Eisendstadt, S. N. *From Generation to Generation.* New York: Free Press, 1971. A classic describing the role of ceremonies in structuring relationships among groups of youths, and between adults and the young. Many implications for our current situation.

Gennep, Arnold. *Rites of Passage.* Chicago: University of Chicago Press. A seminal 19th-century work articulating the basic issues about rites of passage in a provocative and lucid style.

Lesko, Nancy. *Symbolizing Society.* New York: Falmer/Taylor, Francis, 1988. A study of ceremonies and values in a modern Catholic high school. Many insights applicable to public schools.

Wynne, Edward A. *Planning and Conducting Better Ceremonies in Schools.* Bloomington, IN: Phi Delta Kappa, 1990.

1. Inventory the ceremonial life in your school or classroom. Describe the relationship between such activities and the school or class's proclaimed purpose or goals. Are the existing ceremonies likely to stimulate appropriate emotions (e.g., dedication, good humor, community, and reflection) regarding goals?

2. Are some important school or class policies not now recognized in ceremonial form? What ceremonies should be invented or adapted to communicate such policies? What forms of ceremonial creation and redesign, if any, are necessary?

In speculating about ceremonial improvements, you might consider the following possibilities:

✦ Ceremonies marking the beginning and end of the school year. The beginning ceremony might be aimed at stimulating commitment and could invite pupils, faculty, and parents to identify significant personal and collective educational goals. (On such occasions, should pupils bring in flowers? Should they recite pledges? What special things should teachers do?) The end-of-the-year ceremony might help participants identify constructive educational goals for their summers, e.g., read 10 books.

✦ Ceremonies to memorialize significant, deceased, recent or past heroic figures or events.

✦ Public induction ceremonies for new principals or teachers.

✦ Commitment ceremonies, where students and faculty commit themselves to some important school or public-service activity.

✦ Gratitude ceremonies, to express thanks for significant services to the school or students, e.g., thanks to particular donors of gifts, to taxpayers in general, to parents, or teachers.

3. Are the talents of faculty, students, and parents now properly mobilized to enrich ceremonial occasions? Remember, there are songs to be sung, costumes to be designed and made, food to be prepared and served, press releases and recitations to be written, posters to be constructed, instruments to be played, flags and banners to be designed and made, and schedules to be developed. There's room for everyone to make a unique contribution.

CHAPTER 11

A Final Word

The Greek scholar Lucian (c. 120-200 A.D.) recited the following education principle: "Educators mimic farmers, who shelter and enclose their plants while they are small and young, so they may not be injured by the breezes; but when the stalk at last begins to thicken, they prune away the excessive growth and expose them to the winds to be shaken and tossed, in that way making them more fruitful."[1]

Many readers may find our proposals of interest, but may still be reluctant to adopt our whole package. This is understandable and appropriate. By this point, readers are informed enough to pick and choose among the proposals we have offered, relying on their own experience and values. Our closing remarks will stress the crucial role of sentimentality in shaping our current public and professional orientations regarding education.

There is an important contrast between *sentiment* and *sentimentality*, a contrast that will provide readers with novel and powerful insights. You can use these insights to assess the value of our preceding proposals, as well as the many other proposals for education reform.

SENTIMENT AND SENTIMENTALITY

It may seem strange that a book on education reform concludes by discussing sentiment and sentimentality. We live in an era in which the paramount forces appear to be rationality and analysis. The achievements of science and industry have dramatically changed human life. The efficiency of transportation and communication have increased immensely during our lives. Important medical discoveries have continued the long-range trends towards prolonging the human life span. Our comparative national affluence has enabled us to construct a complex and pervasive formal education system that provides pupils with steadily lengthening exposure to education. Computers are delivering on their promises to increase human productivity. Whatever the deficiencies in our economic system, it has displayed far greater efficiency than some previously popular models, e.g., state socialism or the unmanaged capitalist economy that antedated the Great Depression in the U.S.

Most of these notable achievements were attained through the application of science, stressing logic and analysis. In a sense, the achievements are the outcome of containing sentiment and emphasizing rationality. Against such a backdrop, how can one justify concern over the place of sentiment or sentimentality in education?

The simple fact is that children have feelings. This reality may be gratifying or distressing, but it is inescapable. Adults who intimately relate to children must emphasize the need to share, express, and direct such feelings. The critical role of feeling in education is intensified by the remote and diffuse nature of the end product we desire from education: effective adults. Given such obscurity, education is inevitably affected by vague, ambiguous intentions, such as the hope of attaining some undefinable forms of equality, or extinguishing other persisting human deficiencies. Education, unlike economics, cybernetics, electronics, business, medicine, or biology, must emphasize the stimulation and expression of sentiments, such as love for learning and for our country.

Sentiment is an inherently uncertain force. While we can make forecasts about the efficacy of certain approaches, we cannot ensure precise and uniformly effective outcomes. Because of the inevitability of sentiment, education is really much more complicated than fields like medicine or economics. Again, for education to work well, large numbers of people must harmonize their sentiments about complex issues for long periods of time. And it is harder to generate such harmonic, persisting emotions than to coordinate the use of technology like the telephone, or a new test for cancer. As a result, the large-scale application of pure rationality to education may be inappropriate, and surely is stress-provoking. To escape such stress, adults are likely to substitute sentimentality for either reflection or wholesome sentiment. Or some adults will try to entirely suppress the role of sentiment in education. That process is equally unsatisfactory, since feelings are to education as fuel is to automobiles. In the end, we must face an unfortunate truth. Education problems must be resolved through the mobilization of an appropriate but cumbersome mix of sentiment and rationality.

How is wholesome sentiment different from destructive sentimentality? *Sentiment* simply means one is moved, or affected, by serious emotions, e.g., love, hate, fear, pride. It is a truism that such emotions are inherent in healthy human life and are important motivators for human conduct. *Sentimentality* means the excessive cultivation of emotional stimulation, a predisposition to allow our emotions to ride roughshod over reason and experience, instead of cooperating with these critical forces. Sentimentality glories in the feckless, undisciplined expression of feelings. In our era, this weakness has especially affected education. The affliction is partly due to the notable efficiency science and rationality have displayed in many other fields of human endeavor ("If we can put a man on the moon, then why not . . .?"). It is too distressing to contrast the important, but limited, triumphs of industry and science with the tragic limitations of human emotions and our human existence. The contrast is especially dramatic in education, where we must stimulate and release emotion while simultaneously applying considerable rational thought. This is a demanding recipe.

HAPPY-THINK

One friend put it to us simply. Too many contemporary Americans have a special vulnerability to "happy-think." The phrase means the inordinate, sentimental insistence on good feelings. It is true that the Declaration of Independence did laud the pursuit of happiness. But few of its signers ever imagined that right of pursuit implied the right to attainment.

The prevalence of happy-think does not mean afflicted persons always think happy thoughts. However, they do assume any disruption in happy-think is unwarranted, a violation of personal liberty. As a result, in many quarters there is little patience with information or ideas about education that disrupt happy-think. Such intrusive reflections are taboo. Repressing upsetting information inevitably makes things even worse. Conversely, in education many utopian and sentimental ideas are received with inordinate tolerance. This accounts for the short life of many education fads.

Schools, we have said, do and should involve our emotional life. In general, teachers should love children and the society in which they will live. Parents and children should be encouraged to like and love their schools. Despite such sentiments, our views are also highly unsentimental. Many good things are now happening in education, and more good things can and should happen. However, we are obdurate foes of happy-think.

To paraphrase the English philosopher Thomas Hobbes, "Man is the wolf to man." In other words, men and women have deep-set, powerful instincts that often lead them to act against the best interests of their fellows. The recognition of such distressing human potential flies directly in the face of the premises of happy-think. One critical task for education is to moderate and redirect such threatening human capabilities.

These wolfish tendencies are often expressed by collective or institutional action. Indeed, even the romantic Jean-Jacques Rousseau recognized that capabilities for evil often existed in human institutions. However, unlike Rousseau, we do not see men and women as innately good, and only their institutions as potential wolves. Instead, the selfish institutions that surround us, whether they are nations, businesses, unions, ethnic or religious organizations, professional associations, or public-interest groups, are not alien beings. They merely reflect the amalgamated aspirations of their members.

The matter is not entirely bleak. For example, economists have demonstrated that market economies are often able to harness such selfish drives to generate collective benefits.

Furthermore, selfish aspirations are not the sole motives for human action. Human misconduct often coexists with a remarkable medley of admirable and noble acts and motives. Despite this admixture, a disposition towards selfishness always will be an important part of human motivation. Serious, nonsentimental conceptions of education must include a clear recognition of this persisting proclivity.

These views are not novel. They would have been presumed by the authors of *The Federalist Papers*. They pervade the writings of Sigmund Freud and are most clearly expressed in his *Civilization and Its Discontents*. The concepts of hubris and tragedy are ancient. Such concepts recognize that overweening pride and significant flaws are inherent in human action. The theme of redemption, prevalent in many religions, provides another important insight. The theme suggests a widespread perception that human beings are strongly disposed to wrongdoing—and in need of being redeemed.

There is ample contemporary evidence to support such premises. America now has the largest, most costly and elaborate education system, ranging from preschool through college and graduate school, in human history. We possess a civilizing force of unprecedented scope. Yet, despite the breadth of this institution, many signs point to the continuing vitality of human selfishness. The dreary statistics about the long-term increases in youth disorder are not news. Turning to other areas of social distress, we can identify increasing public concern with topics such as child and spouse abuse; declining commitments to parenting by adults: rising rates of divorce; pollution and global warming; and a variety of interethnic tensions. Whatever the specifics of such topics, the problems rest on a common theme: the human pursuit of narrow self-interest. Such selfishness may arise in small groups, such as parent/child or husband/wife relations, or in conflicts between large institutions and groups, such the tensions between conservationists and industrial developers and their customers.

Conflict, tension, envy, and disruption are inevitable concomitants of personal and group life. There will probably be persisting efforts to redirect such tendencies, and novel medical remedies or original academic courses that will try to extinguish these disorders. We can see improvement and even notable victories—and surely problems and failures. However, we wonder whether dramatic, all-out aspirations for change might just make matters worse.

From Its Beginnings

American education, from its beginnings to the present, has continuously been adapting, with necessarily mixed success, to the realities of our dynamic society. Adaptation has involved questions of ideology, interest-group conflict, resource allocation, and necessarily imperfect forecasting. If there is any special cause for increased distress in our era about education, it is the spread of sentimentality. Policies that would not bear serious intellectual consideration have attained excessive influence in education, due to their sentimental appeal. These policies support the prevalence of happy-think.

We have offered a variety of prescriptions for improving school and classroom management. These prescriptions have worked well for many teachers in the present and past. They can also help other educators and their pupils. But we reject sentimentalism. Our prescriptions will only work if educators apply diligence and reflection. Furthermore, even with diligence and reflection, some pupils and their families will not adequately respond. Teaching can only be probabilistic. We must do our best, and pray our failures will be helped by other persons and institutions.

Notes and References

Introduction

1. Wynne, E. A. (1987). *Chicago area award winning schools, l987.* Chicago: University of Illinois at Chicago.

Chapter 1

1. Read, M. (1968). *Children of their fathers.* New York: Holt, Rinehart and Winston.
2. Powell, A. G., Farrar, E., & Cohen, D. (1985). *The shopping mall high school.* New York: Houghton-Mifflin.
3. Wynne, E. A. (Ed.). (1984). *Developing character: Transmitting knowledge.* Posen, IL: ARL, p. 4, and National Center for Health Statistics, Department of Health and Human Welfare (1991). Personal communication.
4. Ferderner, L. (Ed.). (1991). *Youth indicators, 1991* Washington, DC: Government Printing Office, p. 128.
5. Ogle, L. T., Alsalam, N., & Rogers, G. T. (1991). *The condition of education 1991* (Vol. 1). Washington, DC: U. S. Department of Education, 1991, p. 78.
6. Congressional Budget Office (1986). *Trends in educational achievement.* Washington, DC: Congressional Budget Office.
7. Cummings, W. K. (1980). *Education and equality in Japan.* Princeton, NJ: Princeton University Press, p. 111.
8. Goleman, D. (1990, December 25). The group and the self. *New York Times*, pp. 13, 15.
9. Youth for Understanding (1989). *Towards understanding those mystifying Americans.* Washington, DC: Author.
10. Wynne, E. A., & Hess, M. (1986). Long-term trends in youth conduct and the revival of traditional value patterns. *Educational Evaluation and Policy Analysis, 8,* 294–308.
11. Swidler, A. (1979). *Organization without authority.* Cambridge: Harvard University Press, and Kozol, J. (1972). *Free schools.* Boston: Houghton Mifflin.
12. Cremin, L. (1961). *The transformation of the school.* New York: Vintage, p. 348.
13. Gallup, G., Jr., & Castelli, J. (1989). *The people's religion.* New York: Macmillan, p. 4.
14. Goldman, A. L. (1991, Apr. 10). Portrait of religion in the U. S. *New York Times*, p. 1.

Chapter 2

1. Marius, R. (1985). *Thomas More, a biography.* New York: Knopf, p. 225.

2. Bowen, J. (1971). *A history of western education* (Vol. 1: The ancient world). New York: St. Martins Press, p. 153.
3. Cohen, Y. (1964). *The transition from childhood to adulthood.* Chicago: Aldine, p. 47.
4. Tyack, D., & Hansot, E. (1982). *Managers of virtue.* New York: Basic Books.
5. Yulish, S. M. (1980). *The search for a civic religion.* Landover, MD: University Press of America.
6. Gurr, T. R. (Ed.). (1989). *Violence in America* (Vol. 1). Beverly Hills, CA: Sage, introduction.
7. Schlesinger, A., Jr. (1986). *The cycles in American history.* Boston: Norton.
8. Freud, S. (1938). *Civilization and its discontents.* London: Hogarth.
9. Krathwol, D., Bloom, B., & Masia, B. (1964). *Taxonomy of educational objectives, handbook II: Affective domain.* New York: David McKay, p. 79.
10. Rousseau, J. J. (1974). *Emile.* New York: Dutton, p. 56.
11. De Pencier, I. B. (1967). *The history of the laboratory schools.* Chicago: Quadrangle Press, p. 59.
12. Le Vine, R. A., & White, M. (1986). *Human conditions.* New York: Routledge & Kegan Paul, p. 69.
13. Wynne, E. A. (1987, March). Competitive sports—inevitably controversial. *Journal of Physical Education, Recreation and Health, 58,* 80-86.
14. Wilson, J. Q. (1991). Human nature and social progress. Bradley Lecture, American Enterprise Institute, May 9.
15. Durkheim, E. (1961). *Moral education.* New York: Free Press.
16. e.g., Klapp, O. (1969). *The collective search for identity.* New York: Holt, Rinehart and Winston.
17. Hartschorne, H., May, M. A., & Shuttleworth, F. K. (1930). *Studies in the organization of character.* New York: Macmillan.
18. Kohlberg, L. (1981). *Essays on moral development* (Vol. I: The philosophy of moral development). New York: Harper & Row, p. 31.
19. Rushton, J. P., Brainerd, C. J., & Preisley, M. (1983). Behavioral development and construct validity. *Psychological Bulletin, 94,* 18–38.

Chapter 3

1. Coleman, J. S. (1968). The concept of equal educational opportunity. *Harvard Educational Review, 38,* (1), p. 22.
2. Maryland State Commission on Values Education (1979). *Statement of purpose.* Annapolis, MD: Maryland State Department of Education.
3. Cicero (1974). *De Officia [On Duties]* (H. Edinger, Trans.). New York: Bobbs-Merrill, p. 105.

4. Mullis, I. V. S., Owen, E. H., & Phillips, G. W. (1990). *Accelerating academic achievement.* Washington, DC: Office of Educational Research and Improvement, U. S. Department of Education, p. 75.
5. Office of Education Research and Improvement (1988). *Youth indicators, 1988.* Washington, DC: Government Printing Office, p. 70.
6. Honeywell, R. J. (1964). *The educational works of Thomas Jefferson.* New York: Russell & Russell, p. 26.
7. Bowen, J. (1981). *A history of world education* (Vol. 3: The modern world). New York: St. Martins, p. 250.
8. Parry, V. J. (1969). Elite elements in the Ottoman empire. In Wilkinson, R. (Ed.), *Governing elites* (p. 72). New York: Oxford University Press.
9. Quick, R. H. (1896). *Essays on educational reformers.* New York: Apppleton, p. 43.
10. Lerner, B. (1991, March). Good news about American education. *Commentary, 91,* 19-25.
11. Ogle, L. T., Alsalam, N., & Rogers, G. T. (1991). *The condition of education, 1991* (Vol.1). Washington, DC: U. S. Department of Education, p. 24.
12. Slavin, R. E. (1988, Spring). Synthesis of research on grouping in elementary and secondary schools. *Educational Leadership, 46,* 67–77.
13. Drebeen, R., & Barr, R. (1988, November). The formation and instruction of ability groups. *American Journal of Education, 97* (1), 34–64.

Chapter 4

1. Ryan, K. (Ed.). (1991). *The roller coaster year: The stories for first year teachers.* New York: Harper Collins.
2. Ibid.
3. Grant, G. (1982, January/February). The character of education, and the education of character. *American Educator, 18,* 37–45.

Chapter 5

1. Etzioni, A. (1989, December 17). Fixing the schools is not enough. *New York Times.*
2. Fullinwider, R. F. (1990). *The ends of political and moral education.* Unpublished manuscript, Harvard University, Cambridge, MA.
3. Sizer, T. (1985). *Horace's compromise.* Boston: Houghton Mifflin.
4. Kidder, T. (1989). *Among schoolchildren.* Boston: Houghton Mifflin.
5. Matthews, J. (1988). *Escalante, the best teacher in America.* New York: Holt.
6. Grant, G. (1988). *The world we created at Hamilton High School.* Cambridge, MA: Harvard University Press.

7. Bloom, A. (1987). *The closing of the American mind.* New York: Simon and Schuster.
8. Maslow, A. H. (1970). *Motivation and personality* (2nd ed.). New York: Harper and Row.
9. Kramer, R. (1991). *Ed school follies: The miseducation of the American teacher.* New York: Collier/Free Press.
10. Purkey, W. W. (1978). *Inviting school success.* Belmont, CA: Wadsworth, p. 3.
11. Stevenson, H. W. (1987, October). America's math problems. *Educational Leadership, 45* (2), 5–6.
12. Stevenson, H. W. (1987, Summer). The Asian advantage: The case of mathematics. *American Educator, 11*, p. 30.
13. Mecca, A., Smelser, N., & Vasconcellos, J. (Eds.). (1989). *The social importance of self-esteem.* Berkeley, CA: University of California Press.
14. Coulson, W. (1991, January). Pop psychology of the sixties. *Religious Life*, pp. 3–5.
15. Everhard, R. (1985). Feeling good about oneself. *Sociology of education, 58* (4), p. 158.

Chapter 6

1. Bandura, A. (1977). *Social learning theory.* Englewood Cliffs, NJ: Prentice-Hall.
2. Biehler, R. F., & Snowman, J. (1986). *Psychology applied to teaching.* (5th ed.). Boston: Houghton Mifflin.
3. Coleman, J. S. (1974). *Youth: Transition to adulthood.* Chicago: University of Chicago Press.
4. *The Boston Parents' Paper* (January, 1990), p. 5.
5. Green, T. F. (1984). The formation of conscience in an age of technology (John Dewey Lecture, 1984). Syracuse, NY: Syracuse University Printing Service, p. 4.
6. Coles, R., & Genevie, L. (1990, March). The moral life of America's school children. *Teacher Magazine.*
7. Walberg, H. J. (1988, March). Synthesis of research on time and learning. *Educational Leadership*, p. 76–81.
8. e.g., see Wittrock, M. C. (Ed.). (1986). *The handbook of research on teaching* (3rd ed.). New York: Macmillan, and Ornstein, A. C., & Levine, D. U. (1989). *Foundations of education* (4th ed.). Boston: Houghton Mifflin.
9. Lanckton, A. (1992). How seventh- and eighth-grade teachers perceive their role as moral educators. Unpublished doctoral dissertation, Boston University.
10. Simon, S. B. (1971, December). Values clarification vs. indoctrination. *Social Education*, 902–905.
11. Hirsch, E. D., Jr. (1985, Summer). Cultural literacy and the schools. *American Educator*, 8–15.

12. Berkow, I. (1990, August 20). Sports in the Times. *The New York Times*, section C, p. 9.

Chapter 7

1. Moline, J. N. (1981). Classical ideas about moral education. *Character*, *2*, (8), p. 8.
2. Kozol, J. (1967). *Death at an early age*. Boston: Houghton Mifflin; Holt, J. (1967). *How children fail*. New York: Pitman; and Silberman, C. E. (1970). *Crisis in the classroom*. New York: Random House.
3. Lewis, C. S. (1947). *The abolition of man: How education develops man's sense of morality*. New York: Collier/Macmillan Books, p. 29.
4. On the other hand, the poet Ogden Nash wrote: "Hope that in the human breast does spring is fond of wine or beer, or anything designed to help a hope to spring."
5. Delattre, E. J. (1988). *Education and the public trust: The imperatives for common purposes*. Washington, DC: Ethics and Public Policy Center, p. 89.
6. Nord, W. A. (1991). Teaching and morality: The knowledge most worth having. In D. D. Dill and associates (Eds.), *What teachers need to know*. San Francisco: Jossey-Bass.
7. Bennett, W. (1977, August 15). Let's bring back heroes. *Newsweek*.
8. Vitz, P. (1986). *Censorship, evidence of bias in children's books*. Ann Arbor, MI: Servant Publications.
9. Kilpatrick, W. K. (1985). *The emperor's new clothes: The naked truth about modern psychology*. Westchester, IL: Goodnews Press.
10. Aristotle, *The Ethics*.
11. Coleman, J. S. (1974). *Youth: Transition to adulthood*. Chicago: University of Chicago Press.
12. Power, F. C., Higgins, A., & Kohlberg, L. (1989). *Lawrence Kohlberg's approach to moral education*. New York: Columbia University Press (pp. 7, 25).
13. Hand, D. (1989, April 9). Morality lessons? Hear, hear. *New York Times Special Report on Education*, p. 53.
14. Counts, G. S. (1932). *Dare the teachers of America build a new social order?* New York: John Day.
15. Wynne, E. A. (1976). Learning about cooperation and competition. *Educational Forum, 40*, 279–288.

Chapter 8

1. Capon, R. (1965). *Bed and board*. New York: Simon and Schuster, p. 94.
2. Botsford, G. W. (1965). *Hellenic civilization*. New York: Octagon Books, p. 478.

3. de Honey, J. R. (1977). *Tom Brown's universe*, New York: Quadrangle/New York Times Books, p. 139.
4. Sizer, T. (1984). *Horace's compromise: The dilemma of the American high school.* Boston: Houghton Mifflin.

Chapter 9

1. Lortie, D. (1975). *Schoolteacher.* Chicago: University of Chicago Press, p. 97.
2. Longford, E. (1969). *Wellington: The years of the sword.* London: Weidenfels & Nicholson, p. 121.
3. Waller, W. (1932). *The sociology of teaching.* New York: Wiley.

Chapter 10

1. Polybius (1979). *The rise of the Roman empire* (I. Scott-Kilvert, Trans.). New York: Penguin, p. 347.

Chapter 11

1. Bowen, J. (1971). *A History of Western Education, vol. 1, The Ancient World.* New York: St. Martins Press, p. 153.

Index